KING WILLIAM'S TONTINE

In a time before bonds, treasury notes, or central banks, there were tontines. These were schemes in which a group of investors lent money to a government, corporation, or king, similar to a modern-day loan syndicate. But unlike conventional debt, periodic interest payments were distributed only to survivors. As tontine nominees died, the income of survivors correspondingly increased. Morbid perhaps, but this was one of the earliest forms of longevity insurance in which the pool shared the risk. Moshe A. Milevsky tells the story of the first tontine issued by the English government in 1693, known as King William's tontine, intended to finance the war against French King Louis XIV. He explains how tontines work and the financial and economic thinking behind them, as well as why they fell into disrepute. The author concludes with a provocative argument that suitably modified tontines should be resurrected for twenty-first-century retirement income planning.

Moshe A. Milevsky, PhD, is a professor at the Schulich School of Business and a member of the Graduate Faculty in the Department of Mathematics and Statistics at York University in Toronto. Visit his website at www.MosheMilevsky .com.

"I frequently saw Moshe after he had spent the day researching this book in the bowels of the British National Archives. He was covered in as much dust as Howard Carter after he first entered Tutankhamun's tomb. This shows the thoroughness with which this fine book was written. The timing could not be better either. Lorenzo de Tonti's concept of sharing longevity risk in a pool has a key role to play in retirement income plans of the future. There will be no more entertaining study of Tonti's brilliant idea."
– Professor David Blake, Director of the Pensions Institute, Cass Business School, London

"Professor Moshe Milevsky's book explores a particularly interesting time in the origin of government debt. While the book focuses on the 1693 tontine that King William used to finance England's war with France, the book also offers a witty and pleasurable romp through the history of tontines. Finally, the book shows how the tontine principle can be used to improve today's pensions and annuities."
– Jonathan B. Forman, Alfred P. Murrah Professor of Law, University of Oklahoma College of Law

"There is no more important topic than how our aging planet will confront and manage longevity risk, or the risk of outliving our resources. *King William's Tontine* offers a smart and humorous investigation into how our forefathers addressed the problem and Moshe A. Milevsky's plan to update the solution for generations to come."
– Olivia S. Mitchell, Professor, Wharton School, University of Pennsylvania

"Moshe Milevsky has given us a royal tour of the history of the tontine, full of revealing insights and many anecdotes, and has related the tontine to present-day retirement policy challenges brilliantly."
– John Piggott, Professor of Economics, University of New South Wales

"Who could have guessed that a slightly macabre financing scheme invented by a seventeenth-century Italian businessman might hold the key to retirement security for today's workers? In this charming and witty book, Moshe Milevsky, today's leading authority on annuities, blends economic history and financial engineering to promote a new way – actually centuries old – of enabling savers to retire on a secure income."
– Laurence B. Siegel, Gary P. Brinson Director of Research, CFA Institute Research Foundation

King William's Tontine

*Why the Retirement Annuity of the Future
Should Resemble Its Past*

MOSHE A. MILEVSKY

York University, Toronto

CAMBRIDGE
UNIVERSITY PRESS

CAMBRIDGE
UNIVERSITY PRESS

32 Avenue of the Americas, New York NY 10013-2473, USA

Cambridge University Press is part of the University of Cambridge.

It furthers the University's mission by disseminating knowledge in the pursuit of
education, learning and research at the highest international levels of excellence.

www.cambridge.org
Information on this title: www.cambridge.org/9781107076129

© Moshe A. Milevsky 2015

First published 2015

A catalogue record for this publication is available from the British Library

ISBN 978-1-107-07612-9 Hardback

"Old age, which is exposed to so many accidents and which too often is resented by those eagerly awaiting the death of the old, will be protected from vicissitudes. The Tontine will oblige those whose interest it is to prolong the life of the old, to treat them with respect and care because of the advantage they will find and will hope to increase ... It will motivate husbands and their wives to take extremely good care of each other."

Lorenzo de Tonti (1653)

In another glorious English year called 1693,
there lived a little prince William Duke of G.
He had very great dreams at the age of four,
to be a brave soldier in his uncle's French war.
The King from Orange had a constant frown,
and the people wanted little William crowned.
Thanks to a horse and a broken collarbone,
sweet loving mother Anne got lifted to the throne.
Adorable and cute the clever boy was so swell,
but nurses and doctors worried he wasn't well.
One August after celebrating the age of eleven,
he became quite ill and was called up to heaven.
Gone was the William named in a funny tontine,
and the hopes of future Stuart kings and queens.

Zoe R. Milevsky (age 10)

Contents

Preface: In Memoriam for Jared

Spare a moment of pity for an old fellow named Jared who was first mentioned in the early chapters of the Bible, in the book of Genesis. You have certainly heard of his famous grandson Methuselah, aka the oldest living person in the Bible. Methuselah, of course, is synonymous with longevity, old age, and great genes. Entire tomes have been dedicated to Methuselah and his drawn-out life. Books such as *The Death of Methuselah*, by Isaac Bashevis Singer, or *Back to Methuselah*, by George Bernard Shaw, have made him one of the most famous literary figures – or pensioners – in Western history. The Oscar-winning British actor Sir Anthony Hopkins played him in the movie *Noah* and the great American writer Samuel Langhorne Clemens (aka Mark Twain) penned a story with Methuselah as the central character. No fine essayist passed him by.

For those of you who aren't familiar with the story, it is said that Methuselah lived to the astounding age of 969. That is 11,628 months, or 353,685 days on earth. It is no surprise that his diet, genes, many probable marriages – and even his investments – have been the subject of intense curiosity for centuries. And yet, his grandfather Jared – a man I suspect most of you have never heard of until now – lived to the equally unbelievable age of 962 years. Yes, you guessed it. He was the Bible's second-oldest literary figure. Second place garners no books, Nobels, or gene patents, hence the pity.

It was quite the family, though. Methuselah's grandson Noah – the famed sailor and nautical zookeeper – lived 950 years, which is slightly less than two decades short of Methuselah's remarkable feat, placing him in the number-three position. Noah (aka Russell Crowe) needs no introduction or any more fame. (Hey, just try booking him for a speaking engagement these days.) Moving on to number four in the biblical Guinness book of records we find Adam. Yes, the first. Adam lived to 930 and has no small part in human history, quite likely regretting the long nap he took in the Garden of Eden and not keeping a closer eye on his rib cage. But poor old Jared was the Bible's second-oldest person, missing his grandson's record leisure-shattering retirement by a mere seven years, or approximately 0.7% of his own life span. Jared lived and lived and then died, in almost complete obscurity.

Did Jared have any idea he would last that long?

This book is inspired by Jared's extended and very obscure plight. Jared is my euphemism for any retiree or pensioner who will shatter no records or become the subject of any books, documentaries, or scientific projects. They will live far longer than their parents ever did – perhaps not as long as their grandkids – but will have to find some way to pay for it all. Jared represents the hundreds of thousands, possibly millions, of elderly around the world who will reach extremely advanced ages, and nobody will consider it a big deal.

In all actuarial likelihood, you are a Jared.

Yet no insurance company, retirement system, or pension plan can afford to support all these Jareds, especially considering how little we have collectively saved for retirement. So, how will society pay for it all? I believe that (part of) the answer to Jared's dilemma is to dust off the history books and revisit a most popular and fascinating arrangement that has lain dormant for centuries. It is called *The Tontine Scheme*.

Allow me some time to elaborate. You probably have a while ...

Acknowledgments

It took quite a while to complete this project. The book's gestation, in a manner of speaking, lasted longer than an elephant's. When I got started on this mission a few years ago – that is, during the highly optimistic phase – my original intention was to create *the* most comprehensive and encyclopedic reference on the finance, economics, and actuarial theory of tontines, including a broad review of the insurance history and the relevant academic literature, all wrapped up with a passionate advocacy piece arguing that tontines should be resurrected in the twenty-first century. (At least that is what I promised in the book proposal.)

Well, it took me about six months to realize that such an ambitious project was too broad, impractical, and simply unachievable in finite time. I also worried that after all that effort nobody would really care about an insurance policy that has been dead for centuries. Not to mention I came across some excellent (historical) references about tontines, which made me wonder: "What could I possibly add?"

But then, during a visit to the National Archives in London, I stumbled on the details and old documents from the first English tontine launched in 1693 (i.e., King William III's tontine). Here was something different that might provide me with a new and unique entry point to the topic. I thought it was a great place in history from which to launch the journey, even though according to most insurance historians it isn't considered the most successful tontine.

I then rescaled my objectives to offer readers a careful and rigorous but entertaining appreciation of tontines and their colorful history as well as to explain why the underlying tontine sharing principle, or simply "tontine thinking," is quite relevant in twenty-first-century retirement income planning.

The fuel that kept this project going were the many comments after a brief article I wrote about the possibility of resurrecting tontines, published in the *Wall Street Journal*, cited as Milevsky (2013). With an inbox full of encouraging emails, I was satisfied that I wasn't the only person who cared about these long-forgotten products. The final "kick in the pants" came from Professor William Sharpe, when I was at a conference he was co-organizing at Stanford University in the summer of 2014. His first words to me were: "Hey Moshe, when are you going to finish the tontine book?" Well, I felt like a young graduate student being admonished by his thesis supervisor. I went into full production mode and for the next six months I was living, eating, and breathing tontines.

As far as help is concerned, I would like to acknowledge financial support from a Schulich Research Fellowship (during Fall 2013), which gave me the time off from teaching to delve into the topic and visit the National Archives and library in London. A research grant from NETSPAR (awarded during Winter 2014) as well as ongoing funding from the IFID Centre at the Fields Institute helped with many of the direct and indirect costs.

The members of the editorial team, including Nishanthini Vetrivel at Newgen Knowledge Works, as well Karen Maloney, Kate Gavino, Phil Good, and Chris Harrison at Cambridge University Press, have been a pleasure to work with. The editor of the *Financial History Review* – where parts of Chapter 4 previously appeared – Stefano Battilossi, was very encouraging and forced me to think carefully about the historical context behind the first English tontine.

This project would have been impossible to complete (let alone survive) without able help from research assistants. I would like to thank Rejo Peter (YorkU), Dajena Collaku (YorkU and IFID), Minjie Zhang (YorkU), Daniel Tut (YorkU), and Alexa Brand (IFID) for help with many aspects of the manuscript. I am also indebted to staff at the British Library as well as the National Archives in London and, in particular, Paul Carlyle and Gavin Walsh. Also David Raymont, the librarian at the Institute and Faculty of Actuaries (UK), alerted me to documents pertaining to King William's tontine that I had not been aware of. He was extremely sympathetic about the entire project. I also thank David Raymont for permission to use the cover image of the list of tontine nominees.

Moving on, I would like to thank the many individuals who offered advice and comments during the research and writing of this book. In particular, I would like to call out Lowell Aronoff, David Blake, Jorge Bravo, Forrest Capie, Narat Charupat, Jonathan Forman, Ed Furman, Steven Haberman, Faisal Habib, Huaxiong Huang, David Laster, Sandy Mackenzie, Jonathan Milevsky, Anthony Neuberger, Jens Perch Nielsen, Ermano Pitacco, Steven Posner, David Promislow, Joshua Rauh, Mike Sabin, Bill Sharpe, Pauline Shum, Bob Toth, Steve Vernon, and Geoffrey Wood.

A collective thanks is due to seminar and academic conference participants at the IFID Centre (Toronto, Summer 2012), IME Congress (Copenhagen, Summer 2013), Cass Business School (London, Summer 2014), the Society of Actuaries Living to 100 Conference (Orlando, Winter 2014), Stanford Center on Longevity (Palo Alto, Spring 2014), NETSPAR International Pension Conference (Venice, Summer 2014), Longevity 10 (Santiago, Fall 2014), and ETH Risk Center (Zurich, Fall 2014). I am grateful for their suggestions, but I alone am responsible for all errors.

A special thanks goes out to my colleague, friend, and mentor Tom Salisbury, for the many educational and entertaining conversations we have had over the last quarter of a century about probability, mathematics, and finance, and more recently about tontines. I'm fortunate that I was able to "infect" him with the tontine "bug." A number of ideas about the optimal design of tontines and the concept of the "natural" tontine (which I discuss in Chapter 8 and label Jared's tontine) were jointly developed. He was also kind enough to read the manuscript and offer great suggestions for improvement.

Finally, no thank you is complete without acknowledging my lifetime partner, supporter, promoter, and mate. As with my (eleven) previous books and numerous articles and papers, she diligently read, commented on, and helped improve every aspect of this project. Thank you, my dear Edna.

Permissions: Some of the material in this book has appeared (in early or "raw" form) elsewhere. The relevant permissions have been obtained and noted wherever texts or tables appear verbatim. In particular, a much shorter version of the story from the early part of Chapter 2 was published in *Research Magazine* in the fall of 2013. Also, a summary of the high demand for annuities in Chile, which is described in Chapter 8, appeared in *Research Magazine* in May 2013. I thank the editor, Gil Weinreich, for permission to use extracts from both. An academic version of Chapter 3 was recently published in the *Financial History Review*, in 2014. The main idea presented in Chapter 8, which is the structure of a "natural tontine," was first described in my joint paper with Thomas Salisbury (available as SSRN at http://ssrn.com/abstract=2271259). The Gompertz mortality model and annuity pricing formula is mentioned briefly in the appendix, but is described in much greater detail in Milevsky (2006, 2012).

The figures of King William III and William Henry Duke of Gloucester are used with permission from the National Portrait Gallery, London. The cover image is used with permission from the Institute and Faculty of Actuaries, London.

King Billy, Protestant Hero of England

1693: REIGN OF WILLIAM III AND MARY II

In the early days of 1693, at just about the same time American Puritans in New England were burning witches, half a world away, King William III of England (see Figure 1.1) was in the midst of battle with another sort of devil, the Catholic King Louis XIV of France, also known as the Sun King.

The hostility between the English king – who was actually Dutch in origin – and the infamous Sun King extended far beyond the few years since William had ascended to the English throne jointly with his wife, Mary. In fact, before winning the triple crown of England, Ireland, and Scotland, Prince William of Orange had spent the first thirty eight years of his life on the European continent under the constant threat of French aggression. The French and Dutch had been going at each other for centuries. In fact, there was a persistent rumor that King Louis XIV had actually once tried to kidnap King William, back when he was still the Prince of Orange, so there was no love lost between the glamorous Frenchman and the dour Dutchman.

But in early 1693, while basking in the glory of his victory at the Battle of the Boyne in Ireland, King Billy, as he was nicknamed, was atop the English throne. And the forty-two-year-old monarch intended to settle the score with Louis once and for all by combining the best of the Dutch and English fleets. His vision and lifetime objective as the leader of the House of Orange was to secure a protestant Europe for generations.

Now, good intentions, strategic generals, and motivated troops are *necessary* but not *sufficient* conditions for waging a successful campaign against your enemies. Wars need money. In fact, when it comes to military campaigns that can change the tide of history, one requires very large sums of money. And this, alas, was something King William III didn't have in early 1693. To the point, he wanted the English to pay and fund his war, but

Figure 1.1. King William III. By John Faber, Jr. Copyright © National Portrait Gallery, London. Asset # D9228. Used with permission.

they weren't thrilled about the idea, placing him in a foul frame of mind, I might add.[1]

Indeed, it might have helped his cause if King William III had been a suave and easygoing political charmer, like his predecessor, Charles II – the popular king who was known as the Merry Monarch. Charles II's debauchery made the French court seem tame and boring in comparison. Imagine Bill Clinton as king in the late seventeenth century. But King Billy was callous, aloof, and the antithesis of charming.[2] Moreover, he was

---

[1] The historical source for information about King William is Claydon (2002) and Kiste (2003).

[2] See Somerset (2012) as well.

living in a foreign land and reigning under knotty constitutional dynamics. He was a lifelong asthmatic suffering from constant poor health and hated the weather in London. He was also childless and without a legitimate heir. His (mostly political) marriage to his wife, Queen Mary II, by all contemporary accounts, lacked romance and passion. In fact, while we're on the topic of family, William's sister-in-law, Anne, gave him much grief. And his father-in-law, James, would probably have killed William if he could get his hands on him. Actually, as all English schoolboys and schoolgirls are taught, William of Orange invaded (or was invited to) England – triggering the Glorious Revolution of 1688 – and exiled his father-in-law off to France.[3]

In the last decade of the seventeenth century, King William's main priority and existential preoccupation was to secure the funds he needed to pay his troops and continue his campaign against France. William – who was a military commander and master strategist – still had outstanding debts to settle from his previous battles, including the 21,000 men he had hired to accompany him to England in 1688. Money was tight, and King Billy was in a bloody bind.

I must admit that the story of an English monarch in need of money might sound a bit distant and incredulous to anyone in the twenty-first century. But then again, even Queen Elizabeth II, who ascended the throne in 1952 and has a personal net worth of more than £300 million ($480 million), has monarchical financial problems and disputes with Parliament over who should pay for what. In early 2013, a parliamentary committee questioned her household's (over)spending, and for a brief period in 2013, the queen applied for welfare – yes, welfare! – to pay for the upkeep on some of her palaces.[4] Presumably, the future King Charles III (her son), the subsequent King William V (her grandson), or even future King George VII (her great-grandson) will have similar run-ins with Parliament.

But three centuries ago – when the beginning of our story takes place – the Crown's finances were even more precarious, precisely because they were subject to the whims of Parliament, which controlled all the purse strings. Yes, the monarchs owned land and were entitled to live in castles – and the Orange family owned large tracts in the Netherlands – but cash flow and income weren't easy to obtain, especially to finance a war. The now-common practice of making the monarch accountable to the English

---

[3]   More on the Stuarts in Chapter 4.
[4]   See the article in the *Independent* from September 24, 2010, "Queen Tried to Use State Poverty Fund to Heat Buckingham Palace."

Parliament directly – and the English people indirectly – was one of the great constitutional achievements of the late seventeenth century.

Sure, a millennia or two ago, kings could do as they pleased and seize whatever they wanted or desired, whenever they wanted, but not so by the end of the seventeenth century. If a monarch needed more money – whether to wage war or provision mistresses – he needed Parliament to authorize and approve the additional funds. Now, of course, Parliament couldn't really order the "creation" of money by printing, as it does today. Its only source of revenue was taxes, including land tax, custom tax, and excise tax, as well as taxes on salt, wine, spirits, tobacco, and even births and marriages. Requisitioning or raising additional funds today requires increasing taxes, and, naturally, as the elected representatives of (some fraction of) the people, Parliament is reluctant to do so, especially for wars that aren't widely supported.

So, I now get to my main story.

William got his money from Parliament in the end. And in its attempt to raise funds to fight William's war against the French, the English Parliament authorized something virtually unheard of within the empire; something that was to change the economy forever – a financial revolution according to some: *they decided to borrow money by issuing long-term government debt.*

The plan was that creditors would voluntarily lend (aka invest) a minimum of £100 each toward the war effort, and the government – not the king or any one person, the actual *government* – committed to pay interest on this £100 note for the next ninety-nine years. The Act of Parliament authorizing the ninety-nine-year loan was called the Million Act, which, as you guessed, was an attempt to get 10,000 Englishmen to (lend £100 or more each and) contribute £1 million to fund King William's war. To put this number in perspective, £1 million in the year 1693 would be equal to between £100 to £500 million today, depending on wage and price inflation assumptions in 2015.[5] Relatively speaking, this was a large sum of money.

At this point you must be wondering to yourself: "That's it? They borrowed money to fight a war? Is that revolutionary? Heck, the U.S. federal government owes $18 trillion in the year 2015, for heaven's sake!"

Well, part of the answer is that yes, this sort of scheme was a big deal in the last decade of the seventeenth century. Up until 1693, to be precise, the

---

[5]   From a different perspective, the annual cost of supplies for the entire British army of 65,000 men in the year 1692 was £1.8 million. So, the Million Act would raise half the budget for one year of the army (Gregory and Stevenson 2007, 162).

English *as a people, governed by Parliament* had never borrowed long-term funds the way it is practiced today. Yes, individuals had borrowed money for millennia, kings and queens had borrowed money, and even corporations – which did exist, mind you – had borrowed money, but not a nation.

To be perfectly honest, the real interesting story here is *how* Parliament implemented the borrowing scheme known as the Million Act and the type of debt they issued and committed the country to paying. This wasn't your grandfather's savings bond.

At a broad level – and I'll get into much more detail later – the way the scheme worked was that in exchange for each £100 investment, the government committed itself to pay 7% interest until maturity of the so-called bond. So, the lenders were receiving interest payments of £7 per year for ninety-nine years, which sounds and smells awfully like a very long-term bond. But – *and this is key* – if and when investors owning the individual bonds died, they couldn't – I repeat, could not – bequeath the share or bond units to their children, friends, or loved ones. Instead, the £7-per-year interest they would have been entitled to had they still been alive was forfeited and distributed to the other investors who were still alive. For the sake of example, if twenty years later half of the original £100 investors had died and half were still alive, then each surviving investor would now receive £14 interest in that year, which is double their first year's interest payment. In thirty years, if three-quarters of the original investors had died, then all surviving investors would receive £28 interest (or a payout yield of 28%) in that year alone.[6] And in the end, in theory the longest-living survivors would get all the interest income on the proverbial table. Think of the last hand in a poker game. Winner takes all.

This, ladies and gentlemen, is a *tontine scheme* – and it was the first time it was launched nationally in England. King William III used tontines to fund and pay for his war.

If this is the first time you have heard of a tontine, you might recoil in horror.[7] "Does this mean that your interest or tontine dividends increase as your friends and neighbors die?" Well, the short answer is yes. No doubt you weren't praying for their well-being.

You might be surprised to learn that tontine schemes were extremely popular for about 200 years, from the late seventeenth century – when it was

---

6   The £7 interest per share is divided by 0.25, which is the percentage of survivors, resulting in £28 interest paid to all surviving shares. So, when only 10% of the pool remains, survivors receive £70 in interest. I explain the math in much more detail in Chapter 2.

7   "Tontine" rhymes with "tall queen."

launched nationally in England – to the late nineteenth century. This was the golden age of tontine schemes. Large tontine schemes were launched in Italy, the Netherlands, Denmark, and France all around the same time. The English Parliament formally joined the tontine festivities – to help King William fund his war – in 1693.

It is worth noting that at just about the same time the first parliamentary tontine was sanctioned and got under way under King William III, across the English channel King Louis XIV oversaw the launching of the first French state tontine (to much greater success, I might add) in Paris.[8] I presume the thinking in London was – just as with French fashion, cuisine, and clothing – if they were popular in France, then why not offer them in England?

Perhaps you can relish the irony here. The English needed money to fight a war and kill Frenchmen. So they engaged the same financing method employed by the French, who were fighting a war trying to kill Englishmen – by borrowing money and paying interest that would grow – as other people died. Macabre, no? If there were bond underwriters at the time, I can just imagine the sales pitch. As long as the investor stayed alive – and away from the battlefields – their investments would yield lively returns. I doubt there was a Goldman Sachs at the time, but I suspect they would have had a hand in this sort of bond business.

But – and here is where I'll join a moral battlefield of sorts – in this book I try to convince you that there is merit in this sort of tontine scheme and that they should be brought back from the dead. Yes, I know this is an uphill battle, and I'm not proposing to resurrect King William's exact version. I'm calling my proposal Jared's tontine in honor of the world's second-oldest literary figure. More importantly, I argue for why these sorts of schemes may make more economic sense than you might think at a first passing.

A Recap

Let me sum up here again. It is little known – even among professional economic historians and central bankers – that less than a year prior to the charter of the Bank of England (which took place in July 1694), the earliest attempt by the government to borrow money for the long run wasn't by issuing bonds, notes, or bills, which is the preferred and familiar method used in the twenty-first century. Rather, the first instrument of English

---

[8]   The first French state tontine was launched in 1689 (Jennings and Trout 1982).

national debt was in the form of a tontine scheme – a product that today has virtually disappeared from our lexicon and landscape.[9]

This book is about tontine schemes in general, the first English government scheme in particular, and why they may not be as bad as you might initially think.

In broad terms, a tontine can also be viewed as a type of life annuity or lifetime pension where "annuitants" receive "income" as long as they are alive, and the payments increase as other annuitants die and leave the tontine pool. In theory the longest-living survivor gets all the dividends until he or she dies and the obligation or instrument is extinguished.

When I describe tontine schemes to friends and relatives, the first question (or joke) I hear revolves around people killing each other to get their interest payments. In fact, quite a few movies and books have been penned with this plot. The truth is that there is little evidence of any of these sorts of shenanigans taking place. You might be surprised to know that the exact opposite was observed. Tontine nominees – that is, the people on whose lives the payments are based – lived much *longer* than the population average and had *lower* mortality rates compared with individuals who didn't participate in a tontine. It appears as if being a member of a tontine scheme kept them alive! Why this might be the case is a mystery – or perhaps not – that I address later, but for now, rest assured that the incentive to murder was not as great as you might expect, especially since most tontine schemes capped payments at some point.

Still not convinced of the economic soundness of this scheme – or that anyone ever tried to borrow money in this peculiar way? Well, none other than Alexander Hamilton, the first secretary of the U.S. Treasury, suggested a similar tontine scheme in the year 1790 – in a series of letters to George Washington and a proposal to Congress – to help pay off and eliminate the massive debt from the Revolutionary War. I'll get to the American plan later on, as well.

---

[9] This is not to be confused with the group savings and microcredit policies in French-speaking regions of present-day Africa, called Rotating Savings and Credit Associations (ROSCA). There are also a variety of community-based savings and loan schemes marketed under the tontine label in (present day) Malaysia where they are legal, regulated by the Cooperatives and Consumerism Ministry of Malaysia and referred to as "kootu" or "chit funds." An hour's flight away from Kuala Lumpur, in Phnom Penh, Cambodia, "tontine kittys" as they are known in Cambodia, are quite popular but apparently illegal. Although these unique schemes are interesting and rather complex they have absolutely nothing to do with classical tontines covered in this book. Life and death play no role in the payout function and that is all I have to say on this matter.

Tontine schemes – like the character in the popular children's book *Where's Waldo?* – exhibit an odd and peculiar habit of appearing in unexpected and critical places over the last few centuries. Some historians have argued that tontine schemes were partially to blame for the bankrupt treasury preceding the French Revolution. In the United States, private tontine schemes managed by insurance companies were accused of fraud and eventually banned by regulators in the early twentieth century, leading to the creation of collective pension plans and Social Security.

Moreover, some of the greatest scientists in the last 300 years, from the astronomer Edmond Halley, the mathematicians Abraham de Moivre, Leonard Euler, and Friedrich Gauss, to the world's first and most famous economist, Adam Smith, opined, wrote about, and made an appearance in the tontine business.

I should add again, however, that this book is more than just an interesting story about a somewhat peculiar insurance product that existed a few centuries ago. For those of you who are appalled by the idea of benefiting from others' deaths, I will ask you to suspend judgment until the very end. Despite the fact that tontines have been extinct or (according to some) illegal for almost 100 years – and I'll get to that, as well – I am going to argue for the resurrection of tontine schemes, or what I prefer to call the tontine sharing principle, or better yet, "tontine thinking."

I will try to convince you that "tontine thinking" might help resolve one of the biggest challenges facing society today – no, not religious wars between neighbors – the challenge of making your retirement funds last for as long as you live. Remember, one of the by-products of a tontine scheme is that members get income for as long as they live. This helps insure against the unexpected and increasing cost of living a long life, which can be just as important as insuring against the devastating damage – to a family – of a short life. I will discuss the demise of Defined Benefit (DB) pensions, the cost of long-term guarantees, and point out that "tontine thinking" is already being used in places you wouldn't expect, but it is hidden and obscure. My point is as follows; Why not bring it back into the open?

I don't seek to resurrect King William's exact version of a tontine since we have learned quite a bit in the ensuing three centuries, but the foundations were there 320 years ago. And some aspects of his design were quite innovative and worthy of reproduction. I'll elaborate on this as well.

But *why* would someone want to do this? Why bring back an investment and insurance product that has lain dormant for centuries? The *Encyclopedia Britannica*, VHS tapes, pagers, and typewriters were all great ideas and innovations in their time, but the world has moved on. Why bring back tontines? Well, let me start with one good reason.

TAKE LONGEVITY RISK OFF MY BOOKS

If you happened to wander into an industry or academic conference focused on the topic of retirement or pensions – as I do on occasion – you will notice that nowadays, most of the speakers mercilessly and repeatedly pound away on one theme. Notwithstanding the daunting long-term challenges we face in society – from religious warfare, climate change to water scarcity to income disparity – the one phrase that comes up repeatedly at pension conferences is *longevity risk*. This term, which, I confess, I'll use quite a bit, as well, is roughly defined as the fear that a person or retiree will live longer than was expected. I'll offer a much more refined definition later on in the book, but for now think of longevity risk as the symmetric opposite of *mortality risk*, which is the chance of dying at a younger age than expected. The key word here is *expected*.

The presentations at these conferences usually begin with a slew of World Bank or IMF or Society of Actuary statistics that are supposed to surprise and astonish the audience – although, by the hundredth time you see the numbers, the shock factor is gone – namely, that we are living decades longer than our grandparents and parents ever did. You are likely to hear statements claiming that in the early twentieth century life expectancy at birth was fifty years, but by the beginning of the twenty-first century, it had increased to eighty years. This, of course, translates into a growth rate of four months per year or one day more of life for every three days we have already lived. The probability of living to triple digits has gone from close to zero a century ago to a fifty-fifty coin toss today according to (optimistic) demographers. And for a married couple, the odds are closer to three-quarters. So, by the twenty-second century, the experts claim, we will all survive to the age of 122 – which is the age of the oldest verified[10] woman, who lived and died a few years ago in France, Jeanne Louise Calment.[11] I'm not saying I agree with any of these statements. But you do hear them over and over again.

Regardless of the statistical accuracy of these forecasts – which is something else I'll discuss at much greater length later on – any normal person hearing these things would consider it good news. After all, who doesn't

---

[10] Biodemographers are still awaiting validation of the centenarians listed in the book of Genesis.

[11] There is a cute story about Jeanne Louise selling her apartment in Paris to a (young) lawyer in the 1970s on the condition that she could continue to live in it for the rest of her life. In exchange, the lawyer agreed to pay her a fixed sum per month (a life annuity, in lieu of the purchase price.). Needless to say, he died well before she did and he never got her apartment. Whether Jeanne Louise lived to 122 or "only" 110 is the topic of some controversy, according to professor Leonid Gavrilov and professor Natalia Gavrilova from the University of Chicago. Either way, she did live a very long time.

want to live longer? But these aren't ordinary audiences. These are pension administrators, insurance company executives, actuaries, risk management experts, and government regulators who – to misquote the great writer F. Scott Fitzgerald – worry about things different from you and I. The common thread linking this band of worriers together is their financial liabilities.

Directly or indirectly, those in attendance are responsible for paying retirees a fixed, known, guaranteed income for the rest of their lives. The longer retirees live, the more they have to pay. So if the longevity forecasts are true and the longevity risk materializes, these responsible and prudent folks will have to set aside more money to pay claims and will require more business capital to support their activities. All this can be extremely expensive.

No matter how you phrase it, a fact that at first hearing should be good news for everyone – hey, isn't a long life a blessing? – is perceived as scary news for the pension and retirement business. But it doesn't have to be. That's my main point, which I'll get to later.

To be specific, DB plans – for example, the pension plans of police officers, firefighters, teachers, and government employees – have promised to pay their retirees a monthly paycheck for the rest of their lives. So longevity risk would imply they are on the hook for longer (than expected). Likewise, life insurance companies have promised to pay annuities for life, and for them, too, longevity risk means they must mail checks for longer (than expected). In fact, even reinsurance companies – which are the entities that insurance companies use to protect and insure themselves – are worried and concerned about longer lives.

All this activity is taking place in an environment in which more and more private sector pension plans – such as Motorola's, General Motors's, and Verizon's – are transferring their longevity risk to insurance companies. These insurers are promising to make the payments to retirees instead of the primary companies where the retirees worked and earned their pensions.[12] So the large corporations might be reducing their longevity risk – but now the insurers have more of it.

Don't get me wrong, these insurance specialists also worry about the other side of the coin, which is excessive and unexpected deaths and epidemics – from something like an Ebola or SARS epidemic – but they have

---

[12] See, for example, the article by Rob Kozlowski in the industry publication *Pensions & Investments*, on September 29, 2014, "Motorola Wraps Up Buyout at Light Speed," in which this trend of transferring longevity risk from industrial corporations to insurance companies is described in much greater length.

been worrying about those matters for centuries, ever since life insurance companies came into existence. The concern around longevity risk is much more recent. Stated differently, owing to improvements in medicine and the awareness of nutrition and hygiene, mortality rates around the world are *expected* to decline – that is, less deaths this year compared with last year – by 1%. But what if the *realized* number is closer to 2%? Everyone lives longer. Who will pay for all of this?

These conferences and gatherings I mentioned are more than just a club of worriers building on one another's phobias. Most speakers at the events come with a briefcase full of solutions. That's the point of these gatherings. Whether they are pitching complex insurance solutions, reinsurance treaties, or capital market instruments like longevity bonds, the common denominator is "We can help take the longevity risk off of your financial books."

Yet another group of experts have suggested that companies simply dump their pension's longevity risk onto the backs and wallets of the retirees themselves. They suggest giving retirees the money and letting them worry about how to make it last. You might be in one of the plans called a Defined Contribution (DC) pension. Nothing is guaranteed. The trustees and managers of those plans don't attend these sorts of conferences. They don't have to worry (but you, as an individual, do). But, even in the DC world, the insurance industry is aching to swoop in and offer life annuities to the retirees who have the longevity risk on their personal balance sheet. I'll get to the messy problems with that strategy later as well. But then the insurance company has to worry about longevity risk.

The underlying assumption here is that somebody somewhere has to guarantee something. Ultimately there is a risk that has to be borne by a third party – which then implies that someone has to worry about this risk, reserve for this risk, and *charge for this risk*. But my question is: do we really need this?

Enter the Modern Tontine?

Perhaps a better solution to the problems posed by longevity risk is to offer retirees themselves a choice of two products or systems. Let's make the risk explicit and see how people react to this risk. If individuals aren't aware of what is being guaranteed, they are less inclined to pay for it anyway.

For the same $100,000 nest egg, for example, we could give (rational) people a choice between a life annuity that pays them $500 per month for the rest of their lives, guaranteed – no matter what happens. This guarantee is backed by the insurance company, which is then (partially) backed by the reinsurance company, which is then (partially) backed by capital markets. They have to worry about longevity risk and find ways of managing longevity risk.

Or the retiree can be offered a variant of (but not exactly the same as) King William's tontine. They would start off receiving the same $600 per month – which is *more* than what a life annuity would provide – in exchange for the same $100,000 nest egg or retirement account. If people die as expected and on time, then the payments would stay at $600 per month. But, if *realized* mortality deviated from *expected* mortality rates, the $600 would move up or down. I'll talk about the mechanics of how this might work much later in the book, but for now contemplate the choice.

Would you rather have the safer $500 per month or the risky $600 per month? Okay, well, what if the tontine starts at $650 per month? And then goes up or down. I'll get to the choice of tontines versus annuities later on as well. King William's tontine offered people a similar choice. Yes, there are many details to complete and fill in, but this is a preview.

Spoiler alert. The underlying concept I'm "selling" in this book is that a pool of retired people with similar demographic factors could share and absorb the longevity risk among themselves using "tontine thinking" or the tontine sharing principle.

I'll surprise you with a statistic of my own, namely, that you don't really need that many people to make this a viable retirement income plan. The 1,000 or so participants in King William's tontine were more than enough to create a reasonably stable retirement income plan. This is thanks to something called the Law of Large Numbers (LLN), which was first noticed by Astronomer Edmond Halley and formalized by Mathematician Abraham DeMoivre – two giants of science who were active in the late seventeenth century and early eighteenth century, and actually had a minor role in King William's tontine. More on them, later.

Part of the agenda for this book is to argue that by reintroducing transparent, simple, and nondiscriminatory tontines, we can actually give retirees better and more informed choices. This is why King William's novel financial scheme is relevant to the twenty-first century.

OVERVIEW AND OUTLINE OF THIS BOOK

Chapter 2 explains how a (generic) tontine scheme actually works in much greater detail as well as some of the economics and finance behind tontines as a form of debt. You will read about the famous Scottish economist Adam

Smith and his clever psychological insights on why tontines were a better way to borrow money compared with *life annuities*. I discuss exactly how tontines differ from the more familiar life annuities – which are the basis of all defined benefit pensions and social security programs. In this chapter I lay the foundations of "tontine thinking" or the tontine sharing principle and why the economics of this idea are so powerful.

In fact, informal tontine schemes were launched long before the English Parliament voted to use them for funding purposes in 1693, and Chapter 3 reviews one of the earliest, yet informal, schemes in Elizabethan England as well as a surprising participant in such schemes. This chapter also reviews what is known about the Italian financier Lorenzo de Tonti – who proposed the idea to King Louis XIV and after whom tontines are named – and his attempts to promote the scheme. Lorenzo was quite the colorful character and an imaginative entrepreneur, but he got into a bit of trouble toward the end of his life. His two children took the family name to America. More on them to follow.

Chapter 4 gets to the core of the story with the background, rationale, and specific design of King William's tontine. By the way, the first English tontine of 1693 was named King William's tontine by John Finlaison – a person who will make an appearance in a number of places in this book.[13] John Finlaison was a statistician and economist in nineteenth-century England, whose official position was (first) Actuary of the National Debt. He was the founder of the British Institute of Actuaries. Today, actuaries are indispensable to the insurance industry but didn't yet exist in the late seventeenth century. The so-called Million Act, which was likely drafted and discussed in late 1692 but only passed by Parliament in January 1693, was of course the attempt to raise a million pounds to fight a war against King Louis the XIV of France. As mentioned, France itself used tontine schemes in the late seventeenth and early eighteenth century to raise money to fight its war against England. In this chapter I provide some historical context and color. As well, I discuss some of the financial options that were attached to the tontine, which gave every single participant a very interesting *option to annuitize* – the relevance and importance of which will become clear later on. Chapter 4 is the "historical" core of the book, which discusses some of the other fixed-income investments that were available in the last decade of the seventeenth century.

Chapter 5 takes a closer look at the more than 1,000 nominees to King William's tontine and uncovers something rather puzzling, which I alluded

---

[13] So, the book's title isn't my idea.

to earlier. The public concern with tontine schemes is that investors will be incentivized to murder each other to increase their payments. But there is little, if any, evidence of these shenanigans at advanced ages – like centenarians trying to kill each other – to try to win the tontine. No, instead of excessive deaths, it appears that not enough people were actually dying in tontine schemes.

Although mortality rates – especially for children – were very high in the late seventeenth and early eighteenth century, the nominees of King William's tontine lived a *very long* time, much longer than their peers and friends who hadn't been nominated to the tontine. More than 50% lived for thirty-seven more years after joining the scheme and 30% survived more than fifty-five years. These survival rates might not seem like much in 2015, but they were astonishing given mortality rates at the time. The oldest surviving nominee of King William's tontine lived to the ripe old age of 100. Yes. You read that correctly. She died in 1783 in Wimbledon, ninety years after the scheme was originally set up and she was selected as a nominee. Centenarians aren't a twenty-first century phenomena.

This brings up the question: Does being nominated to a tontine keep you alive? Or, perhaps, was there something more suspicious taking place? I discuss a concept that economists label anti-selection and whether that can explain the puzzling survival rates.

In the same chapter, I also shine light on the darker side of tontine schemes, which is partly to blame for their poor reputation and eventual decline. I review some of the accusations and complaints that were leveled against their promoters, including accusations of fraud and deceit.

Chapter 6 looks more broadly at tontine schemes – what I refer to as debt tontines versus equity tontines – over the ages and around the world. Some tontines were bonds and some tontines were stocks. I'll explain this in more detail. Then, we cross the Atlantic Ocean to examine the American experience with tontines, which were exported from England in the seventeenth century. As I mentioned, in 1790, the first U.S. Secretary of the Treasury Alexander Hamilton actually proposed a tontine scheme to help reduce the crushing national debt incurred during the revolution. He suggested the U.S. government replace high-interest debt with new bonds in which coupon payments would be made to a group as opposed to individuals. The group members would share the interest payments evenly among themselves, provided they were alive. Hamilton claimed – in a letter to none other than George Washington – that a tontine would reduce the interest paid on U.S. debt and eventually eliminate it entirely. Congress decided to pass on Hamilton's proposal (and recall that Hamilton himself resigned in disgrace upon admitting an affair with a married woman). But the tontine idea itself never died.

A few decades later, U.S. insurance companies began issuing tontine insurance policies to the public in the mid-nineteenth century that became wildly popular. These policies weren't quite the British and French tontines discussed in earlier chapters – and I'll explain how they differed. But one thing is for certain, by the start of the twentieth century, historians have documented that half of U.S. households owned a tontine insurance policy, which many Americans used to support themselves through retirement. Let me say this again just to be clear. Long before mutual funds, stocks, and bonds, it was tontine (insurance) policies that were the most popular type of retirement savings instrument in the United States – until a number of insurance company executives ruined it for everyone. The shenanigans and abuse around tontine insurances made headlines and made political careers. In the end, the influential New York State Insurance Commission banned tontine insurance in the state, and by the second decade of the twentieth century, most other states followed. Tontine insurance is now illegal in the United States (and much of the developed world) and this chapter addresses the legal issue head-on. My argument in a nutshell is that the insurance ban does not apply to King William's sort of tontine. I'll explain why.

In fact, a number of countries (today, in the twenty-first century) have adopted "tontine thinking" or the sharing principle in the design of their pension plans, which is something I cover in Chapter 6, as well.

Chapter 7 looks at optimal design issues. I roll up my sleeves – so to speak – and take the opportunity to discuss (more formally) some of the economic and financial problems with the traditional design of tontines – like the fact that the last few remaining survivors receive an enormous income, which doesn't seem very fair. While there were a number of flaws in the design of King William's 1693 tontine – and many good reasons why it wasn't a huge success – there are quite a number of valuable and motivating design features that are quite relevant for today. There is much to be learned from the mistakes of the past, but they can also serve as an inspiration for the future. This chapter is the technical "core" of the policy aspects of the book where I advocate the creation of something called Jared's tontine, which allows for an equitable and efficient sharing of longevity risk.

Finally, in Chapter 8, I conclude with a nontechnical review of how someone might explain, promote and justify tontine schemes for the twenty-first century. More importantly, I argue in favor of reintroducing (a modified version of) tontines given the immense pressure faced by individuals, pension plans, and government programs to help fund an increasingly long and uncertain life span. The taint of tontines can be mitigated with suitable adjustments to alleviate problems encountered during the last few centuries. Indeed, given the insurance industry's concern for longevity risk capacity, and its poor experience in managing the risk of guaranteed lifetime withdrawal benefits (aka GLWBs). I argue that tontine insurance is a triple-win proposition for individuals, corporations, and governments, and I provide some examples of tontine schemes (albeit with different names) around the world that are operating on a large and small scale.

My other agenda in writing this book – besides telling a good story about an intriguing period of late seventeenth-century financial history – is to offer some (graduate) lessons on the topics of actuarial present value, portfolio and investment choice, and financial option pricing, as well as insurance and pension economics. Indeed, perhaps an alternative title for this book could have been: *Tontinomics* (but, alas, my staid publisher would have none of that. Cambridge "will not publish books with titles that are not a word" I am told). Either way, and regardless of the title, I do hope you enjoy the tale.

A NOTE ON ANCIENT TIME AND MONEY

Flying over the international dateline can be a disorienting affair. Aside from the exhaustion that follows a ten- to fifteen-hour transpacific flight and the jet lag that comes from skipping multiple time zones, you also have to contend with a possible missing day. When you fly from east (say, San Francisco) to west (say, Sydney) you might end up leaving Monday night and arriving at your destination on Wednesday morning, skipping Tuesday for good. Your cell phone might have a tough time adjusting to this, as well. It's not just humans that are confused!

Well, that oddity is nothing compared with what it was like to cross the Channel from England to the Continent in 1693, when a large part of our historical narrative takes place. While a boat ride from Dover (England) to Calais (France) might have lasted a day or two at most, you actually arrived ten days *after* you left. Yes, the total trip time was 24 to 48 hours, but the arrival was ten calendar days later. Think of crossing the international dateline ten times in one flight and missing ten days along the way. It certainly sounds weird if this is the first time you read about it.

You see, back in the late seventeenth century, the English (still) adhered to the Julian calendar while the Continent had already switched over to the Gregorian calendar, which is the system we all use today and is named after Pope Gregory XIII. Although the Julian (named after Julius Caesar, but no longer used today) and the Gregorian calendars have the same number of months, there is a ten- to twelve-day gap between them. So, for example, if it was March 1 in England, it might be March 11 in France. I'll explain why and how this came to be in a moment.

To make matters even more confusing, in England the year began on March 25 and not January 1 like it does today. So, what all of this means is that a date listed as March 1692 (England, Julian) might actually be April 1693 (Gregorian) to a Frenchman, Spaniard, or German. The date depended on where you were, which sounds like something out of the theory of general relativity but was a fact of life.

The reason for this discrepancy between the two calendars had to do with summer weather during Easter – which the Catholic Church disliked. Bear with me and I'll explain what I mean by this, but for now I presume you see the problem as it relates to historical events taking place in England during the late seventeenth century. Every time I mention a date in this book you will be wondering, *Okay, when exactly did this take place?*

To avoid confusion or having to write two different dates on an ongoing basis, the convention I will adopt is one that is quite common for historical writing. When dealing with events taking place exclusively in England – for example, the date of February 3, when King William's tontine subscriptions began – I'll be referring to the Julian calendar. All events taking place everywhere else (for example, France) will use the Gregorian (new) calendar. Regardless of whether I'm referring to England or anywhere else, I will always make sure to use the proper (Gregorian) year. Henceforth, if and when you see the year 1693 (or any other year), rest assured that it will be the period from January 1 to December 31, even though some documents in England might have labeled the months from January to March, the year prior.[14]

Why this headache? Well, until 1582 the western world was (happily) using the Julian calendar. Dates were aligned across (relevant parts of) Christiandom. Everyone was on the same diary page, so to speak. But a problem was starting to creep into the calendar because of the extra February 29 added during leap years. There were simply too many of them over the course of a century and the calendar year was getting too long relative to the seasons. The (Julian) custom was to add a leap year every

---

[14] This can be maddening at times. An English newspaper with a date in late February 1693 would really be early March 1694, depending on the dating convention. Some authors use the convention 1693/1694 as an alternative. Perhaps all of this is overkill and more than the reader cares to know about dating in England.

four years, and the length of the (Julian) year was exactly 365.25 days. But because the solar year was slightly shorter, the vernal equinox was slipping back in time and was on March 11 by 1500. This, then, was delaying Easter into the summertime when it should have coincided with spring. Remember, the sun and seasons don't really care about the calendar, and something had to be done to move Easter back into the spring time.

Solution: delete some extra days from the existing calendar and eliminate a few leap years from the future calendar.

Bear with me here. The most important difference between the Julian and Gregorian system is in how they treated February 29. The old Julian system added them exactly every four years like clockwork. The new Gregorian system adds them every four years *except* for years that are exactly divisible by 100, also known as the centurial years. Those years do not have a February 29 added. Therefore, the year 1700 had a leap year in England (Julian) but not in the Continent (Gregorian).

Now, some readers might wonder; what about the year 2000? Wasn't that a leap year? Well, that is the exception to the new Gregorian rule. Centurial years are not leap years unless the year is divisible by 400. So the year 2000, the year 2400, and so on, will be leap years.

The first countries to adopt the Gregorian calendar were (heavily Catholic) Spain and Portugal. In those countries and a few others that followed, ten entire days were eliminated from the calendar. People went to bed on the evening of Thursday, October 4, 1582 (Julian), and woke up the next morning on Friday, October 15 (Gregorian). In those countries there was no October 5, or 6, all the way to October 14, 1582. Nobody was born on those days and nobody died then either. It is quite the accomplishment when you think about trying to coordinate this, and Pope Gregory XIII gets the credit (and name) for pulling it off.

Not all countries went along with (Catholic) Gregory and his new calendar. The Protestant countries, in particular England, the few U.S. colonies, and (what is today) Canada, didn't make the switch in 1582. As you might know, the Catholic pope wasn't very popular in England. So in those places the date of Thursday, October 4, 1582 (Julian), was followed by Friday, October 5, 1582 (Julian), and so on, for almost two centuries. Hence the gap across the Channel.

By the time the UK switched from Julian to Gregorian, the gap between the two calendars had now grown from ten days to eleven days. This is because of the extra leap year that the "Julians" had added (in the year 1700) that the "Gregorians" had avoided. But eventually even the English surrendered to the new system. On the evening of September 2, 1752 (Julian), the British went to sleep and woke up the next day to September 14, 1752 (Gregorian), skipping eleven days overnight. Needless to say, no (British) tontine nominee died on September 3, 4, or any other day until September 14. The dates didn't exist. This is an odd little curiosity that is only of interest to people working in a specific time frame (from 1582 to 1752), but that is exactly our historical period.

Now that we have (old) English *time* out of the way, let's move on to (old) English *money*. In the late seventeenth century the English were using a system of pounds, shillings, and pence (or penny). There were 12 pence to a shilling and then 20 shillings to a pound, so every English (or British) pound was worth 240 pence. Today, of course, the shillings are gone and there are only 100 pennies to the pound, but in those days the pound was a very large sum of much smaller pieces.

A British pound in the year 1693 was worth much more than a British pound today, owing to both inflation and the time value of money. Compounding £100 for 320 years at (a minimum) 2% real interest rate leads to almost £56,500.[15] At 3% real interest the £100 would grow to £1,282,070. Yes, millions and a very big difference between 2% and 3%. So, given all that would have transpired with markets and money over the 320 years, one never really knows what inflation-adjusted interest rate to use when you move money across centuries. It is part science and part art.

Perhaps a better sense of what money would have been worth today is to examine what people were paid at the time. According to historians, the average industrial wage for a laborer in the late seventeenth century was about £16 per year.[16] So the £100 tontine minimum investment was about six years' worth of salary and definitely not a trivial sum. Today, if the average industrial wage (in 2015) is approximately £30,000, then the equivalent (present-day) cost of one share of King William's tontine would be £180,000 (equivalent to almost US$300,000). So, whether the £100 in the year 1693 is worth millions, a few hundred thousand or a mere fifty thousand pounds today, the tontine was most definitely an investment for the rich.

With that out of the way, let's move on to how a tontine really works.

---

[15] The formula is $100(1.02)^{320} = 56500.84$.

[16] See C. G. Lewin (2003), which is quite relevant to the topic of this book, a source for some of the material I discuss later and covers pensions and insurance in more depth. It is a great reference for students of insurance and pension history.

Tontine's Economic Origins: Cheaper Debt

THE FINANCIAL PATH TO LONG-TERM BORROWING

To properly appreciate tontines and the rationale for their existence, one needs to understand the process by which monarchs borrowed money prior to the modern era. Imagine for a moment that you are the king of England sometime during the seventeenth century and that you need £1 million rather urgently, to build some boats, or perhaps wage a war against a mortal enemy or to support your many (illegitimate) children. Now, being that the Middle Ages are over and the Divine Rights of Kings is no longer in fashion, you can't just pilfer the money from your loyal subjects. Sure, you might be able to tax your citizens – which is a far more palatable form of confiscation – but that process takes time to implement and it certainly won't generate the million pounds very quickly. Like anyone who has needed large sums of money in a hurry, you really have no choice but to *borrow* the money.

Now – whether you are a seventeenth-century king or a twenty-first-century commoner – there are essentially three methods by which to structure such a loan and eventually pay back your creditors:

1. You repay the principal you borrowed plus the interest accrued, all at the very end of the term of the loan in one big bullet payment.
2. You make periodic interests payment on the loan and then return or payback the original principal at the very end.
3. You use the common method used to finance your home and car, which is you make relatively constant payments that blend interest and principal over time, so that the entire loan is paid off by the very end. This is known as amortizing the loan.

As you might discern, method number one – pay all the interest and principal at the very end – isn't very appealing or practical. Eventually, when the loan term is over and it is time to pay it all back, you will have an even bigger "problem" than you do today. Method number two is more palatable, although it still creates the "problem" of paying off the large original principal at the end of the term. Finally, method number three is the most appealing and easier to implement because it spreads your "problem" over time. If you amortize the loan and – as the king of England – combine it with a fiscal policy of taxing your citizens and subjects, you can use the tax payments to pay off the loan and diffuse your obligations.

Needless to say, there is an unspecified and nefarious fourth alternative by which you borrow £1 million using any of the first three payment methods described above and then basically default on your financial obligations and leave your creditors (angry and) impoverished. Of course, you can't employ the borrow-then-default strategy for long. Your creditors and citizens might soon rebel and at the very least they will quickly learn not to lend you (or your relatives) any more money.[1] Kings have done this from time to time, including the infamous Stop of the Exchequer in 1672, when King Charles II (who was the uncle of King William III) defaulted on his debts to goldsmith bankers in London.[2] This action irreversibly damaged the Crown's personal credit and was one of the factors that led to Parliament taking over the nation's financial obligations. I will return to the problem of default and credit risk later on.

These three methods might sound rather abstract, so here is a detailed example to understand the magnitude involved. I will use and reference these numbers again when I (eventually) get to tontines, so it's worth familiarizing yourself with them.

For example, if you (the king) borrow £1 million for a term of twenty-five years, and manage to negotiate an interest rate of 6% per year (which is 0.5% per month), you can agree to pay it back using one of three methods. You can dispense £5,000 per month to your creditors – which is the 0.5% monthly interest rate times the million pounds – and then return or payback the entire £1 million at the end of the twenty-five years. This was method (2) described above. In contrast, method (1) involves not

---

[1] Unless you are the government of Argentina in the twenty-first century.

[2] See Roseveare (1991, chap. 2), Horsefield (1982), and Nichols (1971) for a general discussion of borrowing by King Charles II and his brother James II, prior to the glorious English revolution. I want to emphasize again that the monarchy borrowed money, and large sums of it, prior to the tontine loan of 1693. But, these were closer to "personal" loans and most certainly were not backed or guaranteed by the English Parliament or people. The king owed the money.

making any interest payments for twenty-five years and then paying back the entire loan with interest at the end of the term. Alas, with the power of compound interest the outstanding loan will have grown to £4,465,000 by the end of the twenty-five years.[3] So, as I mentioned, with method (1) you will have replaced a relatively small "problem" with an even bigger one in twenty-five years.

Alternatively and much more practically you can *amortize* the loan over twenty-five years and pay it back in equal installments that blend interest and principal. This, mind you, is method (3) noted above and something every modern homeowner with a conventional mortgage has learned to do.[4] Namely, to cover the £1 million loan, you agree to pay exactly £6,443 every month for twenty-five years.[5] For now, trust me that this number works out. The extra £1,443 that you pay in the first month, above and beyond the £5,000 (interest based on the 0.5% per month) reduces the outstanding principal. A blend of interest and principal neutralizes the entire £1 million by the end of the twenty-five years. There will be no bullet or final payment to make and outgoing cash flows are quite smooth over time. The business of "smoothness" is important and something I'll return to much later on (in Chapter 7). From a purely financial basis, all three loan methods must have a present value of exactly £1 million so that you pay back the loan eventually. The amortization method can also be described as a *term certain annuity*. The constant payments of £6,443 per month are a 300-month annuity whose present value is £1 million.

Needless to say, all this is a refresher of undergraduate Finance Theory 101, which you might be well acquainted with. In fact, the formula that links the monthly (£6,443) payment, the interest (0.5%) rate, the term (300 months) of the loan, and the amount (£1 million) borrowed, can be expressed mathematically as follows:

$$P = \frac{rB}{1 - 1/(1+r)^n} = \frac{(0.005)1000000}{1 - (1.005)^{-300}} = 6443.014$$

[3] The formula for the amount you owe is £1 million multiplied by the (1.005) monthly interest rate factor, to the power of 300 months.

[4] Until the mid-1930s during the Great Depression in the United States, home loans were structured using method (2), under which a large bullet payment was due at the end of the term. The administration of President Herbert Hoover made it easier for banks to offer amortizing mortgages, the way they are structured today.

[5] The present value of 6,443 for 300 months at a rate of 0.5% is exactly equal to one million.

In this formula[6] – which I promise is the first of only two formulas in the entire book – the letter P denotes the monthly payment, the letter B denotes the amount borrowed, the letter r denotes the interest rate charged, and the letter n denotes the number of periods or months over which the payments (P) will be spread in order to pay off the loan (B). Note that if the interest rate were doubled – from 0.5% per month to 1.0% per month – the corresponding (monthly payment) number on the left-hand side of the formula would be 10,532.24 instead.

There are many variations on the theme of constant monthly payments. You might make interest-only payments for a few years (which is £5,000) and then larger (than £6,443) monthly payments for the remainder of the twenty-five years to compensate. Or you could make much larger (than £6,443) payments for many years and perhaps pay off the entire loan before the twenty-five years are over. These are all valid alternatives but unnecessary complications for the purposes of understanding tontine loans – which is my eventual objective here.

It is worth noting that the idea of *amortizing* a loan and paying it off slowly over time – as opposed to interest only and then principal – is a more recent phenomenon. In fact, this amortization innovation – and it was innovative when it was introduced in the sixteenth century – was done partially to obscure or hide the actual interest rate that was underlying the loan.[7] Recall that usury, or borrowing money, was illegal and highly restricted for much of the previous two millennia so borrowing via amortization served some nonfinancial purposes, as well.

Another complication I would like to bypass at this point is the issue of interest rates underlying the loan. While all three examples above assumed a rate of 6% per year (or 0.5% per month), in practice the structure of the loan might impact the interest rate, as well. So, for example, if you (the king) weren't expected to make any interest or principal payments for twenty-five years, I suspect the "market" (i.e., the lenders or creditors) might charge you a higher rate, compared with a situation in which you make steady and constant payments during the next twenty-five years. A bond trader on Wall Street would note that the duration *of* the loan would impact the interest rate charged *for* the loan. As I said though, let's keep things simple

---

[6] A number of financial scientists were aware of this formula and generated tables of "present value factors" in the mid-seventeenth century. See Poitras (2000, chap. 5).

[7] See Geisst (2013) for a discussion and very thorough review of the history of usury and debt.

for starters. Interest rates are constant. Bear with me here; I'll get to tontines in a moment.

Who Do You Borrow from and at What Rate?

Regardless of the terms of the loan, you (the king) could source or borrow the money from either one unique individual creditor or from a company (like a bank) or from a syndicate of people, each contributing a small amount to the loan. If the loan were syndicated, the group of people sharing the burden of the loan would invest £1 million and would allocate the £6,443 monthly payments among themselves. Sharing payments and therefore risk is a very important concept here, because as I alluded to earlier, borrowers (even kings) could default. The danger or hazard was spread among the syndicate. Investors and lenders were aware of the importance of investment diversification – even though they might not have described it in those terms – well before twentieth-century portfolio theory.

For example, if five people contributed £200,000 to the loan syndicate (and the underlying interest rate was 6% per year, which is 0.5% per month), they would split the monthly payouts – which the king would be paying – of £6,443 for a total of approximately £1,289 each, over twenty-five years. Naturally, the bigger or larger the syndicate size, the less each member would contribute. Obviously, the monthly payouts – if we can call them that – from their individual contributions to the loan syndicate would be lower, as well. In an extreme case, if a total of (say) 10,000 investors each contributed £100 toward a million pound loan, then each investor would be entitled to (a mere) £0.6443 per month, or £7.732 per year. Recall, the underlying interest rate was 6% per year, but the extra £1.732 (approximately) above and beyond the £6 is the amortizing portion explained above.

I would like to emphasize the distinction between the underlying interest rate (0.50% per month) and the so-called cash yield, which is 0.6443/100 or 0.64% per month. The former number (0.50%) represents a true economic interest rate – often called the *internal rate of return* (IRR) – and the latter (0.64%) number is simply a blended measure of ongoing revenue or cash flow. Okay. Enough said about the interest technicalities.

Let's go back to method (2), which I described above. It calls for interest only during the twenty-five-year term and then a final payment of principal at the end. This might also be an option for the syndicate of lenders. In that case, the group of 10,000 shareholders would split £5,000 each month, for a £0.5 dividend, and then receive their original £100 investment back in twenty-five years. There are many ways to structure a syndicated loan to a king, and you will learn about one final innovative way of doing so in a moment. (Hint: It's called a tontine.)

I'll pause here with a note on terminology. When one person lends money to another person I'll call it an outright loan and the amortized payments a blend of interest and principal. In contrast, when a syndicate or group of people band together and do the same, for most of this book I'll use terms like *investors*, *shares*, and *dividends*. This might be a slight abuse of notation considering that I'm referring to fixed-income bond-like products, but in reality these syndicate units were really treated like – what we today might call – mutual fund shares. The individual rights to payment could be sold, traded, or bequeathed (or lost.) So, I will stick to investors, shares, and dividends as opposed to borrowers, promissory notes, and interest payments, unless I need to differentiate between the two.

Of course, none of this is hypothetical or imaginary. Royalty borrowed money, syndicates lent the money, and payments were made. But – and this is key – most kings in the seventeenth century would have been lucky to pay (only) 6% interest on their twenty-five-year loans. I'll delve into this topic – actual interest rates – in Chapter 4, but for now, suffice it to say that 6% was a bargain.[8] A more realistic interest rate for a twenty-five-year loan might have been 12% per year (1% per month), and even that inexpensive rate would only apply to the best of monarchs.

Now, if you run the same numbers under a 12% interest rate, the amortized (fixed payments for twenty-five years) loan would result in payments of £10,532 per month, which is 63% more than the £6,443. Once again, the present value of the £10,532 per month over a period of twenty-five years is also £1 million. The reason you need the higher payments to achieve the same present value is because the underlying interest rate is higher (12% versus 6%).

This again is undergraduate Finance Theory 101 based on equation 1, which is also taught in business schools everywhere in the twenty-first century. But I must admit that it wasn't an easy exercise or calculation for merchants and bankers to compute in the seventeenth century. In fact, many people (in the twenty-first century) without advanced training in finance would be hard pressed to work out or solve for the embedded interest rate (the IRR) on a twenty-five-year, million pound loan in which the annual payments are £6,443 × 12 = £77,316 or £10,532 × 12 = £126,384 or any number in between. To do this properly, you have to invert the main

---

[8] For those interested in the history of interest rates during the seventeenth century, for example, see the classic reference book by Homer and Sylla (2005, chaps. 11 and 12).

Table 2.1. *Different ways of borrowing £1 million over twenty-five years*

	6% Nominal annual interest			12% Nominal annual interest		
	Balloon loan (i.)	Interest only (ii.)	Amortize (iii.)	Balloon loan (i.)	Interest only (ii.)	Amortize (iii.)
Monthly Payment	N.A.	£5,000	£6,443	N.A.	£10,000	£10,532
Terminal Payment	£4,465,000	£1,000,000	N.A.	£19,788,500	£1,000,000	N.A.

Note: In all cases, the present value (PV) of the loan is exactly £1 million.

formula I presented earlier and solve the interest rate. It's not unreasonable to suggest that some (unsophisticated) lenders might view an annual payment of £77,316 as implying a 7.73% interest rate, when in fact the underlying IRR really is 6.0%. Remember, again, the difference between "cash or payout yield" and true interest rate.

Smoke and mirrors aside, working out the monthly payments on the loan – or the implied interest rate you are really receiving – is only half the problem. The borrower has to get subscribers (lenders, investors) to actually make the loan. And if the 12% interest (a promise of £10,532 per month) wasn't enough, he might have to offer an even greater interest rate, especially during times of turmoil and stress. Sure, the king could borrow the money and make no payments at all for a while (zero interest?), but then he would have to (eventually, somehow) payback the original £1 million plus some accumulated interest. So, there always was an underlying interest rate. Hopefully all of this is clear.

Here is the bottom line. Kings wanted to borrow money at the lowest possible interest rate, but lenders and investors wanted to get the highest possible rate, as well as to get compensated for any risks they might be taking. Table 2.1 provides a summary of the different ways in which a twenty-five-year loan can be structured under two (6% and 12%) interest rates. It is a review of the numbers I presented earlier. Note the difference between (i.) balloon loan, (ii.) interest-only loan, and (iii.) amortizing loan, all with different cash flow patterns over time. There is nothing new here.

So, I finally get to the raison d'être of the tontine annuity scheme proposed by Lorenzo de Tonti, a man you will learn much more about in Chapter 3. The last few pages all boil down to the next sentence. The original intent of a tontine was to make it *easier and cheaper* for the king or queen or Parliament (or any other government entity) to borrow money. At a cynical level of abstraction, the intent of the tontine annuity loan was to borrow at (say) 6% and make it look as if you were really paying (say) 12%.

In some sense the intent of the tontine annuity was to fool investors by introducing an element of lottery or bet and thus appealing to their *gambling instinct*. Investors or syndicate members *might* accept a lower interest rate than they should have otherwise using a conventional loan structure, but their financial and economic loss was compensated by the "fun of the game" or distorted by unrealistic expectations about their longevity. Yes, this is not a very logical or rational explanation and would be anathema to what economists call the efficient market hypothesis (EMH), which argues that markets in aggregate can't be fooled.

The rationale for tontine-based financing versus a conventional loan is a behavioral economics argument pure and simple. Alas, I am getting ahead of myself here. First I still must explain how tontines work, exactly, and how they are related to amortizing loans.

CAN AMORTIZATIONS FOOL INVESTORS FOR LIFE?

Think back to the above-mentioned syndicate. Assume that (market, fair) interest rates are indeed 12% and that you (the king) should rightfully be making payments of £10,532 for the next twenty-five years on a million pound loan. See Table 2.1, again, for reference. But imagine now – to save a few pounds – that you offered the following deal to the syndicate. You would agree to make payments of (only) £10,200 per month. But instead of making the payments for exactly twenty-five years, you would pay each member of the syndicate his or her dividends for as long as they were still alive – even if it was longer than twenty-five years! If a member of the syndicate lived for fifty years, he would get double the payments. If he lived for seventy-five more years, he would receive triple the payments, but if he died tomorrow his heirs would get nothing! Now you (the king) would be taking a chance that your syndicate members would all live a very long time – and we will get to that risk in a moment. The question at hand is whether syndicate members would accept the £10,200 per month *for life* instead of the £10,532 for twenty-five years that you should be paying (assuming interest rates of 12% per year).

Astute readers – and certainly astute investors – would refer to the formula displayed earlier. They would invert the relationship linking the payment (10,200) and the interest rate (1% per month) and solve for the implied time horizon, denoted by the letter n. Doing so would actually show that the break-even horizon, or implied time horizon, is exactly 395 months or approximately thirty-three years.

$$P = \frac{rB}{1 - 1/(1+r)^n} = \frac{(0.01)1000000}{1 - (1.01)^{-395}} = 10,200$$

The key here is to locate (via trial and error) a number for the exponent (n) so that the left-hand side exactly equals 10,200. So, if the member of the syndicate thought they would live (much) longer than thirty-three years, this sort of deal might be appealing. Perhaps only (young, healthy) members might sign up for such a syndicated loan! Either way it's unlikely that you (the king) would save much money by borrowing money using the method I just described as opposed to the amortizing loan over twenty-five years. And if you tried to push the monthly payments for life too low – say, to £8,000 instead of £10,200 – the syndicate would balk at the offer.

The interest they should be charging you (the king) is 1% per month, and so the £8,000 wouldn't even cover the interest, let alone any repayment of principal. Offering to make constant payments for life instead of over a fixed time horizon is unlikely to fool people and will probably not reduce your overall cost of borrowing.

We Are Still Not There

No, as you might have guessed by now, this arrangement isn't a tontine. What I have just described is a conventional life annuity loan, pure and simple. And it isn't imaginary or hypothetical. This is (also) how money was borrowed at the time, and I'll tell you more about the history in Chapter 4. It's unclear whether the king would win or lose from this deal, because of the *longevity risk* that your syndicate might live longer than expected. Moreover, the syndicate members themselves might balk at this arrangement if they worried about not living the full number of years needed to break even.[9] This method of borrowing was an interesting variation on the amortization schedule. DB pensions are structured this way. Fixed payments for life.

The tontine annuity loan – finally, we are there – is similar to borrowing money via a life annuity structure, but one in which there is an added small

---

[9]   I'll abstain from the temptation to make a whole bunch of jokes about the king's perverse incentive to murder his subjects under such a scheme, but I return to the topic of nefarious activities in Chapter 5.

twist, a twist that I suspect you have by now guessed or remember from Chapter 1. You (the king) make dividend payments for as long as syndicate members are alive, but when they die the *payments are redistributed to other members* of the syndicate who originally lent the money. Unlike a conventional life annuity where the king is exempt from making payments to annuitants upon their death, with the tontine annuity, the payments will continue regardless to other members of the syndicate. On the flip side, under this sort of structure the king can predict with reasonable accuracy what the outflow might be. He only has to concern himself with forecasting how long the longest-lived syndicate member will survive as opposed to the entire statistical distribution of deaths. I get back to the embedded longevity risks (many times) later on in Chapter 7.

Now that we have arrived at our destination, there is some terminology to clarify. Mechanically, the tontine annuity loan had three participants. There was the *investor* (who purchased and owned the shares), the *annuitant* (who received the ongoing income payments), and the *nominee* on whose life the payments depended. In many cases the annuitant and the investor were the same (older, male) person while the nominee was a separate (younger, female) individual. Occasionally the investor was also the annuitant and the nominee. That is really the simplest case. The investor could bequeath or transfer the shares to anyone and payments would continue to the new individual, as long as the nominee was still alive.

The tontine annuity loan would be defined by its subscription price (say, £100), its *guaranteed* cash yield, which was the monthly (or annual) payment that investors would receive as long as their nominee was still alive. In contrast, the *actual* or realized cash yield depended on the number of other nominees that were still alive at the time of payment. Each surviving member was guaranteed to receive their lifetime pension, which would increase (proportionally) as the other beneficiaries died. There was a guaranteed payment and the actual payment, which could only be higher.

A Detailed Example of Cash Flows

Going back to the million pound loan, imagine that the sponsor of a tontine (e.g., the king) offered to pay a guaranteed dividend of £8,000 per month to a syndicate of investors. Yes, this number is quite low compared with the £10,200 or £10,500 payments discussed above, but this is a tontine loan. The £8,000 would be paid to the syndicate as long as at least one of the nominees, each selected by the individual syndicate members, was still alive. Let's further imagine a syndicate of five investors advancing £200,000 each, expecting at least £8,000 / 5 = £1,600 per month (a cash yield of 0.8% per

Table 2.2. *Tontine paying £8,000 to a syndicate of five investors*

Number of surviving nominees	Monthly payment to annuitant
All Five Alive	£1,600
Four Alive	£2,000
Three Alive	£2,667
Two Alive	£4,000
Last Survivor	£8,000

Note: Each member of the syndicate invests £200,000, which entitles their annuitant to a guaranteed £1,600 per month as long as their nominee is still alive.

month or 9.6% per year) as long as their nominee lived. The five syndicate members will obviously earn more than the guaranteed £1,600 if and when the nominees selected by other members die. Table 2.2 provides a summary of the different payout possibilities.

Notice that the guaranteed £1,600 per month, or 19,200 per year on an original investment of 200,000 is equivalent to a guaranteed cash yield of 9.6%. Think of this as the worst-case scenario. Even if every other nominee is still alive, the syndicate member would be assured the 9.6% payout per year.

The investor whose nominee was the last survivor would be entitled to the entire £8,000 per month, or an astounding £96,000 per year, which, on a 200,000 investment, is an actual cash yield of 48% per year. This is not 4.8%. This is 48% per year. The catch is that your nominee must be the last survivor among the group of five. Even if your nominee was among the last two survivors, your monthly payment would be £4,000, which is £48,000 per year and a cash yield of 24% per year.

The individual investor might accept the inferior deal because of the enticing or alluring possibility that their nominee will be among the last remaining survivors and earn the entire £8,000 dividend.

ADAM SMITH'S BEHAVIORAL ECONOMIC INSIGHT

From a financial economic (supply side) point of view, an interesting question is whether the tontine can actually be a cheaper way to borrow. In a perfectly functioning capital market people can't be fooled. They would properly solve for the total interest rate and say: "Hey, the king is only paying the syndicate £8,000 per month, when he should have been paying us £10,532 per month." I could imagine the more quantitative member of the group – likely a banker from Amsterdam or Geneva – saying: "Assuming twenty-five years of payments, this leads to an implied interest rate of 8.42% when we should be charging him 12%, given his risk profile." As a whole, the syndicate might not agree or like the terms. But individual members might think that as long as the person they nominate is healthier (than average) and a few other nominees die early, the monthly dividend will grow over time and exceed what it would have been under the 12% interest rate they should have charged.

In the language of modern behavioral economics, the tontine is a cheaper form of debt – for the seventeenth-century king – because of the psychological biases ingrained in us all. Namely, we look at the possibility of that very large dividend we might receive – if our nominee is still alive – and we allow that (lottery ticket dream?) to cloud our better judgment. Sure, this may sound rather vague and psychological, but one of the greatest and earliest economists said the exact same thing. I believe this was precisely what the Scottish economist Adam Smith (1723–1790) had in mind when he wrote in *The Wealth of Nations*, [Book V, Chapter III, Part V].

> from the confidence which every man naturally has in his own good fortune, the principle upon which is founded the success of all lotteries, [the tontine] annuity generally sells for some-thing more than it is worth. In countries where it is usual for government to raise money by granting annuities, tontines are upon this account generally preferred to annuities for separate lives.

If you read between Adam Smith's lines, I think he is saying that governments would save money – compared with issuing regular debt or annuities – by using tontine financing. And there you have it. The greatest economist ever, Adam Smith, endorsed tontines.

It Never Was about Retirement Pensions

As you can tell by now, the tontine annuity loan was never about creating products to help individuals manage the risks (financial cost) of living a longer life than expected. It was never designed as longevity insurance, and it certainly wasn't created as a pension for the syndicate, although I'm sure some investors purchased it for these reasons and it was promoted as a sort of longevity hedge by Lorenzo de Tonti himself. It was only much, much later on that the tontine annuity concept was co-opted by insurance companies and pension funds. For now I'll summarize as follows. The tontine annuity loan was designed *in theory* to fool people into lending money at a lower interest rate than they would have otherwise demanded or insisted on. Whether or not this worked in practice is a topic for another chapter. I'll return to some of the behavioral benefits of tontines, as a way to overcome a phenomenon known as the "annuity puzzle" later on as well.

TONTINES vs. ANNUITIES: THE STOCHASTIC PV

Without getting too technical, Figure 2.1 provides graphical indication of the difference between a (King William style) tontine and a (more familiar, modern) life annuity. It plots the present value of the cash flows or income you will receive on a 100 unit (dollars or pounds or euros) investment, weighted by the probability of getting those cash flows or payments.

Here is how to interpret the charts, which are called "densities" or a "density" in the language of probability theory. Both curves (or densities) are centered around the value of 100 units, which is the amount of money that it costs in this hypothetical example to purchase the investment. The tontine pays (a guaranteed) yield of 5.6% or 5.6 units per year, per 100 investment up front. The annuity offers a yield of 7.54% or 7.54 units per year. These are the economically fair payouts for the two different instruments, meaning that if you didn't really care about risk, you would be indifferent between the two. The expected discounted value of both cash flows over time is the same. The only reason you might choose one versus the other is personal preferences for risk and consumption. Another way of thinking about Figure 2.1 – which was generated under the assumption that 1,000 people have purchased the tontine – is via the old joke that asks: What is more valuable? $1,000 worth of gold bars or $1,000 worth of silver coins? Answer: They are worth the same. But the gold bugs will select one and the silver lovers will pick the other. It is as simple as that.

Notice that the right-hand tail of the tontine density is much "thicker" compared with the annuity density, since there is a chance that you will live a very long time (and others will not) and you will end up earning much more than 100 units in present value. With the tontine there is also a chance that you will die (early) and regret not having purchased the annuity (instead), which would have paid 7.54 units instead of the 5.6 units.

This is why the left-hand tail of the density picture for the annuity is under the tontine. Think of each point on the vertical y-axis as the corresponding probability of receiving a benefit whose present value is the horizontal x-axis. So, if somebody were to ask you: "What are the chances

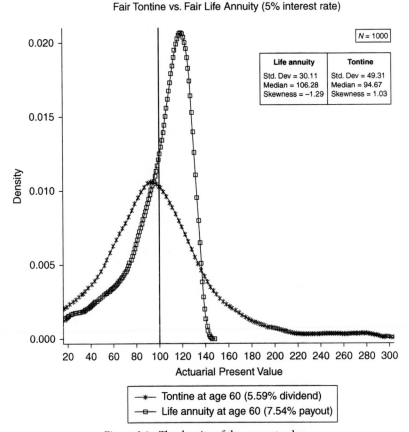

Figure 2.1. The density of the present value.

I'll get 60 (dollars, euros) or less back from the tontine?" The answer is the area under the curve from 60 to the left – which is about 20%. If somebody asks about the probability of getting less than 60 back from the annuity, the answer – that is, area under the annuity density to the left of 60 – is about 15%. The left tail is "worse," but the right tail is "better" when buying a tontine. If all this talk of densities and tails is too abstract, for now simply ask yourself: Do I understand the difference between a tontine and a life annuity? That is really all that is needed at this point.

The next section offers yet another way to think about the risk exposure or the liability from issuing (i.e., borrowing money) using the tontine principle.

LAST ONE TO DIE PLEASE SHUT OFF THE LIGHTS

Remember that when an insurance company or pension plan promises to make annuity payments to a group of retirees, each individual death (is welcomed and) reduces their obligations just a little bit. Each death represents one additional payment that doesn't have to be made. Every year the company or fund monitors deaths very closely, and they start to worry if realized mortality rates are lower than expected. In the big scheme of things, if the average age of death for retirees increases from (say) age eighty to (say) age eighty-five, this will have an enormous impact on the liabilities. Multiply the extra five years of (average) payments by the hundreds of annuitants or pensioners and you arrive at a fairly large sum. Longevity risk, as it is referred to, is quite scary for a pension fund or insurance company.

But with a tontine scheme, the situation is quite different. The individual patterns and timings of death will have absolutely no impact on the issuer paying the bills. The king, city, or government really does not care whether "on average" retirees live to eighty or retirees live to eighty-five. They don't care (so much) about the average of *who dies when*. They only worry about (or plan for) when the last person (finally) dies, which is when their obligations will terminate. Here is my main point. The age at which the last nominee will (finally) die is relatively invariant to the size of the tontine pool. The chances are that your "longest liver" will be a centenarian. That's all that matters. Let's examine this longevity risk issue in greater detail. You will see that whether you have a pool of 100 or 1,000 or 10,000 nominees, the oldest "liver" will survive to roughly the same age. And if the longest "liver" (yes, this sounds awkward) actually survives another year or two, this will take place so far in the future that its impact today (in discounted terms) is quite small. Table 2.3 makes this point in a more rigorous manner.

Here is how to read and interpret Table 2.3. Start with the second column, which displays the results assuming a tontine scheme with (only) one nominee. In this case the sponsor of the tontine is scheduled to make payments until the one nominee dies. No, this isn't really a tontine – since there is only one person in the scheme – but it helps set the stage for what follows. According to the results listed in the table, there is a 50% probability this (one) sixty-five-year-old nominee will die at or before the age of 86.3, a 90% probability he will die at or before the age of 97.5, a 99% chance that he will die at or before the age of 104.2, and so on. By the way, these numbers have been calibrated or based on mortality rates for (typical, healthy) sixty-five-year-olds. As you can see, there is a 99.99% probability this (one) nominee will be dead before the age of 111. Stated differently, the

Table 2.3. *At what age will the last nominee die?*

Probability confidence level of ...	Size of initial tontine pool of sixty-five-year-olds			
	N = One nominee	N = 100 nominees	N = 250 nominees	N = 400 nominees
50.00%	86.3	105.0	106.6	107.4
90.00%	97.5	108.1	109.3	109.9
99.00%	104.2	111.0	112.0	112.4
99.90%	108.2	113.2	114.0	114.4
99.99%	111.0	115.0	115.7	116.0

Note: Assumes Gompertz mortality with parameters (m = 88.72, b = 10). Explained in Appendix A.

probability the last surviving nominee from this tontine (consisting of one person) survives to the age of 111 – and the sponsor has to make payments for more than forty-six years – is 0.01% or 1 in 10,000. The chances are slim, and after forty-six years your obligations to this one annuitant will be over.

Now what happens when the tontine pool is increased to 100 people? As you can see from the same table (in the third column), the probability that the last remaining survivor lives to become a centenarian is quite high. In fact, there is a 50% probability that the last remaining survivor will live to age 105. In fact, if you want 90% confidence, then you (the sponsor) better plan to 108. If you want 99.99% confidence, then you (the sponsor) better plan for fifty years of payments, to the age of 115.

Notice the trend in the table as I increase the initial size of the tontine. With only one nominee, the range between 50% and 99.99% is age 86 to 111. But once you have 400 nominees the range decreases. Now it is between age 107 and age 116, which is a much smaller range of uncertainty. And although I didn't display this in the table, if the tontine was set up with a million people, the age at which the final person would die is somewhere between 115 and 120.

For those readers who are interested in *how* these numbers are computed, the key is to compute the probability that everyone is dead by a certain age and then subtract 1 from this number to arrive at the probability that at least one person is alive.[10]

---

[10] If p denotes the probability of survival to a given time t, then $(1-p)$ is the probability of death by t. Now, given the assumed independence of these events, $(1-p)^N$ is the probability that all N nominees are dead by time t. So, $1-(1-p)^N$ is the probability that at least one person is alive. This, by definition, is also the probability that the sponsor is still making payment to the tontine pool.

Here (again) is the main takeaway from all of this. When you have a reasonably large enough pool of nominees in the tontine scheme, you will probably be making payments (to someone) until they are 110 to 115 years. So, whether your pool consists of 100 nominees, 250 nominees, or 400 nominees, the odds are high that you (the sponsor) will be "on the hook" for fifty years, assuming everyone starts at the age of sixty-five.

But – and this is critical – whether the last one lives to the age of 114 or 115 or 120 doesn't really make a big difference! Remember, you (the sponsor) have to make the entire payment until the last nominee dies and the discounted value of a $1 payment fifty years from now isn't that far from the discounted value of a $1 payment forty-nine years from now. *You aren't exposed to that much longevity risk when you run a tontine scheme.*

As I said earlier, now compare this with an insurance company or pension fund that commits to make annuity payments to annuitants for as long as they are still alive. As the individual nominees drop out of the pool (i.e., die) the sponsor's liabilities decline in a corresponding manner. Each individual death makes a difference. But (again) with the tontine, the pattern and timing of individual deaths make little if any difference. The only thing that matters is when the last nominee dies, and that is relatively easier to predict. To conclude, a tontine system poses little longevity risk to the entity standing behind the tontine. But in the life annuity business the risk is ever present.

3

A Most Curious Will(iam) and Older
Than You Think

LIFE AND DEATH IN ELIZABETHAN ENGLAND

In the year 1581, in the county of Lancashire in the northwest part of England, a wealthy landowner by the name of Alexander Houghton died without legitimate heirs to inherit his wealth and continue his title. Alexander Houghton was a nobleman with a large estate, a household with more than thirty servants, and substantial income from his properties and investments. Alexander loved the arts, theater, and music and supported a troupe of players from a local acting company in Lea Hall, Lancashire.

Although Alexander's half brother and brother-in-law inherited a part of the estate, he left provisions in his will that the younger servants and employees be given permanent employment with his relatives and that they be granted permanent financial support. All in all, Alexander left a substantial fraction of the estate to his devoted servants and employees. As anyone who has watched and enjoyed the PBS television show *Downton Abbey* can attest, the relationship between master and servant was quite close in England, having been developed over many years and generations.

However – and this is where things get interesting – Alexander Houghton didn't quite hand over a lump sum of money to his favored group of servants. Rather, he set up a long-term arrangement, which was equivalent to a strange sort of retirement pension.

First, the will specified that the annual rents from properties contained in the estate, amounting to about 330 shillings per year, be distributed among eleven of his most favored employees. It appears that the oldest was to receive 66 shillings per year, the next oldest 40 shillings per year, and so on, all the way to the youngest, who was to receive 13 shillings per year for life. These sums might seem trivial by today's standards, but in the mid-sixteenth century the average industrial wage was 125 shillings a year.[1] So, even 13 shillings per year was a very nice pension annuity, especially for the youngest one, who was only seventeen at the time.

The income or cash for the pensions, paid to the servants, was to be sourced from the annual rent charges on property owned by Houghton in the village of Withnell, which is part of Lancashire. The trustee of the will was given explicit instructions to collect the approximately 330 shillings every year and distribute them to the annuitants, that is, the beneficiaries of Alexander Houghton's generosity.

Now, at this point, you might be wondering why I would start the long journey ahead of us with a benevolent and childless English landowner who was kind enough to grant a pension to his devoted employees when he died. There is nothing shocking or surprising in this arrangement, and last wills and testaments have been used to perpetuate the deceased's wishes since ancient Greece and Rome.

But, you see, Alexander Houghton added a minor provision to his will that made his generosity unlike any other pension – and is at the logical core of the main thesis of this book.

I will quote directly (in more modern English) from his will.[2]

> The portion of those that die shall be equally divided among those that shall survive, so that the final survivor among them shall have for his life the whole rent from the property.

Effectively, when one of the eleven servants died, the income he or she would have been entitled to – instead of going to spouses and children, which is quite common in today's pension – would instead be distributed to the other servants who were still alive. In other words, the pension of those still living would increase as other members of the group died off. The entire 330 shillings would be paid out to the group each and every year, regardless of how many annuitants were still alive. Only when the final annuitant died would the 330 shillings revert to the estate.

Why Alexander Houghton chose this particular structure – you die and I win – to disperse the assets in his estate isn't quite clear. At first glance, this might appear to be a most unfair arrangement. Why should the survivors

---

[1]   Lewin (2003).

[2]   My source for the information about Alexander Houghton (sometimes spelled Hoghton) and the provisions in his will is Bearman (2002).

benefit from the death of others? Shouldn't the income continue to a spouse or perhaps beneficiaries? In fact, the morbid reader might worry about possible shenanigans to accelerate the demise of others (aka moral hazard), which is something I address in a later chapter.

When you think about it carefully and through the prism of economics, there are some good reasons why a pension *should be* structured this way. Most importantly, it is much easier to budget and forecast how much a pension will actually cost the provider or sponsor in any given year. In the above case, it was exactly 330 shillings each and every year, as long as at least one servant was still alive.

I will try to convince you – multiple times within this book – that Alexander Houghton was "onto something" when he structured his will (and their pension) this way. But even if you disagree with the merits or fairness of such a scheme, it was Alexander Houghton's will after all and he was free to do with his wealth, income, and property as he pleased.

Of course, we will recognize Alexander Houghton's arrangement as a *tontine annuity*, named after the famed Italian entrepreneur Lorenzo de Tonti (1602–1684) of whom I promise you will learn much more later on.

Alexander Houghton structured his will's income provision as a tontine scheme. As you might note from the dates at the beginning of this story, Alexander Houghton wrote his last will and testament (and likely died) in 1581, initiating a tontine scheme among his eleven servants almost a century before King William's first national tontine in 1693, and even before Lorenzo de Tonti invented and named tontines in the mid-1650s.

In the first of many surprises, I note that private tontine schemes – of which I will describe others – were quite popular in England. In fact, tontines were extremely popular in England during the seventeenth and eighteenth centuries. Tontines were referred to in official documents as life annuities with group survivorship benefits, or graded annuities. Perhaps the Italian Tonti was scooped.

FINANCING THE MERCHANT OF VENICE

But the bigger surprise lies in the actual beneficiaries to Alexander Houghton's will, and in particular, one of the eleven servants named William. William was seventeen years of age in 1581 and was quite fortunate to benefit from his master's largess of 40 shillings a year for the rest of his life. From the will, it appears that William was employed as an entertainer, musician, and actor. It is not clear whether he was part of the acting troupe that Houghton supported, or whether William entertained other employees and servants. A pension of 40 shillings a year for life was extremely valuable – recall the average industrial wage was 125 shillings – so one might surmise that William was quite the entertainer.

What we do know for certain was his last name: Shakeshafte. This makes him one William Shakeshafte, and – hold on now – the person most historians today believe was *William Shakespeare!*[3] The dates work out perfectly, and the surname Shakeshafte was the name of William's paternal grandfather and a common variant he used.

So, it seems Shakespeare likely spent part of his teenage years entertaining in the household of Alexander Houghton, after his early childhood at Stratford-upon-Avon. Indeed, his connection to the region of Lancashire has been linked to his Catholic and popish sympathies, which is a subject of much controversy in his plays.

Then, soon after his employer died in 1581 – and the will's generosity was put into action – William married the then-pregnant Anne Hathaway in 1582, had twins, moved to London, and the rest, as they say, is history.

Let's pause and enjoy this for a moment. It appears one of the first documented tontine schemes in history involved the greatest playwright and author in English history. It is not, therefore, unreasonable to assume that the income from the tontine helped finance the creation of *Hamlet*, *Macbeth*, and, my personal favorite, *The Merchant of Venice*.

William Shakespeare died at his home in Stratford-upon-Avon at the age of fifty-two, having received his tontine income for almost thirty-five years, quite possibly outliving the other ten servants who were much older than him in 1581, perhaps even winning the tontine by the time of his death in 1616.

This, mind you, was the year Lorenzo Tonti became a teenager somewhere in central Italy. So, here is the first of many myths I plan to dispel about tontines. Tontines were probably not invented by Tonti. Perhaps this is yet another example of Stigler's Law of Eponymy stating that no scientific discovery is named after its original discoverer.

---

[3] As per Hamer (1970), Sir Edmund Chambers who is the leading Shakespearean scholar of the twentieth century, was one of the first to argue that William Shakespeare was in fact William Shakeshafte, although anything to do with Shakespeare's work and identity are quite controversial. See, more recently, Bearman (2002) for an opposing view.

LORENZO TONTI

Figure 3.1. The promoter.
Source: History of Life Insurance, by Terrence O'Donnell (1936, 160). Artist unknown.

LORENZO DE TONTI: THE PROMOTER

Unfortunately, very little is known about the life of Lorenzo de Tonti (see Figure 3.1) – also known by the name of Laurent or Lawrence – especially his younger years. As of yet, nobody has written a thorough biography (or even obituary) of the man who invented the notorious financing scheme, which is in the title of this book.

Most of the information in this particular section is based on the monograph written by the historians R. M. Jennings and A. P. Trout in 1982.[4] They reviewed his letters and communications, which are stored in the Parisian archives and focused on the French origin of tontines. Another

---

[4] Jennings and Trout (1982, chap. 2).

(earlier) source is E. W. Kopf, who wrote an article in 1927 on the history of annuities, and T. O'Donnell, who wrote a comprehensive book on the history of insurance in 1936, which is where the only picture we have of Lorenzo de Tonti is taken from.[5]

By most accounts, Lorenzo was born in (what today would be called) south-central Italy around the year 1602.[6] How and where he spent his childhood is unknown, but it seems he studied medicine (or at least an early seventeenth-century version of medicine) because he is referred to as a physician from Naples in early documents. But Lorenzo was much more than just a doctor and must have been quite the politician, as well. In the 1640s he was communicating with and offering financial advice to the French Cardinal Mazarin, who was the de facto leader of France while young Louis XIV was still a child. Sometime during 1650 Lorenzo de Tonti became governor of Gaeta, which is a city approximately 100 kilometers to the north of Naples.

For his service, Governor Tonti was promised a pension from Cardinal Mazarin of 6,000 livres per year, which in the mid-seventeenth century was a small fortune. By his early thirties, Lorenzo was on the fast track to success with political connections, an entrepreneurial spirit and the ear of important people in power.

As an informal financial consultant to the French monarchy, via Cardinal Mazarin, he hoped to earn a commission or percentage of any profits his proposals might generate. Over the years, he offered proposals on how to organize successful state lotteries and how to create companies that trade and would import from East India. Being a doctor, he even offered public health suggestions on how to prevent the plague from entering France. He certainly wasn't lacking in ideas or self-confidence.

Somewhere around 1653, Lorenzo made his most ambitious proposal yet, the modified form of life annuity called the tontine. As I explained in Chapter 2, the tontine was designed to help governments or cities or municipalities borrow money (i.e., debt financing) at the lowest possible interest rate but with the widest possible participation. Lorenzo envisioned a cheap and easy way for the government of Louis XIV to borrow and help finance its military.

His proposal, which was eventually published under the title: *Edict of the King for the Creation of the Royal Tontine Society*, laid out a plan in which investors would pay 300 livres per share and thus gain access to a so-called

[5]   Kopf (1927).

[6]   This is difficult to confirm, and his birth date is only an estimate.

tontine society. As members of the society, investors would self-select into one of ten distinct classes based on the age of their nominee. The first nominee class would include all children under the age of seven, the second class would include nominees between the age of seven and fourteen, the third class would include nominees between the age of fourteen and twenty-one, and so on. The last (oldest and tenth) class would consist of nominees above the age of sixty-three.

According to Lorenzo de Tonti, the tontine society would offer great riches to everyone involved, including the king, investors, their family members, the promoters, and so on. He was a dazzling promoter for certain.

The Financial Details Were Nebulous

According to the plan – which is the basis of all tontine schemes developed ever since – each year the French government would distribute 5% interest to the annuitant, which is 15 livres per 300 livre share, assuming their nominee was still alive. And, upon the death of a nominee, their corresponding interest would be reallocated to surviving members of the same class. So, the death of a five-year-old nominee, for example, would only impact the dividends of those investors who had selected nominees in the first (age zero to seven) class.

Lorenzo not only designed the plan, but he also made predictions and forecasts of the number of investors who would likely subscribe to the tontine. He made repeated reference to the sum of 1,025,000 livres, which would be distributed to the classes each year. Of this total, 100,000 would be allocated to each of the ten classes in proportion to the number of survivors. This is the tontine sharing principal. The extra 25,000 would go to supporting the expenses and overhead for the tontine society. You can think of the extra 25,000 in terms of the (modern) management expense ratio. Of the 25,000 fee, half would go to the collectors and tellers. The other 12,500 would be "divided into equal parts by the comptroller general and those he would appoint." Presumably a large part of this would go to Lorenzo Tonti himself.

Working out the math, each one of the ten classes was expected to contribute 2,000,000 livres, which at 5% interest corresponds to the 100,000 payment. Multiplying this sum by the ten individual classes results in a projection of 20 million livres raised by His Majesty, on which they would pay 5.125% interest, with 5% to the investors and 0.125% (or 12.5 basis points) going toward overhead and management expenses.

Based on a 300 livre entry price and 20 million principal, Tonti was projecting that 66,667 individual shares of the tontine would be purchased by the investing public – which is wildly optimistic to say the least. Over the next century of (many) tontines issued in France, it is doubtful that a total of 66,000 shares were ever sold.

One of the additional technical problems with Tonti's proposal was the awfully low interest rate that was being offered to the older ages (of nominees) in the tontine society. It made no financial sense at all. For example, the tenth class in the tontine, consisting of those above the age of sixty-three, was asked to forfeit 300 livres in exchange for 5% interest only. At a very basic level, they would never get their original investment back and they would have to live at least twenty years (think of 15 livres per year on a 300 investment) to get their money back. Now, granted, perhaps Tonti was channeling the economist Adam Smith, who argued that everyone believed they would outlive everyone else, but 5% was truly pitiful. The only class for which 5% made any sense at all was the younger ages.

Lorenzo's original plan was extremely naive and simplistic on multiple levels. Indeed, the tontines launched by the French government (much, much later) had a higher interest rate for older nominee ages precisely to compensate for the fact that they were not expected to live much longer. In some sense the French went from a stingy plan to an overly lucrative plan. I provide more details on the French tontines in Chapter 5.

His Proposal Makes for Interesting Reading

Notwithstanding the skimpy financial and economic foundations and some of the bombastic predictions, the fifteen-page proposal makes for some amusing reading. The document is called a Royal Edict, which was probably written and composed by Lorenzo himself, in the form of a royal proclamation.

The document – which was recently translated from French and reprinted in the encyclopedia edited by S. Haberman and T. A. Sibbet (1995) – consists of roughly fifteen pages describing the mechanics, rationale, and even the risks of tontines. Think of it as a seventeenth-century version of an investment or stock prospectus, but without the Securities and Exchange Commission (SEC) to look over the shoulder of the promoter. As I mentioned earlier, some of the claims made were fantastical.

The Royal Edict started by describing the number of classes, the amount that would be paid to each class, and the mechanics of how payments would be made. With the financial details out of the way, the Royal Edict went on to make arguments for why it would be a good idea for citizens to join the tontine.

> Old age, which is exposed to so many accidents and which too often is resented by those eagerly awaiting the death of the old, will be protected from vicissitudes. The Tontine will oblige those whose interest it is to prolong the life of the old, to treat them with respect and care because of the advantage they will find and will hope to increase ... It will motivate husbands and their wives to take extremely good care of each other. (p. 14)

So, according to Lorenzo, owning a tontine share that is dependent on your own life would encourage the people around you to take better care of you, so they can benefit from the income, which is quite cynical. The same section goes on to offer a form of career guidance.

> It is often the case that mothers and fathers ... go against their children's nature and force them to embrace professions which do not suit their inclination and potential. This sometimes throws young people into despair, the inconvenience of which can be remedied by the Royal Tontine, by the means of which parents can buy several shares for their young children who when they reach the age of discretion will then own enough capital to release the burden on their families and who will be able to provide for themselves in the profession of their choice. (p. 14)

In other words, by purchasing shares for your children you can feel better about not forcing them to go to medical, law, or engineering school, because once they win the tontine they can do anything they want with their lives – emphasis on lives, of course. The document reads like a late-night infomercial for investments in gold shares, silver coins, or alpaca farms, all pitched by a smooth-talking promoter (sitting on a yacht sipping champagne).

The Royal Edict was more than just a piece of advertising. It was also concerned with administrative matters, such as how to ensure nominees were alive. The document states:

> If any of the investors were to die and his inheritors or others were fraudulently to replace him by someone else, we order that those guilty be condemned to a ten thousand pounds (livre) fine, one third of which to be paid to the Hotel-Dieu of our beloved town Paris, one third to the Investors of the class, to be shared in proportion to their dividends and a third to the informer; alternatively, that they receive corporal punishment if they are unable to pay. (p. 9)

A so-called whistleblower that uncovered fraudulent behavior would be entitled to one-third of the fine imposed on the investor trying to replace a dead nominee with a fraudulent live one. And if the outlaw couldn't pay, he would be whipped! Tonti was quite the disciplinarian.

The Royal Edict did display a prescient concern for what today might be called (government) credit risk, especially familiar to readers of the book by noted economists C. M. Reinhart and K. S. Rogoff, published in 2009, called *This Time Is Different: Eight Centuries of Financial Folly*. Toward the end of the edict, Lorenzo wrote:

> The only possible criticism remains the worrying eventuality, as suggested by the examples of the past, that His Majesty would divert the funds destined to [making payments on] The Royal Tontine. Our answer is that there is always a risk to take in any investment, whether investing in overseas trade or in the banks, or securing a loan with interest.... It is manifest that the risk mentioned above simply could not happen because of the damage that the King would cause to His affairs. (16)

In this Lorenzo's forecast and fear were quite prophetic, as I describe in Chapter 5. Many of the payments on French tontines of the eighteenth century ended up being delayed and debased.

WHERE DID THE ITALIAN GET THE IDEA?

There are some historians who have asserted that Lorenzo got the idea for the tontine from a charitable bridal scheme that was quite popular in (what is now known as) Italy, called *montes pietatis*. The way the scheme worked was as follows. When a daughter was born, her parents would invest a sum of money with a *monte* – which is an early type of bank or savings and loan – in her name. The money would be invested and cared for by the *monte*'s management for a period of eighteen years, after which money would be given to the named girl as a type of dowry. This sounds like any other investment account held in trust for a child. But the rules associated with the *montes pietatis* was that if the girl (i.) married before the age of eighteen, or (ii.) died prior to the age of eighteen – perhaps tragedies of equal magnitude to a parent – the investment would be transferred to a younger daughter. Finally, and this is where the tontine element emerges, if there were no surviving (younger) daughters, the money would revert to the *montes* fund and would be redistributed to other survivors. This charity-based scheme wasn't limited to only medieval Italy. They were popular in Germany in the sixteenth century. In fact, there was a proposal made in Nuremberg to force all parents to save money for the children's future by requiring them to make provisions for them when they were born.

All of these schemes existed well before Lorenzo proposed and promoted the Tontine scheme, although it's a far stretch to argue that *montes pietatis* are anything but distant cousins to the seventeenth-century tontine. The link is tenuous.

That said, the earlier-mentioned will of Alexander Houghton, and the tontine-like manner in which his assets were redistributed to survivors (and Shakespeare), suggest that the idea of the living inheriting the income and assets of the deceased was a well-established concept. What Lorenzo did was to take these disparate threads and ideas that had been floating around and turn them into a scheme that could finance millions of livre. For that he deserves full credit and perpetual naming rights.

Sadly, the ambitious, arrogant but naive promoter was never able to monetize his tontine, or any other of his grand investment schemes. The French government didn't implement his proposal when he published his edict in 1653. In fact, it took the French government more than forty years to actually implement any form of tontine. Lorenzo never got his lucrative commission on 20 million livres of capital.

In fact, a much worse fate befell him.

THE END: SEVEN YEARS IN THE BASTILLE

Although this isn't the place to get into the minutiae of French, Spanish, and Italian military maneuvering in the mid-seventeenth century, it seems that Lorenzo Tonti placed himself on the losing side of history. The French and Spanish were battling each other over control of (what today is called) Italy, and during one of the revolts or battles in the 1650s, Lorenzo and his family had to flee Naples. He must have antagonized the royal authorities because none other than the queen herself issued written orders to have Lorenzo Tonti and his brother arrested, claiming they were fueling treason in Paris.

And, although he managed to sort out his political problems, his financial concerns continued to plague the Tonti family for decades. His letters to Cardinal Mazarin begged for funding while trying to resurrect the tontine scheme as well as other harebrained ideas.

In the decade that followed matters didn't improve for Lorenzo, and he was never able to monetize his ideas. It has been called one of the mysteries of the seventeenth century, and it is unclear how and why this happened, but Lorenzo de Tonti eventually reached rock bottom in 1668. Around the time Lorenzo should have been contemplating retirement – and perhaps buying a tontine of his own – he and his two sons were thrown in jail.

I'm not talking about some local jail for a night or two. He was incarcerated in the famous French Bastille for almost seven years. Some historians have speculated that this was because of all the money he owed his creditors. Recall that in those days you (or Lorenzo) couldn't declare bankruptcy and walk away from debts. Deadbeats were thrown in prison. However, the royal order placing him in jail indicates a far more severe crime. He must have gotten into some serious trouble, but we don't quite know what crime landed him in the Bastille.

The letters he wrote during his seven years in jail are replete with pleadings for money to support his two sons (with him in prison) and four daughters, the oldest of whom was responsible for the entire family while Lorenzo was imprisoned. Other letters indicate that Lorenzo's wife died while he was in prison and that he was granted few privileges. His earlier connections to the monarchy provided him with little solace. Finally, and quite unexpectedly, in 1675, he was released from the Bastille with his two boys, under the responsibility of one Monsieur de La Salle, a name you might recognize for other reasons, especially if you live and drive in Chicago or Montreal.

Lorenzo emerged from the Bastille a wrecked and virtually bankrupt man. His last decade of life wasn't any prettier and he died at the age of eighty-two (in 1684) in poverty and obscurity. Sadly, the famed governor, doctor, and promoter never lived to see any of his brilliant schemes implemented.

In an odd twist of fate, his two sons, Henry and Alphonse – who were imprisoned together with him in the Bastille – emigrated to America soon after they were released from prison in 1675, together with Monsieur de La Salle. They went on to achieve the notoriety and success that eluded their father Lorenzo.

The younger brother, Alphonse, helped establish one of the first European settlements in Detroit, Michigan. In fact, Alphonse Tonti was the famous Antoine Cadillac's second in command. He took over Fort Detroit when Commander Cadillac was "recalled" back to France by Louis XIV. Oddly, the first Italian (American) born in Detroit was Lorenzo's grandchild, and the Tonti family grew to become an important part of the city.

The older brother, Henry, was even more famous. He is credited with discovering and settling in Peoria, Illinois, and is well known for his part in the de La Salle expeditions (named after the monsieur alluded to above) down the Mississippi. Henry eventually settled in French Louisiana – quite the contrast from his time with dad in the Bastille – and became part of the colonial fabric of Mobile, Alabama.

Today de Tonti Square Historic District in downtown Mobile is on the U.S. national register of historic places and named after French explorer Henry de Tonti. The register lists Lorenzo de Tonti's oldest son's achievements as being the "Father of the State of Arkansas." The cities of Tontitown and Tontiville, both in Arkansas, are named after him. Alas, there is no evidence that tontines were more popular in any of those cities.

Yes. Truth is stranger than fiction. And here ends the story of the Tonti family.

4

The Million Act to Fight a War against France

WHY WAS A DUTCHMAN THE KING OF ENGLAND?

To the non-English reader – or anyone unfamiliar with British history in the late seventeenth century – it might seem rather odd that a Dutchman, William of Orange, became King William III of England. Dutchman wasn't a nickname. He really was born in what today is called Holland, aka The Netherlands, and spent most of his grown life there. Also he didn't inherit the English throne. He seized it.

So why did William (of Orange) invade England in 1688? What claim did he have to the English throne? Why didn't the English people send him packing back to The Hague? Didn't the existing King of England resist?

The answers to these (good) questions are quite relevant to the historical backbone of this book, which is King William III's need for parliamentary approval to borrow money (via the tontine scheme).

For those readers who are unfamiliar with the Glorious Revolution, this is a good time for a crash course on the fifty-year period from 1650 to 1700. Mind you, this isn't a book about English history nor can I do it justice in a few pages. But with King William III in the title of the book, it's quite reasonable to dedicate some space to this intriguing story; a tale that is rather fascinating in its own right. Here is what you need to know.

There are three main characters in this tale. The first is William (of Orange and then King) himself, the second is King James II of England – William's uncle from his mother Mary's side – and the third player is King Charles II, who is the older brother of James and obviously William's uncle, as well. Charles and James were part of the Stuart family or dynasty.

Figure 4.1 provides a snapshot of (only) the relevant members of the Stuart family – at least as far as this book is concerned – as well as their dates of birth and death. In particular, notice the (potentially confusing)

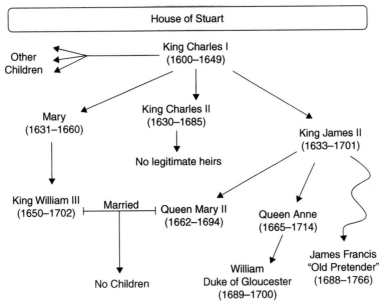

Figure 4.1. Meet the (relevant) Stuarts.

two Mary Stuarts. One was King William III's mother and the other was his cousin, James II's daughter – who then became his wife!

The story really does begin in 1650 when two momentous events take place. First, William of Orange is born (to Mary Stuart) in November of 1650 in The Hague, which is (and was) the home of the Dutch government and Parliament. It is located about 70 kilometers southwest of Amsterdam. Sadly, William of Orange never knew his father – yes, also called William – who died a few months before he was actually born. This might explain some things about his personality – but that is another story.

The second event that took place around the same time – actually on January 30, 1649, to be precise – was less celebratory. Namely, William III's maternal grandfather, King Charles I – whom you recall is also Charles's and James's father – lost his head.[1] Now, I don't mean went crazy or nuts. Rather, his head was actually chopped off. The head loss wasn't the result of a terrible industrial accident or during some bloody battle. The poor fellow was put on trial by Parliament, found guilty of treason, and then beheaded near the

---

[1] Technically speaking, William of Orange wasn't born until a year after his late grandfather lost his head. Also, remember that he was born William of Orange and became King William III, only after he ascends to the English throne, much later.

Banqueting House in Whitehall.[2] Actually, the official charge against him was of being a "tyrant, traitor and murderer; and a public and implacable enemy to the Commonwealth of England." The phrase or legal term used to describe the trial and then killing of a king is *regicide*.[3] And the only time in English history that this happened was with King Charles I – William's grandfather – and it had quite the impact on future kings. English kings and queens certainly didn't treat Parliament casually anymore, which is why they had to ask for money (for their wars) very politely and with deference.

This gruesome event led to about a decade of no king at all, and the country was run by Parliament under a rather brutish and controversial Puritan fellow you might have heard of, Oliver Cromwell. He was later named Lord Protector of the Commonwealth of England, Scotland, and Ireland – although he didn't do much to protect the Catholics in any of those three countries.

Anyway, back to our story. King Charles I's two eldest boys, Charles Junior (who would become King Charles II) and his younger brother, James (who would become King James II), were mere teenagers when their dad was beheaded. They managed to escape from England just in time and would have probably lost their heads as well had they stuck around. They wandered the European continent and spent quite a bit of time in the Netherlands, partially supported and helped by their sister, Mary Stuart – yes, the mother of William of Orange who was a mere child at the time.

Without delving too much into King William III's childhood in the Netherlands, I will note that his private tutor – and the person most responsible for his early education – was coincidently an expert in the pricing of annuities and pensions. His name was Johan de Witt. I'll return to the actuarial aspects of tontines in later chapters, but it certainty is worth noting that King William III was trained in mathematics and finance in the Netherlands by (arguably) the world's first actuary.

Fast-forward a decade to 1660 and the English had tired of being king-less and run by stuffy Puritans. Oliver Cromwell has recently died, and in a bout of nostalgia, the same Parliament that had beheaded his father (King Charles I) invited Charles (Junior) back to England and crowned him King Charles II. At this point young William of Orange was a mere boy of ten.

---

[2] Which today is a famous tourist attraction, naturally.
[3] See the entertaining book *The Kings Revenge*, by Jordan and Walsh (2013) for the story of what happened to the judges and executioners who murdered William's grandfather (and the father of King Charles II and King James II).

This event is known as *the Restoration*, which is quite significant in the English calendar and history. Although England now (after 1660) had a king again, the tension between Parliament and the monarchy always lurked in the background. The king wanted absolute powers – and as much money as he needed – while Parliament tried to rein him in.

Now, as I mentioned in the introduction to the book, King Charles II was a real charmer and a charismatic fellow.[4] He was quite popular with the masses and turned the English royal court into a perpetual party, punctuated by the London plague of 1665 and the great fire of 1666. Generally speaking, though, things were calm in terms of monarchy and politics.

The problem was that King Charles II had no legitimate children of his own to inherit and continue his legacy. Yes, he had more than a dozen mistresses and some twenty illegitimate kids, including his children with the infamous Lady Castlemaine. But his official wife, the queen, never bore him any children. So, when Charles died twenty-five years after the Restoration, in 1685, his younger brother became King James II. By now William of Orange was thirty-five years old and paying close attention to the situation in England.

This is when the problems started to emerge. You see, King James II was the exact opposite of his older brother. He was not very popular with the masses, and he lacked political acumen and strategic charm. Some [unkind] historians have claimed that he was not only foolish but possibly the worst English king ever![5] None of these personality flaws would have been problematic – after all, the throne is hereditary – but for the fact that King James II was also an avowed Catholic in a very Protestant country. That was unacceptable at the time and something the English populace was not willing to overlook.[6] The situation got extremely dicey when King James II (in his foolishness) tried to sack high-level Protestants (in the government and army) and replace them with his handpicked Catholics.

The patient and tolerant English probably would have been willing to wait all this out in hopes that James II's eldest child, Mary – he had no sons at that point, and she was raised as a proper Protestant – would ascend to

---

[4] Two popular TV series in which King Charles II and William of Orange are portrayed is *Charles II: The Power and the Passion* (2003), where William is played by the actor Jochum ten Haaf (oafish, less credible), and *The First Churchills* (1969), where Alan Rowe plays him with greater credibility.

[5] For more information about the Glorious Revolution, its immediate aftermath in England, and the Protestant succession, start with the landmark books by Pincus (2009), Vallance (2006), and Weil (2013), and the very readable Somerset (2012).

[6] "No popery," they chanted in the streets.

the throne and rectify matters. After all, King James II couldn't live forever. It was just a matter of time.

But when James II's wife – who had been barren for ten years – gave birth to a live baby boy in the spring of 1688, all hell broke loose.[7] Remember that (up until recently) boys take precedence on the road to the crown, and this kid would have displaced (his much older sister) Mary. After three years of this nonsense and uncertainty, the English aristocracy had had enough. In the summer of 1688, a group of seven noted and respected English peers sent a letter to William of Orange, who by now had grown up to be quite the military commander, and invited him to invade England and "turf" his uncle King James II.

Why in the world would they invite the nephew William of Orange? Well, he was married to, yes, Mary, the daughter of King James II. As you might have surmised, William (of Orange) was married to his cousin, which made King James II his uncle as well as his father-in-law. See Figure 4.1 (again). That's how it worked in those days.

So, William of Orange – who is a staunch Protestant like his wife, Mary – is invited to England. Note that he had a legitimate claim to the throne via his mother, the sister of James and the deceased Charles, as well as his wife, Mary. Making this Dutchman king of England wasn't as farfetched as it sounds.

He invaded England, sent his uncle (and father-in-law) packing to France, was anointed monarch (jointly with his wife, Mary) by Parliament, and then set about going back to his main hobby – fighting Louis XIV, who, to add insult to injury, still viewed James II as the legitimate King of England.

Here we are. One of the most important slices of English history – the Glorious Revolution in the year 1688 – summarized in 1,000 words leading to the most important takeaway: King William III requires a lot of money to finance his war against Louis XIV. He still has fairly large debts owed to his army of men who helped him invade England a few years earlier. Either way he needs Parliament to allocate him the funds. Remember, the English Parliament can lop off your head if you stick your neck out too far!

THE GLORIOUS AND FINANCIAL REVOLUTION

According to the financial historian P. G. M. Dickson (1967, p. 41), "The English Government at this stage had no system of long-term borrowing to match those of its neighbors and still had to rely on sales of Crown lands

---

[7]   At the time, some claimed that the "birth" was staged and a child was smuggled into the birth chamber to create a male (Catholic) heir.

and rents to cover revenue deficits." So, as part of the early attempts to float long-term debt, prior to the establishment of the Bank of England in 1694 – a story I'll get to at the end of this chapter – the English government experimented with a number of longer-term life-contingent and lottery-based loans.[8] But the absolute first (and most original) attempt revolved around the tontine scheme, which is at the heart of this book.

In January of the year 1693, during the fifth year of the reign of King William and Queen Mary, Parliament passed – and the king gave royal assent to – the Million Act, designed to raise £1 million toward carrying on the war against France. The act itself specified that prior to May 1, 1693, any British native or foreigner – even a Frenchman, presumably – could purchase a tontine share from the Exchequer for £100 as the minimum investment unit to gain entry into the first British government-run tontine scheme.[9] The last decade of the seventeenth century was a rather exciting and vibrant time in financial markets, with an increase in stock market listing and event patent applications.[10] Investment, speculation, and stockjobbing filled the streets.

To quote Dickson again, "Contemporaries were addicted to gambling on a massive scale. It was an age of wagers on the lives of private and public men, the chances of war and the occurrence of natural events, as well as the issue of a horse-race, the fall of dice, the turn of a card." In this type of environment, a tontine scheme appears almost naturally.

For £100, a contributor (annuitant) could select any nominee of any age – including the contributor himself – on whose life the tontine would be contingent. Dividend payments would be distributed to the investor as long as the nominee was still alive. To put the magnitude of the £100 investment in perspective, the average annual wage of a building laborer in England during the latter part of the seventeenth century was approximately £16 and a few shillings per year.[11] Thus the entry investment in the tontine pool

---

[8] For an in-depth analysis of general financial markets during this time period and the origins of the English financial revolution, see Murphy (2009), as well as Roseveare (1991) and Wennerlind (2011). For more information about Dutch influence on the financial revolution and the stock market in general, see Hart (1991) as well as Petram (2014) and the classic by Josef de la Vega (1688).

[9] British History Online, *An Act for Granting to Their Majesties Certain Rates and Duties of Excise upon Beer Ale and Other Liquors*, William and Mary, 1692. www.british-history .ac.uk.

[10] See Macleod (1986) for the increase in patents granted in the 1690s.

[11] Lewin (2003). See also Wagstaffe (1674), who describes an early tontine in the City of London. This tontine wasn't successful or subscribed, but provides (further) evidence of the groundwork and proposal circulating in the City of London in the decade or two prior to 1693.

far exceeded the average industrial wage and the annual dividends alone might serve as a decent pension for a common laborer. The 1693 tontine was clearly an investment for the wealthy, compared with lower-priced shares in French tontines.

King William's 1693 tontine was slightly different from the original tontine scheme envisioned by Lorenzo de Tonti in his edict of 1653. Tonti's scheme involved multiple classes, which effectively reduced the transfer of wealth from older to younger participants. In King William's tontine, each share of £100 entitled the investor to an annual dividend of £10 for seven years (until 1700), after which the dividends would be reduced to £7 per share for the remaining ninety-nine years. These payments and income were to be received tax-free, which stands in contrast to the income from land and a variety of other commercial ventures at the time. In modern (U.S.) terms, one can think of them as tax-free municipal bonds.

Recall that I mentioned in Chapter 1 that King William's tontine paid 7% interest. But, in fact, for the first few years the interest was 3% higher. This might seem like a rather trivial and inconsequential fact, but as a design feature it is quite symbolic. The aggregate payment to the tontine pool declined over time. I come back to the reasons and wisdom of such a structure in Chapter 7 when I discuss the optimal (and what I label Jared's) tontine. For now, it is worth noting that the declining 10%/7% structure was rather unique for any tontine (at the time).

Either way, whether one focuses on the 10%/7% tontine payout rates – or the blended and weighted average close to 8% – these numbers exceeded prevailing (private sector, short-term) interest rates in England at the end of the seventeenth century. Private loan interest rates were officially capped at 6%.[12] The government didn't have to abide by these private sector caps on interest rates and regularly borrowed at higher rates. This situation is the exact reverse of twenty-first-century interest rates, where the (developed country) governments borrow at rates that are lower than most rates in the private sector, although there certainly are exceptions – for example, when Apple borrowed at rates lower than the U.S. government during 2008 and 2009.

According to the economic historians N. Sussman and Y. Yafeh, interest rates (for governments) in England remained quite high – again relative to private sector borrowers – until many years after the Glorious Revolution. In fact, almost a year later (in 1694), when the government negotiated a loan from the (newly established) Bank of England, they paid 8% interest. I'll return

[12] Homer and Sylla (2005).

to the implied or embedded interest rates in some of these schemes later on in this chapter. Also, please note the difference between a *bond* or *loan* paying 8% interest in which the principal is returned at the end of the loan period, and an *annuity* paying a yield of 10% or 8% or 12%. With the annuity the payments are a blend of interest and principal, but with a bond or loan you get pure interest.

The entire £100 had to be paid up-front, that is, it couldn't be paid by installments or over time. The tontine share was purchased – and the money was received – at the Exchequer, which is the government department responsible for collecting taxes and other revenue. Perhaps they actually handed the money to Richard Hampden(or one of his staffers), who was the Chancellor of the Exchequer in 1693.[13] The investor – or very often their agent – was given a "tally of receipt" as well as a paper "Standing Order," which could be sold or assigned to anyone, for the payment of the annuity. The agents who conducted business on behalf of the tontine investors, making and collecting payments, were usually London-based goldsmith bankers. According to records compiled by Dickson, almost half of the tontine subscribers hired goldsmith bankers to manage the process.

Although the main intent was to use the money raised by the tontine to fund the war, the Million Act also introduced a new excise tax on beer, ale, and other liquors for a period of ninety-nine years.[14] The objective was to use this new tax to cover the interest payments on the tontine scheme. This is an early example of funded debt or securitization, by borrowing against future tax revenues.

Finally, in an attempt to reduce nefarious incentives the Million Act stipulated that payments to *annuitants* would be capped when a total of *seven* nominees remained. Their tontine would be converted to a life annuity in which payments stopped increasing as other nominees died. The economic incentive to "knock off" the remaining (few) nominees was nonexistent. The payment to survivors would not change. It was frozen once the number of nominees hit seven. In practice, the deceased's income would instead revert to the government and the Exchequer would "save" on the payments.[15]

---

[13] The well-recognized Charles Montagu became Chancellor of the Exchequer only after Richard Hampden, in 1694. It was Montagu who was Chancellor for the founding of the Bank of England.

[14] The design has been attributed to William Paterson, who is one of the two founders of the Bank of England in 1694, according to Dickson (1967).

[15] Perhaps the issuer of the tontine (i.e., the government) had the incentive to eliminate the remaining nominees, but the nominees or annuitants themselves didn't benefit from the last few deaths.

Now, to put the million pounds they were hoping to raise from the ton-tine in perspective, the number was relatively small compared with the overall budget and fiscal requirements. During King William's war against Louis XIV the government spent a total of £72 million, of which £13.2 million were generated through customs revenue, £13.6 million through excise, and £19.2 million through the (much despised) land tax.

The £6.9 million that was (eventually) raised through various long-term schemes (including those after the tontine was launched) was a relatively small part of the budget.[16] But this was the first time Parliament was guaranteeing these loans, making them public "debts of the nation" as opposed to a particular monarch. The sums might have been small, but the idea was revolutionary.

IN 1693 IT WASN'T YET CALLED A TONTINE

Interestingly, nowhere within the *Statutes of the Realm* (which reproduces the Million Act) was the word *tontine* mentioned, nor was Lorenzo de Tonti ever referenced. Rather, the act – quoted in Raithby (1819) – stated innocu-ously: "And so, from time to time upon the death of every nominee, what-soever share of dividend was payable during the life of such nominee shall be equally divided amongst the rest of the contributors." However, subse-quent writers, such as John Finlaison, whom I mentioned earlier, referred to this as King William's tontine, and by 1789, the tontine issued during the reign of King George III (the last British government tontine) was also offi-cially referred to as a tontine. Interestingly, the first French tontine (issued in 1689) also avoided the term *tontine* and instead made reference to a life annuity with increasing interest from the deceased to benefit survivors.[17]

Just to be clear, King William's tontine was not the first historical instance of a tontine loan or scheme being used for financing purposes. The French launched a tontine a few years earlier, and I'll return to them in Chapter 5. In the Netherlands, which was then called the United Provinces, there was a twenty-year history of tontines. Private investors would often get together and subscribe a capital sum of money that would be invested in stocks (such as the East India Company shares). The income would be paid pro rata to annui-tants as long as the designated nominee was still alive. The Dutch were using tontine financing for municipal and regional finances, as well. In 1670, the cities of Kampen and Groningen floated (small) tontine loans and the cities

[16] Dickson (1967, 50).
[17] Jennings and Trout (1982, chap. 2).

of Middelburg and Delft did the same a year later.[18] In fact, there was a draft proposal or plan (which was never implemented) by the City of London to float a tontine loan in 1674 that sat dormant for two decades and was actually referred to in the debate around the introduction of King William's tontine.

Detailed transcripts of the debates that took place in the House of Commons in mid-December 1692 around the first national scheme, which was King William's tontine are available and noted in the references.[19] In particular, there was lively discourse between Sir Robert Harley, Sir Thomas Clarges, Sir Christopher Musgrave, and Sir Edward Seymour about the merits of such a scheme. Sir Edward claimed, as quoted in Roseveare (1991, p. 88) : "It being but trying an experiment which hath the appearance of reason. And though it has not been tried in this nation, yet it has elsewhere and taken very well." Sir Robert, who was the leader of the Country Party in Parliament, approved but was somewhat skeptical – correctly it turned out – that the investing public would subscribe to the entire fund of one million pounds. Sir Robert Harley would eventually (in 1710) take over as Chancellor of the Exchequer. According to the historian Dickson, the credit for authorship of the tontine proposal is William Paterson, who was also the main promoter behind the Bank of England, which is an institution that probably owes its early existence to the tepid response to the tontine scheme; more on this later.

It is worth noting that the original proposal debated in the House of Commons in December 1692 made reference to a 6% interest rate payable to investors, which was in fact the legal interest cap at the time. Sometime in mid-December the rate was raised (by the Exchequer) to the 10%/7% mentioned above.

Perhaps this was a result of Sir Robert Harley's concern that 6% interest wouldn't entice investors. Was it market forces demanding higher interest rates? Was the response at 6% lukewarm so they raised the rate to 10%/7%? We don't know. In fact, there are a few other puzzling things about the 1693 tontine – which I don't have answers to, and I'll discuss later on – and this is one of them. Why did the final design not match the plan referenced in the House of Commons?

THE OPTION TO CONVERT INTO A LIFE ANNUITY

In fact, to further entice investors to participate in the tontine scheme, the act also included a unique "sweetener" or bonus provision. It stipulated

---

[18] Dickson (1967, 41).
[19] Roseveare (1991, document 9).

that if the entire £1 million target wasn't subscribed to by May 1693, those who had enrolled during the four-month subscription period (starting in February 1693) would have the option of converting their £100 tontine shares to a life annuity, paying £14 per year. Under this alternative, the 14% dividend payments were structured as a conventional, single-premium life annuity with the same life-contingent nominee, but with no group survivorship benefits or tontine features.

This "option to convert" from a tontine to a life annuity – which is a type of derivative security – should be intriguing to anyone with a passing interest in finance or economics.[20]

Why this extra option was added to the Million Act is unclear. Alas, what entices speculators to join a tontine is the large potential payout accruing to the last few survivors, which is the lottery (aka skewness) effect. More participants provide a bigger jackpot, but participants aren't likely to join unless the jackpot is big enough to begin with. So the option to convert was likely added to give investors a possible exit strategy if they were disappointed with the number of subscribers (i.e., the size of the potential jackpot). According to some economic historians, the (exit) option to convert is what doomed the 1693 tontine to failure because 14% is much higher than 10%/7%.[21] In actuality, though, it's not clear how adding an option could reduce the appeal of the tontine. If anything the extra option would increase its value. I'll get into this later on.

The period between the drafting of the Million Act tontine scheme in December 1692 and the date at which the final list was closed in late May/early June 1693 was quite busy and interesting. The London-based promoters of the tontine published an advertisement in late 1692 showing a low expected number of survivors and a correspondingly high dividend payout rate over the next 100 years. These initial projections were likely viewed as unattractive because the resulting subscription rate was much, much lower than the 10,000 target. A few months later, the promoters published a follow-up table showing an even higher expected mortality rate for the group – assuming 10,000 subscribers – and a correspondingly higher projected dividend payout rate for survivors.[22] These projections, together with the actual fraction of the nominees who remained in the tontine, are displayed in Figure 4.2.

---

[20] It is a derivative that depends on both underlying interest rates and mortality rates, in addition to possible credit risk. Even in the early twenty-first century this isn't an easy derivative to price!

[21] See Weir (1989), as well as Jennings and Trout (1982).

[22] Lewin (2003) and Walford (1871).

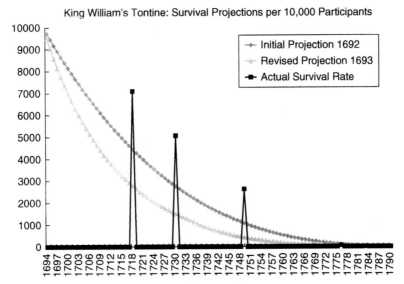

Figure 4.2. Ex post vs. Ex ante.

As it happens, the funds raised by early May 1963 fell far short of the million pound target. In the end, a total of only £377,600 was subscribed and approximately 3,540 people were nominated to the tontine between February and May 1693.[23] The low subscription numbers, and missed target of one million pounds, triggered the option for investors to exchange their tontine shares into a 14% life annuity. But not everyone exercised this option. The plot thickens.

A count of the list of tontine nominees – carefully preserved in the archives of the British Library in London – indicates that a total of 1,013 nominees (representing 1,081 tontine shares) remained in the original 10%/7% tontine, while the other two-thirds elected to convert their shares into the 14% life annuity contingent on the same nominee.

Table 4.1 provides a summary of the timeline of events. To complicate things further, and in an attempt to reach their funding target, the government passed another act in June 1693, which made the 14% life annuity available to anyone, with no restrictions placed on the nominee's age for either the tontine or the annuity. So, whether you were twenty years old, forty years old, or sixty years old, you would purchase a life annuity for

---

[23] Note that one nominee could have multiple shares of £100 contingent on their life. So the number of shares did not equal the number of nominees. The main source here is Dickson (1967).

Table 4.1. *Timeline of major events around the Million Act*

Date	Event
Dec. 1692	Million Act drafted: annuity with group survivor benefits.
Jan. 26, 1693	The act is passed by Parliament and receives royal assent.
Feb. 3, 1693	Tontine subscriptions begin. Payments made to Exchequer.
March 1693	Edmond Halley presents (and publishes) his "annuity value" article.
May 1, 1693	£1 million target not met; 14% life annuity option triggered.
Sept. 29, 1693	1,081 shares remain in tontine; 2,695 convert to life annuity.
Dec. 24, 1693	First payment made to annuitants; three nominees dead already.
Feb. 1694	To reach million target, additional 14% life annuities are sold.
Apr. 1694	Another £300,000 loan on multiple-life annuities authorized.
July 27, 1694	Royal charter for the founding of the Bank of England.
June 1730	514 Tontine nominees are alive; payout is £14.65 per share.
June 1749	267 Tontine nominees are alive; payout is £27.52 per share.
Sept. 1, 1783	Last tontine nominee, Elizabeth St. John, dies; received £1,081.

Note: Compiled from various sources by author.

£100 that would pay £14 every single year for the rest of your life. From the perspective of the twenty-first century, the actuarial pricing and structure of this deal are rather bizarre.

In fact, at first pass, it is puzzling why anyone would stay in the tontine pool instead of switching to the life annuity. On an *expected* present value basis, a cash flow of £10 for seven years and £7 thereafter, is *actuarially* less valuable compared with £14 for life. The expected actuarial present value (APV) of the 10%/7% combination at the 6% official interest rate was worth approximately £142 at the (typical nominee) age of ten, whereas the value of the life annuity was worth about £188. By APV I mean the present value of the cash flows adjusted for the probability of living to various ages. I discussed this in Chapter 2, where I gave a picture of the "density" of the present value for the two instruments: tontines and annuities.

Remember, the original investment was £100. The British government was (really) losing money on these 14% yield annuities. But not everyone was ignorant of this.

ASTRONOMER EDMOND HALLEY OFFERS ADVICE

It's not just twenty-first-century financial logic (and hindsight) that dictates that a 14% life annuity would have been a better deal than the tontine alternative on an expected value basis. In fact, none other than the astronomer

Table 4.2. *Generally comparing tontines to annuities*

Feature	Classical tontine	Constant annuity
Longevity insurance for the buyer.	Pays more if you live much longer than other nominees.	Pays a constant amount for life and doesn't depend on other nominees.
Predictability to the buyer.	Difficult to forecast what annuitant will receive other than minimal interest.	The payout is fixed and known for life.
Exposure to the issuer.	Very little risk other than how long that last nominee survives, which has (much) less risk.	Has to worry about the risk of nominees living longer than projected.
Initial payout rate.	Lower for the tontine.	Higher for the annuity.

Edmond Halley, writing in the January 1693–1694 edition of *Philosophical Transactions of the Royal Society*, opined on the matter,[24] which appears as Halley (1693) in the references, on page #604.

> This shows the great advantage of putting money into the present fund granted to their majesties, giving 14 per cent per annum, of at the rate of seven years purchase for a life, when [even] the young lives at the annual [6 per cent] rate of interest, are worth above 13 years purchase.

The phrase *years purchase* is an early actuarial term for the number of years before the entire investment is returned to the investor. It's another way of quoting a price.[25]

ANNUITY OR TONTINE: WHICH IS PREFERRED?

The choice between a tontine and a life annuity from a statistical perspective, is something I addressed in Chapter 2, and specifically displayed in Figure 2.1. Yet here is a good opportunity to focus on the qualitative difference between the two different ways of guaranteeing an income for life.

Table 4.2 summarizes the choice between the two.

---

[24] The January 1693 edition, according to the Julian calendar used in Britain at that time, would have been after the tontine subscription period closed in May 1693.

[25] See Ciecka (2008a, 2008b) for the history of the first attempt to price annuities, as well as Kopf (1927) and Poterba (2005). For example, if you receive £5 per year for life, it takes twenty years to get your £100 back (ignoring interest), so this would be called a twenty-year purchase.

THE SMART MONEY SWITCHED TO THE ANNUITY

The relative mis-pricing of the tontine (compared with the annuity on an expected present value basis) doesn't necessarily imply that every one of the original 3,000 or so investors would have been better off switching to the life annuity. Indeed, some investors might have a preference for the tontine despite the lower objective expected present value. As an economist might argue, the optimal choice will depend on the other assets and liabilities in the investor's portfolio, as well as on how those assets and liabilities interact (correlate) with the present value of the tontine income stream. The expected internal rate of return (IRR) is just one dimension of the problem.

For example, those investors with a preference for higher relative skewness – and much higher longevity expectations – might have opted for the 10% and then 7% tontine versus the 14% annuity, in order to gain access to the lottery aspects of the scheme. This conclusion is more than hypothetical or conjecture. Recall that more than 1,013 nominees remained in the tontine. Table 4.3 summarizes what is known about this group and the investors who selected them.[26]

First, the amount of money (shares) that were switched from the tontine to the annuity during the period from May to September 1693 was approximately £269,500 (or 2,695 shares), and only £108,100 (which is 1,081 shares) remained in the tontine. These numbers are known with reasonable certainty and appear in multiple sources. The number of investors is slightly harder to confirm with accuracy and is estimated to be 1,015 to the life annuity and 665 to the tontine. In other words, 665 / (665 + 1,015) = 40% of investors stayed in the tontine and 60% switched to the life annuity. Finally, 1,013 nominees remained and 2,525 were switched to the annuity, which is

---

[26] This analysis assumes that £377,600 (which is 3,776 shares) was originally contributed to the tontine scheme prior to the triggering of the May 1693 option to switch. Dickson (1967) as well as Jennings and Trout (1982) refer to this number. The 3,776 share number is consistent with the certificate numbers that appear in Anonymous (1749). In that list, each one of the shares linked to the 267 surviving nominees has an associated certificate number ranging from as low as #61 to as high as #3564. Presumably these were the certificate numbers assigned to the original investors in the tontine as they purchased shares during the February to May 1693 subscription period. Early subscribers were assigned the lowest numbers and the final subscribers were assigned the higher numbers. Recall that only 1,081 shares remained in the tontine by September 1693, so the existence of certificate numbers higher than 1,081 indicates (i.) they were the original tontine certificate numbers and (ii.) that at least 3,564 shares were subscribed. And while one might expect to find some of the 212 certificates with numbers between 3,564 and 3,776 in the year 1749 if indeed that was the original number, it is quite likely that the later subscribers (closer to May 1693) all switched to the annuity and/or died prior to the year 1749.

Table 4.3. *King William's tontine of 1693*

The option to convert from tontine to a life annuity

Investor characteristics	Switched to safer annuity	Stayed in riskier tontine
Total Investment Contributed	£269,500	£108,100
Number of Investors (Annuitants)	1,015	665
Number of Nominees	2,525	1,013
Investors from London	71%	29%
Investors outside London	35%	65%
Average Investment Size	£265.46	£162.56
English Members of Parliament	29	24
Largest Subscriber	Sir Robert Howard	William Tempest, Esq.
Largest Subscription	£4,200	£1,600
Investors with ≥ 10 Shares	95%	5%

Source: Milevsky (2014).

29% in the tontine. Note the larger percentage of investors (40%) versus the smaller percentage of nominees (29%) who stayed in the tontine. This is an indication that the contributors with the larger investments (greater number of shares) switched to the life annuity.

In fact, working backward, the average investment by contributors who switched to the life annuity was £265 compared with a much smaller £162 in the tontine. In terms of their background characteristics, I also have compiled a list of members of Parliament (during the 1692 to 1693 period) who enrolled in the tontine (initially) as well as those who switched to the annuity. It seems that from (at least) fifty-three members who initially enrolled in the tontine, a slight majority (twenty-nine) switched to the annuity. Moreover, the largest single subscriber in the tontine, Sir Robert Howard, had invested £4,200 (forty-two shares) in the tontine and he switched to the life annuity. As a result, the largest remaining investment in the tontine was much smaller, made by William Tempest at £1,600 (sixteen shares.) It is also possible to back out the percentage of investors (annuitants) who resided in the greater London area (including Middlesex, Surrey, and Hertfordshire) and switched to the life annuity. Approximately 29% of this group stayed in the tontine, while the remaining 71% switched to the life annuity. For those who lived outside greater London, the percentages were almost reversed. In this group, 65% stayed in the tontine and 35% switched to the annuity. Table 4.3 also displays the percentage of large investors (defined as those holding ten or more shares) switching to the life annuity: an overwhelming 95%.

Of course, subscribers and investors were not all peers and members of Parliament. At the opposite end of the social spectrum, there were trades-men, artisans, apothecaries, cloth workers, and farmers, as well. A wide swath of people signed up for the tontine, and a majority of them switched to the 14% annuity.

Overall, the data seem to be pointing in the same direction; namely, that the "smart local money" concluded that the 14% life annuity was a better deal than the 10% and 7% tontine and decided to switch. I like to think that many of them acted on the investment advice of one of the greatest astrono-mers of all time, Edmond Halley, after his mid-March presentation to the Royal Society in 1693.

In fact, Edmond Halley and his life table are repeatedly referred to by par-ticipants in the tontine who subsequently complained about the low mor-tality rates, fraud, and so on. But other than the coincidental timing, there is no evidence Halley participated in the tontine scheme or its promotion.

Remember not everyone was convinced. Some investors exercised the option to switch to the *safer* life annuity and some decided to stay in the *riskier* tontine. I estimate that 665 investors stayed in the tontine with their 1,013 nominees (who are all listed in Appendix A). Either way, this is one of the earliest examples of what today we might call *asset allocation with mortality-contingent claims*.

THE CENTENARIAN WHO PICKED THE TONTINE

When the dust cleared in the early summer of 1693, the "bets" had been laid. Table 4.4 provides an indication of who actually remained in the ton-tine scheme. Clearly there was a strong component and representation from London and the surrounding area.

In fact, the longest-living nominee of the 1693 tontine – Elizabeth St. John, who was ten years of age at the time of initial nomination – lived to the age of 100. She survived for ninety more years to 1783. This female nominee spent her senior years in Wimbledon and enjoyed a dividend of £1,081 in her last year of life.[27] Recall that her payout was capped – as explained earlier – once seven survivors remained in the tontine pool. Her

---

[27] Finlaison (1829). The arithmetic is as follows. The £108,100 contributed to the tontine multiplied by 7% interest is £7,567 which was paid out by the Exchequer every year. But since the dividends were frozen once seven shares (nominees) remained, the payment to the last survivor would be only £1,081.

Table 4.4. *Geographic distribution of tontine investors and their shares*

Region	Investors		Shares	
Greater London Area (GLA)	301	45%	503	46%
Southwest	95	14%	169	16%
Central	86	13%	134	12%
North	77	12%	104	10%
East	56	8%	86	8%
Foreign	44	7%	75	7%
Scotland, Ireland, Wales	6	1%	10	1%
Total	665	100%	1,081	100%

GLA: London, Middlesex, Westminster, Southwark, Whitechapel

Southwest: Cleeves, Cornwall, Devonshire, Dorchester, Dorsetshire, Exeter, Gloucestershire, Hertfordshire, Isle of Wight, Somersetshire, Southampton, Wiltshire

Central: Bedfordshire, Berkshire, Buckinghamshire, Cambridge, Ely, Exon, Hampshire, Huntingdonshire, Oxford, Oxon, Surrey, Warwick, Winchester, Worcestershire

North: Cheshire, Chester, Cumberland, Derby, Durham, Gainsborough, Lancashire, Leicester, Lincolnshire, Northumberland, Nottinghamshire, Rutland, Salop, Stafford, Westmorland, Yorkshire

East: Essex, Kent, Norfolk, Norwich, Suffolk, Sussex

Foreign: Belgium, France, Switzerland, Germany, Italy, Netherlands, Spain

final yearly payment (or the payment to the annuitant) was more than ten times the original investment of £100. Note that had she switched over to the life annuity in May 1693 on the advice of Edmond Halley – although likely it was her father who made the decisions and nominated her – and then lived to 1783, her yearly dividend would have been a mere £14. This is a good example of someone who selected the riskier asset – and won.

It is interesting to note that nobody selected to hold some shares in the life annuity and some shares in the tontine. While it would have been impossible to split one share of £100 into a tontine and a life annuity, anyone holding more than one share (in the original tontine) could have diversified and allocated some funds to the tontine and some to the annuity. They didn't, though, according to the careful analysis conducted by Dickson, who reviewed the names of all the investors who switched to the annuity. The lack of diversification is consistent with a recent study that examined investment portfolios during the 1690s.[28] According to Carlos, Fletcher,

---

[28] The article by Carlos, Fletcher, and Neal (2014) in the *Economic History Review* contains details of the stock market in England during the initial years of King William's tontine. In the last decade of the seventeenth century wealthy Englishmen could invest in stocks, bonds, annuities, and tontines. Quite interestingly, very few investors diversified.

and Neal (2014, p. 1), authors of the study, "80% investors who were active in the equity market held shares in only one company." Ergo, perhaps it isn't surprising that investors didn't diversify their mortality-contingent claims.

DIVIDEND PER SHARE COMPUTED

Figure 4.3 provides an example of how the semiannual dividend was calculated. There are very few of these "dividend statements" that have survived for the 1693 tontine, and this particular document is stored in the archives of the Institute and Faculty of Actuaries in London. The booklet of approximately fifteen pages contains the names of all the nominees and is listed as Heyrick (1695) in the references. In fact, the first page of Heyrick (1695) is the cover picture of this book.

The top portion of the document contains the names of fourteen nominees whose "deaths were certified into the Receipt of Exchequer" prior to December 24, 1694. One of these fourteen nominees, named Diana Richers (who is nominee 759 in the list of Appendix A), had two shares linked to her name, which implies that as of December 1694 a total of fifteen shares had been extinguished.

As per the rules of the tontine, the 5% semiannual interest on the £1,500 (dead shares), which is £75, would be distributed to the remaining 1,081 – 15 = 1,066 shares in late December 1694. This extra payment is in addition to the £5 each "live share" was entitled to as an interest payment on the original £100.

The £75 (dead people's interest) is equivalent to 18,000 pence (aka pennies[29]) using the currency nomenclature of the time. Divided by the nondead 1,066 shares is almost 17 pence, or a total of 1 shilling and 5 pence. Adding this extra dividend – which is often called the mortality credit by actuaries – to the £5 that every live share was entitled to receive results in £5 plus 1 shilling plus 5 pence as the total tontine dividend. This is consistent with the "logic" I described earlier in which the fixed amount of interest paid by the Exchequer, which was £108,100 times 10% times ½ = 5,405 is divided by the 1,066 (non dead) shares, leading to £5.07 using modern currency notation.

In practice, though, the dividend paid semiannually was slightly higher because of the way in which the Exchequer treated nominees – via their investors – who hadn't been officially certified as dead (yet), but whose investors had not actually showed up to claim their dividend either. These

---

[29] There were 12 pence to a shilling and 20 shilling to a pound, for a total of 240 pence in a pound.

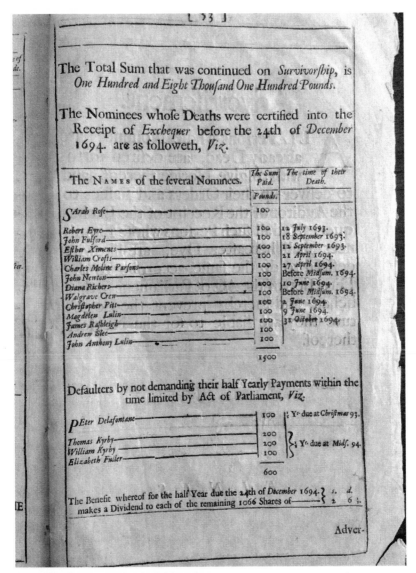

[33]

The Total Sum that was continued on *Survivorſhip*, is *One Hundred and Eight Thouſand One Hundred Pounds*.

The Nominees whoſe Deaths were certified into the Receipt of *Exchequer* before the 24th of *December* 1694. are as followeth, *Viz*.

The NAMES of the ſeveral Nominees.	The Sum Paid.	The time of their Death.
	Pounds.	
SArah Roſe	100	
Robert Eyre	100	12 *July* 1693.
John Fulford	100	18 *September* 1693.
Eſther Ximenes	100	12 *September* 1693.
William Crofts	100	21 *April* 1694.
Charles Moline Parſons	100	27 *April* 1694.
John Newton	100	Before *Midſum.* 1694.
Diana Richers	100	10 *June* 1694.
Walgrave Crew	100	Before *Midſum.* 1694.
Chriſtopher Pitt	100	2 *June* 1694.
Magdelen Lulin	100	9 *June* 1694.
James Raſhleigh	100	31 *October* 1694.
Andrew Slee	100	
John Anthony Lulin	100	
	1500	

Defaulters by not demanding their half Yearly Payments within the time limited by Act of Parliament, *Viz*.

PEter Delafontane	100	½ Yᵉ due at *Chriſtmas* 93.
Thomas Kyrby	200	
William Kyrby	200	½ Yᵉ due at *Midſ.* 94.
Elizabeth Fuller	100	
	600	

The Benefit whereof for the half Year due the 24th of *December* 1694. makes a Dividend to each of the remaining 1066 Shares of ——— 2 6 ½. *s. d.*

Adver-

Figure 4.3. Tontine dividend calculations.
Source: Archives of the Institute and Faculty of Actuaries, London. Copied with permission.

nominees were called "defaulters," and their forfeited dividends were added to the remaining pool, albeit with a lag. In December 1694 the extra dividend (aka mortality credit) was 2 shillings and 6 pence, denoted by 2s. 6d; listed in the lower right-hand corner of Figure 4.3.

Fast-forward to 1730 when the payout rate was now 7%, and another year in which a "dividend statement" is available and a similar process can be observed. The total number of live shares was 544, with an additional 23 shares listed as defaulters. Dividing the 3.5% (semiannual) interest rate times £108,100, which is £3,783.5 in total interest, by the 544 live shares is 6.95 (using modern notation) or 6 pounds and 19 shillings. The actual dividend payout was listed as 7 pounds, 6 shillings, 2 pence (plus another fraction of a pence). The extra 7 or so shillings was due to the defaulters who had not been proven dead or claimed their dividends.

Of course, for those who selected the 14% annuity the calculation was straightforward since every share was entitled to exactly £7 semiannually. There was no need to keep track of defaulters and even the number of deaths wasn't relevant to the payment of dividends. The paperwork (so to speak) was much less onerous for the annuity compared with the tontine.

In sum, whether people selected the 14% annuity or the 10%/7% tontine, one thing was for certain: the government was losing money (i.e., paying too much interest) on these mortality-contingent claims relative to prevailing (private market) interest rates. From a modern finance point of view, the higher rate or yield might have reflected the "riskiness" of lending money to the (young) government relative to the (older) private sector borrowers. It could have reflected a credit yield or a term yield, which is a premium for lending long term. Either way, 14% was a very good deal. Now, let me address how the government managed to find (yet) more money for King William's wars.

A LOTTERY WITH MULTIPLE LIFE ANNUITIES

As noted above, the 1693 tontine didn't succeed in raising anywhere near the sum of money Parliament had anticipated or hoped, which is why many historians have actually labeled English tontines as a failure. In fact, even if the tontine had reached the Million Act target, the sum wouldn't have been enough to satiate King William's war effort. This is why the consultants, projectors, and advisers went back to the drawing board soon after the tontine issue was closed and looked for other sources of funds.

The next scheme the English government floated in late 1693 was the sale of *triple-life* annuities that can be described as something in between immediate life annuities and very limited tontines. These triple-life annuities promised an income to the annuitant as long as any one of *three* nominees who had been named upon purchase were still alive. The investor would pay the usual £100 and, in exchange, he (or she) would receive 10% income (i.e., £10 per year per share) until the last of the three died. This wasn't quite a tontine, in that payments didn't increase when other nominees died, but investors could diversify their risk by selecting more than one nominee. Perhaps this is a tontine's distant (and very tame) cousin. So, for example, the investor could name his three young children as nominees, and, as long as one of them was still living, the annuitant would be guaranteed £10 per share for life.

The government then floated *double-life* annuities paying 12% (which is slightly more) as long as one of two nominees was alive. They rounded out the offering with yet another (familiar) single-life annuity paying 14% for life. This menu of insurance products gave investors quite the interesting choice in late 1693 and early 1694. Do you select the triple-life annuity paying (the safer) 10% yield, the double-life annuity paying 12%, or the (relatively riskier) single-life annuity paying 14%? See Appendix C for the answer.

According to J. J. Grellier, who compiled a record (in 1810) of the national debt from the Glorious Revolution and onward, the government issued or sold a further £107,847 in 14% (single-life) annuities, £170,917 in 12% (double-life) annuities, and £21,235 in 10% (triple-life) annuities. If volume of sales is an indication of acceptance, it seems the double-life annuity was the most popular of the three. By the way, in addition to Grellier, the source for much of the material in this section is from the historian Dickson in the encyclopedic 1967 book, *The Financial Revolution in England*, in which he documents the various options that were made available at the time.

Although there is no evidence that our illustrious astronomer Edmond Halley offered consulting or investment advice on this particular choice, the fact is that in the same article he wrote for the Royal Society and published in 1694, he did analyze the value of double-, triple-, and even multiple-life annuities.

In fact, to add to the complexity and richness of annuity choices – and the demand for insurance quants! – the government followed up with yet another annuity option to raise (more) money. During the period 1695 to 1700 it offered investors who had purchased the original 14% single-life annuities for £100 the choice of converting their life annuities – paying £14 per £100 investment – into fixed-term annuities that would continue to 1792. The investor could swap or exchange the life-contingent payment for a fixed maturity. Obviously, even the youngest and healthiest of nominees was not expected to live for ninety-four to ninety-six more years (i.e., to 1792). In exchange for an additional payment – which the government set at £63 per share[30] – the investor could secure a guaranteed cash flow of £14 for almost a century. At that point there was no need for a nominee. It was a straight ninety-six-year bond (albeit with no maturity value). Many investors (although not all of them) took advantage of the option to convert into what were called the 14% nonredeemable annuities.

If you work out the implied yield, the original £100 per share plus the extra £63 payment would result in a "price" of £163 for a ninety-six-year annuity paying £14, which is a yield of approximately 8.5%. This was (still) higher than prevailing (private sector) interest rates of 6% at the time. Here again, this was yet another annuity investment choice to be made more than 300 years ago.

To add to the richness of annuity choices, independent investors could purchase the reversionary rights to someone else's life annuity (see Table 4.5). What this meant was that in exchange for £63 the investor would be entitled to an income of £14 (which is a payout yield of 14/63 = 22%) until 1792, but it would only begin once the nominee had died! Compare this product with (what today might be called) a deferred income annuity (DIA) or advanced life delayed annuity (ALDA). With a DIA or ALDA, the income starts when the nominee or annuitant reaches an advanced age (say, eighty or eighty-five) and ends at death. With the "reversionary annuity" the income would end in 1792 and begin when the nominee died.

In sum, the 10%/7% tontine investors in 1693 had the option to convert their shares into 14% life annuities. Approximately 60% of them exercised this option and switched to the straight life annuity. Then, a few years later, the same investors were given another (surprise) choice to convert their 14% life annuities into term annuities that ended in 1792. Presumably this generous offer was taken advantage of and employed by the many investors whose nominees were old, infirm, or about to die. During the five-year period (1695–1700) that this new choice was offered (i.e., to remove the life contingency), the Exchequer raised a further £582,000,[31] of course saddling the government with many more years of interest payments.[32]

---

[30] This price was set at "four and a half year's purchase," which is 4.5 times the £14 annual income.

[31] Dickson (1967, 57).

[32] A group of investors (under the title of Million Bank) banded together to purchase the reversionary interest portions and held them separately from the 14% annuities. These were the epitome of long-term investments since they wouldn't pay a penny until the underlying nominee had died.

Table 4.5. *English buffet of annuity choices in the late seventeenth century*

Name	Payout yield*	Features
King William's Tontine	10% (seven years) and then 7% (thereafter)	Optimal for someone with "extreme" longevity expectations.
Single-Life Annuity	14%	Higher yield but only protects one life.
Double-Life Annuity	12%	Longevity insurance for a couple (two nominees).
Triple-Life Annuity	10%	Naming a child as the third nominee, preserving an estate value.
Reversionary Annuity (to 1792)	22%	Pays income once primary annuitant has died – a form of life insurance.
Combine the 14% Life Annuity and the Reversionary Portion	8.5%	A ninety-six-year term annuity.

* Remember that Payout Yield is **not** an interest rate. It is (only) the periodic cash flow divided by the initial payment.

They Need More Money

Although these multiple-life annuities and reversionary annuities proved popular, the government and the war effort required (even) more money. The next scheme launched around 1694 was something called the Million Adventure. (They really did like the word *million* in those days!) The Million Adventure was a lottery scheme run by the government in which they sold or issued 100,000 tickets at a price of £10 each.

I refer those who are interested in this early example of government-sponsored gambling to the extensive 2005 study by A. L. Murphy, in which she examines the Million Adventure and other English lottery schemes around the same time. She notes that before the launch of the Million Adventure, the government tried (but didn't succeed) to pass a bill banning private lotteries and sweepstakes, presumably in an attempt to eliminate the competition before they got into the business. Once the Million Adventure was launched, a ticket in the government-sponsored lottery offered a one-in-four chance of winning something. This is quite generous compared with modern lotteries in which the chances are slimmer. A £10 ticket entitled the winner of the lottery to – yes, here it is again – an annuity for sixteen years. A few select jackpot winners received £1,000 until 1710, while a larger group of smaller winners received the lowest winning payout of £10 for the same sixteen years. Even the non–prize winners (aka blank tickets) were entitled to an annuity of £1. Everyone was a winner!

I would expect that anyone with expertise in the pricing of annuities – whether it be the astronomer Edmund Halley or the mathematician Abraham de Moivre – was quite popular during the closing decade of the seventeenth century. By the start of the eighteenth century, England's national debt consisted of multiple classes and types of annuities.

In fact, according to Grellier, the national debt in 1697 was slightly less than £20 million of which approximately one-quarter (25%) was in an assortment of life and term annuities with various maturities and provisions. It might seem odd for a government to have such a large "annuity liability" on their national balance, when today most debt is in the form of long- and short-term bonds. But if you think about it carefully, the situation isn't much different in the twenty-first century, where a large part of government debt is in the form of (unfunded) social security payments – which are basically annuities.

THE OLD LADY ON THREADNEEDLE STREET

Tontines, life annuities, and lotteries weren't raising the needed funds and King William III was desperate for more money to finance his war against King Louis XIV. He was now willing to try an even more audacious scheme – a bank!

In the summer of 1694, on July 27 (remember, Julian) to be precise, none other than the magnificent Bank of England received its official corporate charter from King William III and Queen Mary II. This charter is possibly their most lasting and impactful contribution to banking for three centuries to follow. They sanctioned the creation of the most important institution in modern financial economy: the central bank. Indeed, if these joint monarchs are remembered for one thing only – and sadly, Queen Mary died just five months after the charter was granted – it should be the creation of the Bank of England.

The concept of a government-sanctioned Bank of England (which was also referred to as Bank of London in some early documents) – like King William's tontine itself – wasn't entirely new or novel. The idea had actually been implemented in other countries, most notably in Sweden (i.e., Sveriges Riksbank). The Swedes – whose rather unique pension scheme I'll discuss in Chapter 6 – can also lay claim to the first central bank in the world, launched in 1668. The Sveriges Riksbank is actually the sponsor of the Nobel Memorial Prize in Economics, first launched and awarded during the Swedish Bank's third centennial in 1968. Nevertheless, the idea of a central (government) bank had never been tried in England, although there were many small regional (city) banks who went about lending money in small sums and without any special privileges. Remember, this was (still) a time well before long-term government bonds.

By all accounts,[33] the main promoter and champion of the Old Lady of Threadneedle Street – a nickname for the Bank of England, originally penned by the caricaturist James Gillray in 1797 – was not a Swede, but a well-known Scotsman by the name of William Patterson.[34]

Despite the precedence of the central bank in Sweden, the Bank of England was modeled on the so-called Bank of Amsterdam (founded in 1609), which was (obviously) in the Netherlands and based not very far from where William of Orange was born and raised. To King William, one of the main uses or purposes of the Bank of England – besides lending him and his government money – was to help transfer funds back to the Netherlands to help pay for the war effort. It is remarkable how much financial innovation – tontines, as well as annuities and banks – were driven by the need to pay for wars.

Now, to be clear, the Bank of England (BoE) in 1694 was a very different institution compared with what it is today. The BoE's mandate and day-to-day operations were different on a number of important dimensions. In some sense, it has little resemblance to today's BoE or any other central bank.

First of all, unlike the BoE today, it was not chartered as a nonprofit public institution. Rather, it started life as a business with slightly more than 1,000 (capitalistic) shareholders who essentially owned the bank and profited handsomely from its activities. The first shareholders (speculators) in the BoE included many of the investors in King William's tontine, and a few other notable names, as well. For example, two of the shareholders in the BoE were the king and queen, who were listed as (jointly, of course) owning £10,000 worth of common stock. Recall that William and Mary didn't participate or invest in the tontine.

In fact, there were exactly 1,272 original shareholders in the BoE (in July 1694), and the numbers ebbed and flowed as investors sold their shares

---

[33] Additional sources for the history and functioning of the Bank of England include Clapham (1945), as well as Dickson (1967) and Grellier (1810).

[34] Although he wasn't the bank's first governor, that honor went to John Houblon. On a related note, today (in 2015) the governor of the Bank of England is (the Canadian) Mark Carney.

in the (secondary) market and new shareholders were added to the roster of investors. By 1701, there were 1,903 shareowners listed in the company records, and by 1751 there were 3,294 voting proprietors.[35] Note that only those shareholders with more than £500 in stock (i.e., five shares) were allowed to vote. The original list of subscribers includes many dignitaries such as Sidney Godolphin (£6,000 in stock), who was First Lord of the Treasury, and Charles Montagu (£2,000 in stock) who was Chancellor of the Exchequer. In early 1695, a certain John Churchill, First Duke of Marlborough (and husband of the famous Sarah Jennings), purchased £4,000 in stock. Many will recognize and acknowledge him as the most successful commander of the army in English history. He bought forty shares in the private sector company that helped finance the wars he was fighting for King William III.

Evidently, the ethical rules regarding conflicts of interest and blind investment trusts – that would apply to every public official today – were utterly nonexistent in those days. People in power, very close to power, or even perceived as having access to power got rich off those connections.[36]

So, the BoE (in 1694) was a private company owned by a collection of connected and powerful people, who profited from the BoE's business and earned dividends for their efforts. The initial public offering (IPO), if it can be called that, raised a total of £1,200,000 of which 25% was paid immediately by the investors, and the remaining 75% was paid in installments. The IPO was fully subscribed after twelve days – a remarkable feat for the time – and the stock immediately started "trading" at par (£100). Anyone could buy or sell shares in the BoE at Exchange Alley in downtown London, where other stocks – such as the East India Co., the Royal African Co., and the Hudson Bay Co. – changed hands among the so-called stockjobbers.

In 1695, which was the first full year of business, the BoE paid a dividend of 6% (i.e., £6 per share) in the first half of the year and then another 4% (i.e., £4 per share) in the second half of the year, for a yield of 10% to all shareholders. In 1696, which was actually a year of financial turmoil in England, no dividends were declared in either part of the year. In 1697, the dividend was 3.5% (at the end of the first six months) and then 4% (at the end of the last six months); there was an additional 20% of profits distributed to shareholders so that subscribers didn't have to make the final installment commitment from the original IPO.

---

[35] Clapham (1945, 284).
[36] Well, perhaps things have not changed that much in the twenty-first century.

During the first few years, the shares of BoE "traded" at a high of £150 per share, and fell as low as £80 during times of (perceived) crises. Yes, it traded like any other stock on the market but was viewed as a premium gilt-edged investment holding. Most people who owned it held on to it for the income, which is no different from today's conservative (widows and orphans) investor.

Indeed, a wealthy investor in the late seventeenth century had to make the same sorts of "asset allocation" decisions we all face in the early twenty-first century. How much should be in stocks? How much should be allocated to fixed income? How much invested in annuities? How much tontines? And so on.

The BoE's main activity was to raise money for the government, by taking deposits and paying (lower) interest on its deposits than it received on its loans, which is no different from how a bank works today. The BoE lent money to the government, including the original £1,200,000 capital subscription, at an interest rate of 8%.

Loans from the BoE to the government very soon exceeded the initial £1,200,000 amount of equity capital that had been contributed by the shareholders. But recall that as a bank, it could make loans that far exceeded its capital through the magic – and it certainly was considered magic at the time – of leverage and credit. It took deposits from the public (paying them a lower rate of interest) and then lent it to the government at 8%. This is the business of banks.

Indeed, this should help shed light on how the BoE managed to pay a first-year dividend of 6% + 4% = 10% when it was only receiving 8% interest from the government (on its loan). Presumably a big part of the story has to do with the fact that it was paying (much) lower interest than it was receiving from the government. Remember from basic finance theory that a (smaller) return on assets (RoA) is perfectly consistent with a (larger) return on equity (RoE) with just the right amount of leverage.[37]

In fact, the BoE had a virtual monopoly of lending money to the king and queen and their treasury, but it also engaged in some other interesting (loan-) related activities. Bank records indicate that the board (which actually was called the Court of Directors) debated whether to lend money against the security of rather peculiar assets.[38] For example, a consignment of tobacco was "not thought fit" as collateral, nor was wine allowed

---

[37] Assuming the BoE paid 6% interest on deposits (the maximum private rate) and the RoE was in fact the dividend payout rate, then a leverage ratio of 51 to 1 would convert an 8% RoA to a 10% RoE. This is all very hypothetical, of course.

[38] Clapham (1945, 113).

as security, but two-thirds of the value of a shipment of cork was accepted as a pledge for a loan, as was coffee and gold, silver, and jewelry. Although nontraditional lending was a minor part of its business – and the goldsmith bankers at the time were opposed to the BoE because it encroached on their "pawnshops" – all this was a rather colorful part of finance in the late seventeenth and early eighteenth centuries.

One thing is for certain. The above is clearly not how the BoE – or any central bank in the developed world – is run or managed today. Today, central banks are sacred nonprofit ventures managed as an extension of government, in charge of monetary policy, stability of currency, and so on. But it was only (relatively) recently, after World War II (in 1946 to be exact), that the government nationalized the BoE and started the process of converting it to the institution it is today.

The relevance to our story is that in 1694 – in the aftermath of the lukewarm public reception to tontines – the government finally found financial success. The IPO raised more than a million pounds in less than two weeks, compared with the many months it took to gather a meager £100,000 for a tontine. It is an early testament to its fame. So, perhaps one can say that it was the tepid response to tontines that launched the BoE.

It is worth pointing out that the BoE didn't take lightly to any competition, especially in its early for-profit years. At the time, there were two major political parties in England, the Whigs (mostly financiers) and the Tories (landowners), so the BoE was viewed as a "Whig-ish" institution and the Tories took any opportunity to criticize and besmirch it. In fact, South Sea Company, which was formed in 1710 and was viewed as a "Tory" company, was intending to compete with the BoE. The story of the South Sea Company – and one of the biggest stock market bubbles and crashes in history – has been the subject of numerous studies and books.[39] The South Sea Company offered to "swap" the English national debt (in 1720) for shares in the South Sea Company, and thus reduce the interest costs to the government.

The impact of the South Sea episode (or affair) on the British economy, financial market and psyche can't be overstated. It had immense and longlasting. implications and is still studied by economists today, as the classic manifestation of a financial bubble and the "madness of crowds." Even Isaac Newton lost money in the South Sea scheme. In fact, the debt incurred by

---

[39] In particular, see the excellent books by Carswell (1960) and Dale (2004), the classic Kindleberger and Aliber (2005), and Temin and Voth (2004, 2013). All of these are sources for the material in this section.

the British government as they tried to unwind and resolve the South Sea crises was recently in the news. In December 2014, George Osborne the chancellor of the Exchequer announced that his government would repurchase and pay off the perpetual bonds (i.e., consols or consolidated annuities) that were issued during the South Sea (1720s) period.[40]

Back to the BoE, even King William himself – who was viewed as sympathizing more with the Whigs than the Tories – complained about the high interest the government had to pay to the BoE. A year after its founding, in April 1695 to be precise, King William III actually appeared before the Court of Directors of the BoE and asked for better terms on a loan – and remember that he was a major shareholder![41]

One final fact worth noting about the BoE, and its power over the subsequent years, has to do with its response to the second (and last) English tontine scheme, which was launched in 1789 – soon after the last nominee of King William's 1693 tontine passed away. I discuss the details of the 1789 tontine at the end of Chapter 5, but needless to say, the BoE was not a big fan. It had come into existence as a result of the lukewarm response to tontines and the Court of Directors didn't take kindly to other methods of government financing. The BoE was willing to lend money to investors to purchase shares in the tontine of 1789 – presumably they were less risky than shipments of tobacco – but it didn't want any additional involvement.

In fact, the BoE was asked by the secretary of the treasury (in 1789) to take over the management of the tontine after it had been subscribed. The response of the BoE was short and to the point: "The Gentlemen of the Bank have very little interest in the tontine and have no opinion to give."[42]

So, it should come as no surprise that in 2015 the BoE is one of the most powerful institutions in the world and tontines have all but disappeared in England and beyond.

---

[40] See the recent *New York Times* article by Castle (2014) for the intriguing details.
[41] Clapham (1945, 25).
[42] Clapham (1945, 187).

Don't Englishmen Die? Anti-Selection vs. Fraud

TONTINE CRIMES IN LITERARY FICTION

In 1718, in the City of London, while the mania around the South Sea Company was unfolding and every stockholder was dreaming of getting rich, a lawyer by the name of Mr. Woollaston was concerned about another matter completely. His fear was that not enough tontine nominees were dying. Let me repeat. The nominees were *not* dying fast enough for his taste! He published a pamphlet, which I'll return to later, in which he complained: "Don't Englishmen Die?"[1]

The common perception or fear – at least among people who have heard of them – is that tontines were banned in Britain and the United States because of the incentives to murder other participants and nominees.[2] Moreover, famous novelists and Hollywood writers have done much to advance this erroneous thesis about the risk of tontines.

Novels and Movies about Tontines

One of the best-known novels – which then became a movie – involving tontines is *The Wrong Box*. It was cowritten by the noted Scottish author Robert L. Stevenson (1850–1894) and Samuel L. Osbourne (1868–1947), who was an American author (and Stevenson's stepson). The story is about an extreme tontine scheme where the last survivor wins the entire fortune, quite different from the one I will advocate (in Chapter 7), in which survivors share ever-shrinking dividends.

---

[1]   Walford (1871, 114).

[2]   This, for example, was a claim made in a recent economics article by Lange, List, and Price (2007), and it has been repeated by various journalists and writers, some of which I mention toward the end of Chapter 7.

The Wrong Box begins toward the very end of the scheme when there are only two surviving members left – each waiting for the other to die, of course. They also happen to be brothers. The comedy (tragedy) revolves around the grandchildren of the tontine (nominee) who are desperately trying to keep one of the brothers alive so they can inherit the tontine funds, while the other brother is trying to kill him. It gets messy, people disappear, and others fall in love. This is a complicated and clever book, which became even more popular when it became the basis of a movie (in 1966) starring Michael Caine, Dudley Moore, and Peter Sellers (yes, all in one movie!). The book and movie increased awareness of tontines – and the first scene in the movie where the tontine nominees are gathered in a room in which the rules are explained is just precious – but Stevenson's tontine has little to do with King William's.

Another example of a tontine (being maligned) in fiction is the two-volume novel by Thomas B. Costain, published in 1955 and simply called *The Tontine*. The story is set in Victorian England, and revolves around a so-called Waterloo Tontine (which is a fiction), established for war veterans. In this novel full of shenanigans, one of the annuitants hires an actor to impersonate and fill in for a dead nominee so they can get their annual dividends. This, perhaps, may not be as fictitious or imaginary in real tontines, as I will soon discuss.

In the book *4.50 from Paddington*, written in 1957 by Agatha Christie, the tontine makes an appearance as the motive for murder. There is a *M*A*S*H* episode and *Barney Miller* episode involving tontines.[3] And, in one of the most recent appearances in pop culture (1996), *The Simpsons* told the story of a tontine in which Grandpa Simpson and Mr. Burns are the last two surviving nominees of a tontine. And, of course, Mr. Burns (ever the villain) gives orders to have lovely old Grandpa assassinated.

With Bad Press, What Do You Expect?

So, with all these crime novels, movies, and cartoons "framing" tontines in this negative way – and giving them such bad press – their negative image should not be surprising. However, there is no evidence that foul play ever occurred in practice. I couldn't find any story or account of nominees in a tontine pool trying to murder another member of the pool, and if you

---

[3] For those readers too young to remember, these are TV series that were quite popular in the 1970s and 1980s. In the *M*A*S*H* episode one of the characters (Col. Sherman Potter) inherits a bottle of rare French cognac as the survivor of a tontine. In fact, I heard a similar story from the son of a WW II veteran whose father was a member of a similar "liquid" tontine scheme.

know of any, I would appreciate if you could let me know. As I mentioned in Chapter 4, King William's tontine froze payments once seven survivors remained in the pool, which would further reduce any incentive for murder.

In theory, could an investor or annuitant – who was actually receiving the income – murder another nominee to (marginally) increase their income? In theory, yes, but could they get away with it? Some of these nominees were quite famous and well protected in their own right. In fact, now is a good point to digress for just a little bit and introduce you to some of the nominees to King William's tontine, who until now have been rather anonymous and faceless.

FAMOUS NOMINEES AND THEIR UNIQUE LIVES

If indeed the "optimal" nominee was a young child who was expected to live for a very long time – and one selected a well-known nominee to avoid verification and confirmation problems – then the most famous child in all of England in 1693 must have been the Duke of Gloucester (see Figure 5.1). And he was indeed one of the 1,013 nominees in King William's tontine (listed in Appendix A). Arguably, of all the nominees for whom we have pictures (from paintings), the Duke of Gloucester must have been the cutest of them all.[4] Here is what we know about him and why he was rather critical to English history and the reign of King William III.

Duke of Gloucester, Heir to the Throne

His Royal Highness Prince William Henry, Duke of Gloucester was the son of Anne Stuart (and George of Denmark), which also made him King William's nephew – and his most favorite one as well. Please refer to Figure 4.1 (back at the beginning of Chapter 4) for a refresher on the Stuart family tree.

William Henry, was born on July 24, 1689, just a few months after his uncle William of Orange arrived from the Netherlands with his wife, Mary, and became king and queen. William Henry was the only one of Anne's children (and seventeen pregnancies) to have survived childhood.[5] As he grew and survived the maladies of the first years of life it was expected that he would (one day) be king of England.

---

[4] In addition, see poem on first page of this book, written by Zoe Milevsky.
[5] His two older sisters, Lady Mary and Lady Anne Sophia, both died (before he was born) prior to reaching the age of two.

Figure 5.1. William, Duke of Gloucester, Artist: Sir Godfrey Kneller.
Source: Copyright © National Portrait Gallery, London. Asset # D11536. Used with permission.

Recall that William and his wife, Mary, had no children of their own. Moreover, Queen Mary died in December 1694, when William Henry was five years old. This placed him one step closer to the throne. King William made him a Knight of the Garter at the age of seven, which was an extraordinarily prestigious and visible honor, especially for a young child. Clearly he had a special place in King William's (rather cold) heart. Anyway, William Henry was well-known in England, being the nephew of a king and the son of a (future) queen, making him an ideal candidate for a tontine nominee.

The public scrutinized all aspects of his life and behavior. Newspapers (such as the *London Gazette*, for example) reported on his whereabouts and pastimes. In fact, reports on his educational progress were given to Parliament every few months and Gilbert Burnet, bishop of Salisbury, was appointed his private tutor.[6] His (eventual) ascent to the throne would further cement the Protestant line of succession, which became so important after the Glorious Revolution.[7]

Sadly, though, William Henry suffered from poor health from a young age. He was born with a slightly outsize head, experienced difficulty walking, often stumbled over his own feet, and needed help climbing stairs. Physicians (many years later) determined that he suffered from hydrocephalus, which is a condition in which there is excessive water in the brain. Alas, it didn't end well for the cute little boy.

William Henry died of pneumonia soon after celebrating (with much fanfare and publicity) his eleventh birthday, in the very early hours of the morning of Tuesday, July 30, 1700. The nation lost the only Protestant heir to the throne. According to the medical historians Holmes and Holmes (2008), his illness wasn't fatal and he might have eventually ruled England when his mother Anne died.

The death of William Henry in 1700 led to the Act of Settlement in 1701, which passed the crown (upon Anne's death) to the distant German branch of the family, resulting in the many King Georges of the eighteenth century. The death of this particular tontine nominee changed the course of history.

In addition to the crowds of (especially Protestant) Englishmen who mourned his death an (anonymous) investor who had named little William Henry as his tontine nominee lost his £100 longevity bet. Since the young prince died five days after the midsummer cut-off point, presumably said investor managed to secure his (half of) 7% dividend (plus any mortality credits) for 1700. So, at the very least he (or she) earned an income of £68.5 from their investment.[8] Alas, this particular investor would have been better-off selecting the 14% annuity. Hindsight is 20/20.

---

[6]   Imagine having to send your report card or transcripts to Parliament for review!

[7]   The source for most of the material in this section about Prince William Henry is from the book on (his mother) Queen Anne, in Somerset (2012).

[8]   The 1693 dividend would have been (at least) £5, plus six years of £10 and the final £3.5 for July 1700. Recall that the interest rate dropped from 10% to 7% in 1700.

The Machado Kids

British heirs to the throne weren't the only famous English names and surnames in the tontine. As you skim the list of 1,013 nominees (in Appendix A) you will find names like Austen, Eyre, Hoere, Middleton, Newton, Pitt, and Slaughter. There is a Thomas Moore (perhaps a relative?) and even a Ruperta, listed as daughter of Prince Rupert, who was a first cousin of King Charles II and King James II. But not everyone on the list of nominees was notable or famous. In fact, most of the names were quite common, such as Smith, Robinson, Rose, Porter, Parker, Martin, and Miller. Moreover, a total of sixty-nine nominees were foreign or listed with a foreign address, and you probably won't be surprised to learn that many of them were Dutch.

One of the most interesting groups of nominees was the Machado children. They were four girls and one boy, each one nominated for one share in the tontine for a total cost of £500, which was no small sum. Antonio Alvarez (also known by his Hebrew name, Moshe) Machado, the father who nominated them, knew something about diversification. He was a trader on the Amsterdam stock exchange, a very wealthy financier, and one of King William's close confidants and friends from his days in the Netherlands. Of the five children he nominated, Jehudith Machado – who was fifteen years old in 1693 – lived (at least) to the age of seventy-one and received tontine dividends for (at least) fifty-six years.

The detailed list of 1,013 nominees is available in Appendix A of this book, together with estimates for how long they lived based on various sources (and assumptions). While it is easy to ascertain the death dates of the famous nominees, the same cannot be said of the commoners. Perhaps the reader might find a relative on the list?

TONTINE AND ANNUITY SURVIVORSHIP BIAS

So, let me be clear, nominees weren't being killed or knocked off by other annuitants. The current ban on tontines in the United States, which is something I address in detail in Chapter 6, had little to do with nominees murdering each other. The ban had more to do with excessive management fees and overreaching insurance regulators. Even in France, tontine annuities were banned in 1763 because they were perceived as an expensive way of funding the national debt and not because of concerns of fraud.[9] This

---

[9] Weir (1989).

is a question of dividend and interest rates paid, not the structure of the tontine per se.

Indeed, if the incentive to murder tontine nominees was powerful enough, one would expect to see evidence in the survivorship data. Older tontine survivors would experience (ex post) shorter life spans compared with regular annuitants or the rest of the population. At the very least one might observe higher mortality rates at advanced ages or toward the end of the tontine's life. In contrast, the fact that nominees with a greater number of shares (and hence more money contingent on their life) died earlier, compared with the remainder of the nominees (in the 1693 tontine), is simply due to the fact that their average age at the time of nomination was higher. Their earlier death is to be expected.

As I alluded to earlier – and as Mr. Coollage complained about – the problem with the death of nominees was the exact opposite. In fact, the survival rates suggest a contrary story. Tontine nominees actually lived *longer than average* – especially nominees who were very young when they were initially named by the annuitant or original investor. It appears that something about being a tontine nominee kept people (or at least their names) alive longer.

Anti-Selection

Of course, most insurance economists would interpret this as early evidence of something called anti-selection, similar to the well-documented phenomena that annuitants live longer compared with the rest of the population, but I argue that it is unlikely to provide a completely satisfactory explanation for high *reported* survival rates among tontine nominees.

Let me get to my main point in this chapter. If indeed tontine participants were involved in any sort of nefarious activities, it wasn't murder but perhaps its opposite – resurrections. In particular, it is possible that tontine contributors would nominate a given child as a nominee and then, if that child happened to die at a young age, the parent would select another (younger) child, possibly even a newborn infant, and name them after their deceased sibling. The nominee's namesake would assume the identity of the nominee and tontine dividend payments would continue from the Exchequer based on the same name but different person. This would have the effect of increasing *reported* survival rates. After all, this was the late seventeenth and early eighteenth centuries when documents used for identification purposes were crude and unreliable. The incentive was certainly there.

Table 5.1. *King William's tontine nominees: survival rates*
after thirty-seven and fifty-six years

Age	# of Nominees	Alive in 1730	Alive in 1749
0–2	96	57 (59%)	33 (34%)
3–5	186	106 (57%)	61 (33%)
6–8	174	93 (53%)	53 (30%)
9–11	181	100 (55%)	52 (29%)
12–14	138	63 (46%)	35 (25%)
15–17	69	32 (46%)	14 (20%)
18–20	50	21 (42%)	7 (14%)
21–23	41	17 (41%)	7 (17%)
24–26	22	10 (45%)	5 (23%)
27–29	14	3 (21%)	0 (0%)
30–32	16	6 (38%)	0 (0%)
33–35	7	3 (43%)	0 (0%)
36–38	7	1 (14%)	0 (0%)
39–41	6	2 (33%)	0 (0%)
42–44	1	0 (0%)	0 (0%)
45–47	3	0 (0%)	0 (0%)
48–50	1	0 (0%)	0 (0%)
51–53	1	0 (0%)	0 (0%)
Avg. Age	11.10	9.83 (46.83)	8.59 (64.59)
Total:	1013	514	267

Source: Milevsky (2014).

Take a look at Table 5.1. Notice the thirty-seven-year survival rate for children aged zero to two in the year 1693 (all ninety-six of them in the tontine) was 59%. In other words, more than half of this group survived to 1730. Moreover, 34% of the original group (of ninety-six nominees) lived for fifty-six years or more years, to 1749.

The data in fact suggest that survival rates were quite high relative to the population in the late seventeenth century. Note that infant mortality rates at the time were on the order of 25% – a quarter of infants died within a few years – and between 30% and 40% of infants died prior to age ten. This implies that the survival probability to age ten was between 60% and 70%. And yet, of the 519 children under the age of ten who were nominated to King William's 1693 tontine, 288 (or 55%) of them survived thirty-seven years to 1730. See Appendix A for the entire list and estimates of how long each individual nominee lived.

A VISIT TO THE LIBRARY AND THE ARCHIVES

As far as the *number* of nominees is concerned, the original 1693 list is available in the British Library and listed in the references here as Heyrick (1694). It clearly shows a collection of 1,013 names and is consistent with the follow-up list and dividend calculations. There is little dispute about that particular number.[10]

As far as future years are concerned, the data are somewhat murkier. The only (later) years in which the names of actual (surviving) nominees are available are 1730 and 1749. These are also available in the British Library and are referred to (blandly) from here on as the 1730 and 1749 living lists. For other years between 1694 and when the final nominee died in 1783, all I have are reports of the total number of surviving nominees or the number of deaths, but not the names themselves. Moreover, as might be expected for the period, many of these reports contradict each other. For example, the number of annual deaths reported in the JHC from 1803 leads to 656 surviving nominees in 1718, which is a 65% survival rate over twenty-five years. In contrast, Mr. Coollage, whom I mentioned earlier, reports a much higher count of 719 nominees, which is a 71% survival rate. In general, it appears that the official House of Commons reports a larger number of deaths and a correspondingly lower number of survivors.[11] A summary of this can be seen in Table 5.2.

Table 5.1 provides a more granular view of the survival rates. It divides the 1,013 confirmed nominees into two-year age bands and examines their survival patterns over time. Remember that many nominees were above the age of thirty, and some as high as age fifty. Clearly, few of them survived to 1730 and 1749. Rather, and not surprisingly, it was the younger nominees who made it to the advanced years. And while the 1730 and 1749 living lists do not provide the best data for a formal comparison with child mortality rates, the list of surviving nominees for each year between 1693 and 1730 – available from the JHC – does provide us with some data for a formal test.

---

[10] The number 1,013 also appears in Walford (1871) and Dickson (1967) and in the JHC (1803). So, it is quite reasonable to conclude that 1,013 is the correct number despite the (incorrect) report of 1,002 nominees in Finlaison (1829), which also appears in Hargreaves (1966), Leeson (1968), Weir (1989), Poitras (2000), and most recently Lewin (2003). I suspect that all of these (incorrect) sources never actually counted the names on the Heyrick (1694) list. Interestingly, Jennings and Trout (1982) correctly list the number of nominees as 1,013 and footnote an alternative account supposing 1,002 nominees.

[11] I tested this "fraud hypothesis" and conducted the statistical tests using the lower number of survivors listed in JHC (1803), which would reduce the bias in statistical terms.

Table 5.2. *Resolving conflicting sources*

How many nominees were in King William's tontine?

Year of observation	JHC (1803)	Walford (1871)	King (1730)	Anon. (1749)	Finlaison (1829)
1693	1,013	1,013	1,013	1,013	1,002
1718	656	719	N.A.	N.A.	N.A.
1730	479	N.A.	514	N.A.	N.A.
1745	303	N.A.	N.A.	N.A.	N.A.
1749	N.A.	N.A.	N.A.	267	N.A.
1783	N.A.	N.A.	N.A.	N.A.	N.A.

Source: Compiled by the author.

Referring again to Table 5.1, even if one relies exclusively on the 1730 and 1749 living list documents listing the actual names of the surviving tontine nominees, it is clear that of the 282 nominees between the age of zero and five in 1693, a total of 163 (= 58%) survived for thirty-seven years to 1730 and a total of ninety-four (= 33%) of the young children nominees survived for fifty-six years to 1749. These survival rates might not appear out of line with demographics of the twenty-first century, but they are highly suspicious for the early eighteenth century.

One of the leading demographic authorities reports that the cumulative mortality rate during the first nine years of life was 27% in early eighteenth-century England.[12] The estimates were obtained by comparing death certificates to baptismal records for twelve different parishes. This would imply that if tontine nominees were representative of these parishes, approximately 70% of infants would survive to the age of ten. In a separate study by the same researchers it was estimated that the survival rate to the age of fifteen years for infants was 70% in the early part of the eighteenth century and 73% in the latter part of the same century.

Once again, recall that almost 60% of tontine nominees survived thirty-seven years to 1730. And, while estimates differ as to the exact magnitude of infant mortality rates, Table 5.3 compares four different sources for year-by-year mortality rates during the period in question. The first column shows the original values reported by Edmond Halley in 1693, whom I introduced in Chapter 4. The second column is extrapolated from the values reported by the demographers I mentioned above. The third is a French

---

[12] Wrigley and Schofield (2002).

Table 5.3. *Child mortality rates in late seventeenth century*

Age	Edmond Halley	Wrigley and Schofield	Simpson, per Deparcieux	Pitt
0 to 1	N.A.	16.70%	32.03%	19.60%
1 to 2	14.50%	7.71%	19.54%	4.48%
2 to 3	6.67%	3.56%	9.29%	4.17%
3 to 4	4.76%	1.65%	5.51%	3.67%
4 to 5	3.68%	0.76%	3.33%	2.96%
5 to 6	3.01%	0.35%	2.76%	1.74%
6 to 7	2.54%	0.16%	2.30%	1.78%
7 to 8	1.73%	0.07%	1.81%	1.66%
8 to 9	1.47%	0.03%	1.66%	1.07%
9 to 10	1.34%	0.02%	1.50%	1.08%
First 10 Years	33.90%*	28.10%	59.06%	36.10%

Source: Milevsky (2014).

mortality table (for comparison), and the final column was used to price the last British tontine in 1789, compiled by Mr. Pitt. They all tell the same story: A third of newborns didn't survive to double digits.[13]

So something smells fishy. Tontine nominees lived a very long time. Before we go any further with our fishing, I must discuss something and deal with some statistical background.

TESTING FOR SHENANIGANS IN MONTE CARLO

To test whether mortality rates for the period in question differed substantially from what was observed among the tontine nominees, I created a Monte Carlo Simulation similar to the one used to create the Stochastic Present Value in Chapter 2 (see Appendix B for more details). Instead of computing the present value of the tontine payments across thousands of

[13] See Alter (1983, 1986) for methodology. Halley's mortality rate ($_9q_1$) of 33.90% is for the age band 1 to 10, because he didn't report mortality rates for q_0. Mortality rates are based on expected (or observed) survivors at age $x+1$ divided by the expected (or observed) survivors at age x, starting at age $x = 0$. The Wrigley and Schofield (2002) mortality rates are based on the quoted survival rates to ages one, five, and ten during the 1650 to 1699 time period and then smoothed exponentially to produce annual rates, which is why the later years are lower. Deparcieux (1746) reports Simpson tables relevant to England. The Chatham Papers were tables included with the 1789 tontine proposal located at the National Archives (catalogue 30/8/277). Even under the most optimistic assumptions, less than 72% of live births survived to age ten.

paths, I focused instead on the date of death and computed the number of tontine survivors in the years 1695, 1697, 1699, 1701, and 1703. I then counted the number of scenarios in which the simulated survivors exceeded the observed number of survivors (rare) versus the number of scenarios in which the simulated survivors were less than the actual number of survivors (quite common).

For example, 986 survivors were reported for the second year of the tontine (in 1695). In other words, twenty-seven nominees (out of the original 1,013) had died in the first twenty-four months of the scheme, which is a mortality rate of 2.6% – or approximately 1.3% per year. But using the mortality rates computed by Edmond Halley and the exact age distribution of all 1,013 nominees, one would expect sixty-three deaths in this twenty-four-month period. The probability of observing (only) twenty-seven deaths when sixty-three were expected is 0.0012% and the null hypothesis (normal death rates) can be rejected at the 10%, 5%, and 1% levels. What this means very loosely speaking is that the chances this is "just a statistical fluke" are less than 1%. Yes, it is possible, but it is very unlikely.

The same low probabilities are observed for the years 1697, 1699, and 1701. The cumulative number of deaths is much less than expected and the cumulative number of survivors is far greater than expected, even when relying on the most conservative source (JHC 1803), which is biased toward reporting a higher number of deaths in Table 5.2.

For example, for 1703, which is ten years after the tontine was established, there are 892 survivors listed, according to the JHC document I referred to earlier. In ten years (only) 121 nominees died. The probability of this event, assuming the Halley mortality tables, is 0.20%. Once again, the null hypothesis (normal death rates) can be rejected at the 10%, 5%, and 1% levels.

There is yet another way to analyze the matter. Although the three primary documents do not have dates of death for any of the tontine nominees (and using Ancestry.com only provided a handful of logically consistent records), there is one possible source that can be used to *estimate* death dates and hence *estimate* implied mortality rates. In this subsection I briefly describe this approach and the results, which are broadly consistent with the earlier claim of possible fraud.

When Did Nominees Die?

On the last two pages of the document listed as King (1730) in the references, there are the names of all the nominees that died or were presumed dead on the eve of the dividend payment of June 1730. Recall that at that point in time there were 514 surviving nominees. The dividend payment per share listed on the third page of the same document was 7 pounds, 6 pence, and 2 shillings.

This list of deceased nominees in King (1730) is not in alphabetical order and does not seem to contain any specific pattern. If, however, I assume that list is given in a chronological order of (reported) deaths, then one can extract or solve for the implied mortality rates by using the information from the JHC (1803) document about the number of nominees that died in each year. There is strong reason to believe that this list was recorded in the order in which the death took place because a few of the death dates for well-known nominees are consistent with this order.

For example, the Duke of Gloucester, William Henry, was the most illustrious nominee of the 1693 tontine and died on July 30, 1700. His name is eighty-seventh on the list of deceased in the "tontine list," which coincides perfectly with the year of death implied by the (so-called) JHC document. Also, the first ten names on the list are consistent with the death order listed in Heyrick (1695).

If, in fact, these 499 names are listed in the order in which they died – combined with their ages in 1693 – then we have a much more robust data set of (censored) life spans that can be used to imply mortality rates.[14] More broadly, the 514 nominees who survived to the year 1730, plus the length of life spans lived by the 499 nominees who did not, together form a rich data set of 1,013. And while the purpose of this chapter is not a demographic analysis, I did examine the implied mortality rate of the nominees aged zero to nine and compared it against some of the mortality rates from that period.

The implied mortality rates for the first twenty-five years of life are converted to survival probabilities in Figure 5.2. This can be compared with any of the four mortality vectors listed in Table 5.3. King William's 1693 tontine nominees died at a (much) lower rate at younger ages. And while this isn't a formal hypothesis test – and the limited number of data points is quite low and imprecise – these results are consistent with the prior analysis. Tontine nominees seemed abnormally healthy and long-lived, which ipso facto raises the possibility of fraud. Moreover, if these numbers form the basis of demographic studies for the period, then some level of caution is warranted.

Ardent economic and actuarial supporters of anti-selection theory might not be convinced by these numbers and will attribute any evidence

---

[14] Using a standardized methodology suggested by Alter (1983).

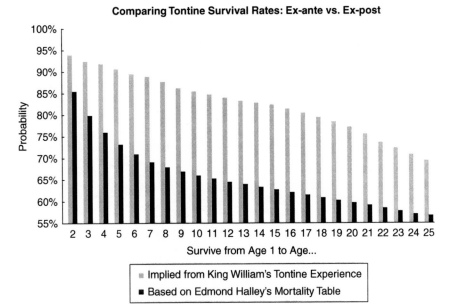

Figure 5.2. Can a tontine promote longevity in children?

of longer-lived nominees to the ability of investors (contributors) to select, monitor, and protect these children.[15] While I agree that the evidence doesn't necessarily imply fraud directly, I would argue that an alternative explanation to anti-selection deserves to be heard. This is especially important considering the fact that actuarial tables used in the eighteenth and nineteenth centuries in England to price annuities were based (in part) on the experience of tontine nominees.

In fact, John Finlaison himself in 1829 did not display mortality rates for ages zero to two in his (famous) report to the House of Commons on the underpricing of annuities even though he (claimed to have had) the entire series of tontine nominee survivorship data. Perhaps he too had doubts about the veracity of his data.[16]

The following (see Table 5.4) is extracted from a letter written by Finlaison in which he compared the "experience" of two groups of tontine nominees; the first English tontine in 1693 and the last one launched in 1789. He was

[15] It is worth noting that even among royalty and nobility the child mortality rate was quite high in the seventeenth and eighteenth centuries. For example, Queen Anne is reported to have had seventeen pregnancies, with five live births including Prince William, Duke of Gloucester.

[16] See Hald (2003).

Table 5.4. *John Finlaison's estimate of remaining life expectancy (female) based on mortality rates extracted from tontine nominee survivors. National Archives Item #T1/3744*

Age	1693 Tontine	1789 Tontine	Months gained
90	2.50	2.87	4
85	2.88	4.12	15
80	4.31	5.62	16
75	6.08	7.69	19
70	8.33	10.12	21
65	11.06	12.88	22
60	13.69	16.04	28
55	16.13	19.44	40
50	18.58	22.87	51
45	21.23	26.27	60
40	24.00	29.73	69
35	26.67	33.19	78
30	29.31	36.50	86
25	31.92	39.96	96
20	34.60	43.02	101
15	37.60	46.04	101
10	41.10	51.19	121
4	44.38	53.63	111

Source: Letter sent by John Finlaison to Dr. Southwood Smith on October 23, 1855.

interested in comparing the life expectancy of the two groups to measure the rate of mortality improvement during the (almost) century that had passed.

These numbers indicate an increase in life expectancy over the century or so, which is not surprising given the reduction in mortality rates at all ages. But notice that Finlaison didn't report values for ages younger than four, despite the hundreds of nominees in that age-group. I take this as further suggestion that he was suspicious of the quality (and accuracy) of the reported death rates.

TOM'S COFFEEHOUSE ON ST. MARTIN'S LANE

In fact, there is much anecdotal evidence in the early eighteenth century that tontine fraud was a major concern. Newspapers in the mid-eighteenth century printed letters from investors complaining about the low dividends from their tontines, relative to what had been claimed when the tontine was launched. Walford (1871) quotes from a pamphlet (attributed to Mr. Coollage) published circa 1720 and entitled *New Proofs in the Supposed Frauds in the Survivorship*. The document reviews the mortality rates computed by Edmond Halley and William Petty and compares them with the much lower mortality rates reported for the nominees of the 1693 tontine. Here is one telling quote which appears in Walford (1871, p. 115).

> Children of six years of age and under are swept away a great deal faster than younger men aged 16 to 30 and 35 years, by reason of the many dangerous sicknesses and infirmities which infancy is obnoxious [*sic*] to. This is the constant, certain, general, course of nature. But in this case you will see it is quite inverted. Where the disproportion but small, I should suspect no fraud, but it is so vast that for that very reason it is incredible.

The pamphlet goes on to accuse specific groups and ethnicities with the lowest mortality rates of being the main source of the fraud and concludes (p. 115) with: "All those concerned in this fund are desired to meet in person or by their agent at Tom's Coffee House in St. Martins Lane, London, at 4 o'clock on Monday the 24th of November, 1718 to consider methods to prevent this fraud." That must have been quite the meeting.[17]

It is worth noting that in the (last) British tontine launched in 1789, the founding act stipulated a long and complicated process for proving that a nominee was still alive. And the act ended with the following ominous warning: "If any person shall counterfeit any certificate or shall personate any nominee with a fraudulent intent, he shall on conviction suffer death." (Quite appropriate for a tontine, one might add.)

If this wasn't enough, in 1808, Parliament passed the British Life Annuity Act. The act reintroduced government-issued life annuities to the public with more appropriate (and actuarially fair) pricing. But the act effectively prohibited the sale of life annuities to nominees under the age of thirty-five.

FRENCH TONTINES, DEFAULTS, AND REVOLUTIONS

Although most of the historical narrative in this book has been focused on English tontines – and primarily King William's tontine issued in 1693 – I would be remiss if I didn't examine or discuss tontines that were offered by the French government around the same time. I'll take a quick pause and jump to the Continent to spend some time in France. As I mentioned at the beginning of Chapter 1, King Louis XIV of France – who was King William's

---

17 And I wish I could have been a fly on that wall.

lifetime nemesis – used money raised by tontines to help finance his wars (against England). In fact, tontines were extremely popular in France, much more so than they were in England even during their heyday in the late eighteenth century. This shouldn't be surprising. Remember that the French have a priority claim to the tontine ever since Lorenzo de Tonti's original proposal (in 1653) was sent to Louis XIV's financial caretakers. I must confess that if tontines have any nationality, then it probably should be French. So, here is a summary of what you should know about French tontines. And if you want to read more about them, I refer you to the extensive work by historians Jennings and Trout (1982), who wrote a scholarly book titled *The Tontine: From the Reign of Louis XIV to the French Revolutionary Era.* (1982). Yes, an entire book just on French tontines, which is also the primary source for the material in this section.

Five years after Lorenzo de Tonti died (in 1684), and almost forty years after his original proposal (in 1653), the French launched their first state tontine in 1689. One might plausibly argue that this was around the same time as King William's tontine of 1693. What is a mere few years in the time before e-mail, phones, trains, and cars? That said, it is quite plausible that the English were influenced by the French in this matter.

Interestingly, while the French government didn't quite like Lorenzo de Tonti's idea (thirty years earlier) in 1653, by 1689 they had warmed up to it – after some changes in the original design. Like the English, they still didn't call it a tontine, though. Talk about adding insult to injury. Lorenzo de Tonti got no royalties or commissions and they didn't even acknowledge his idea.

Overall, the general structure of the French 1689 tontine (actually, they called it a "life annuity with additional benefits of survivorship") was quite similar in concept to the English version, but it differed in a number of administrative as well as economic features. As in all tontines, a pool of investors would contribute (or lend) a sum of money to the king, city, or government. The investors as a group would then be entitled to interest on this money, which would be split among the annuitants as long as their nominee was still alive. Similar to the tontine across the English Channel, there were three parties in the French tontine deal: (i.) the investor, (ii.) the nominee, and (iii.) the annuitant. They could all be the same person, or they could be three distinct people. The shares could be sold to or traded with anyone as long as the corresponding nominee was still alive. There is nothing new here (yet).

In the French version, however, there were some different administrative features. First of all, the entry price or the minimum investment was lower, thus making state tontines accessible to a much wider segment of the general population. Think of the difference between a modern-day hedge fund versus a mutual fund. The former has entry minimums in the hundreds of thousands of dollars while the latter can be acquired with a few dollars, even though they might end up investing in the exact same underlying assets. The (name and) entry price determines the clientele.

In most French state tontines, including the first one issued in 1689, one share in the tontine cost (only) 300 livres compared with £100 for a share in the English tontine. The unit of currency at the time, the livre, was worth much less than a pound. While it is difficult to determine a precise exchange rate between the two in 1689, during the eighteenth century, the average exchange rate between the English pound and the French livre was 24 to 1, according to historians Jennings and Trout. So the currency-adjusted cost of a French tontine share was approximately £12.5. While it is unclear if Englishmen were allowed to buy shares in the French tontine, it's clear that the French tontine appealed to the (less wealthy) masses. And, perhaps as a result, they were much more popular in France. For example, whereas there were (only) a total of 1,013 nominees (and 1,081 shares issued) in King William's tontine, the 1689 French tontine – which I will take the liberty of referring to as King Louis XIV's tontine – had almost 6,000 nominees with more than 12,000 shares issued.

Nevertheless, the total sum raised in the first French tontine was (only) 3.6 million livres, which converted (at the 24-to-1 exchange rate) is £150,450. Like their English counterparts, the French were disappointed by the amount raised in the first national tontine, since they were projecting sums in the 20 million livre range. The relatively small sum they ended up collecting was just slightly more than the £108,100 raised in King William's tontine, but again the participation was much wider in France.

From an administrative point of view, the French imposed some strict and complicated (they were French, after all) verification procedures for confirming the exact age of the nominee as well as their proof of life and age of eventual death. The annuitant or investor needed to produce a notarized stamp to confirm life, and there were penalties for fraud as well as small economic incentives for the heirs to accurately report the death of a nominee. These sorts of rigorous processes were absent from King William's tontine of 1693, perhaps reducing the incidence, as well as concerns, with fraud in France.

There was another far more important economic difference between King Louis's (1689) and King William's (1693) tontines, and that was the amount of interest paid to annuitants. In France, age really mattered. The older the

Table 5.5. *King Louis XIV's first tontine in 1689*

Class #	Age band	Life horizon* (yrs.)	Fair tontine payout rate*	French 1689 tontine rate
1	0 to 5	85	5.08%	5.00%
2	5 to 10	80	5.10%	5.00%
3	10 to 15	75	5.13%	5.56%
4	15 to 20	70	5.17%	5.56%
5	20 to 25	65	5.22%	6.25%
6	25 to 30	60	5.28%	6.25%
7	30 to 35	55	5.37%	7.14%
8	35 to 40	50	5.48%	7.14%
9	40 to 45	45	5.63%	8.33%
10	45 to 50	40	5.83%	8.33%
11	50 to 55	35	6.11%	10.0%
12	55 to 60	30	6.51%	10.0%
13	60 to 65	25	7.10%	12.5%
14	65+	20	8.02%	12.5%

* These are theoretical or model values.

nominee at the time the tontine was initially set up, the higher the payout to the corresponding annuitant. For example, if the (French) nominee was under the age of five when the share was purchased, the payout rate to the annuitant pool was 5.00%, which is 15 livres per year for each 300 livres investment. The 15 livres would be expected to grow over time as (other) nominees died, just like any other tontine. But if the age of the nominee was between twenty and twenty-five at the time of issue, then the payout rate was 6.25%, which is 18.75 livres per year, for each 300 livres investment. Table 5.5 shows the entire range. Remember that the investor could select any nominee of any age – just like King William's tontine – but once the nominee was selected, his or her age would determine the (initial) payment.

The logic here is that the higher the age of the selected nominee, the lower his or her life expectancy. The higher payout rate compensates for the gradual return of the 300 livres over the shorter life span. At the highest age band, which applied to anyone above the age of sixty-five, the payout rate was 12.5% to the pool. As you might intuit, this was really driven by the concept of time value of money and economic fairness. If the nominee at the time of issuance wasn't expected to live a very long time, then the payment should be higher to compensate for the shorter time horizon. This is akin to amortizing the same mortgage loan over ten years versus thirty years. The longer the period of the (same) loan, the lower the annual payments. In fact, by now, many readers would have been puzzled by why King William's tontine didn't have this feature. I'll provide one possible explanation later, but for now I'll note that in France they did things differently.

As you can see from Table 5.5, King Louis's (1689) tontine had fourteen distinct classes or age bands for nominees. These separate classes didn't mix or subsidize each other. For example, when a member of class #8 (i.e., age band thirty-five to forty) died, this would have no impact on payments to the other thirteen classes. In some sense you can think of the French (1689) tontine as being fourteen separate and parallel tontines launched at the exact same time. Each one of the fourteen tontine (classes) was only open or available to nominees in a certain age band. There were no cross-subsidies from one age band to another, which reflects that people at different ages have different death rates. According to the French, it really wasn't fair to treat every nominee equally. In this regard, the French should be commended for their forward thinking and financial sophistication. I'll build on this idea – of not having subsidies across different age bands – in Chapter 8, when I discuss the optimal tontine structure for the twenty-first century.

Now, before one gets too carried away with the apparent sophistication of the French in 1689 relative to the English in 1693, I should note that the fourteen different payout rates per class were *not* determined in a very precise and scientific manner. In fact, whoever set up or priced the French deal (in 1689) used a crude and rather blunt formula. I'll get to what they (probably) did in a moment. They certainly didn't use the main formula that I displayed in Chapter 2, linking payments to interest rates and time horizons. The French get partial credit for thinking properly – older nominees deserve more – but their execution was faulty.

How Should the French Have Done It Properly?

First, let's start with a systemwide or economic interest rate, which at the time in France was 5%.[18] Using (very) modern-day language, I'll assume the term structure of interest rate in France (in 1689) was flat at 5% for all maturities. I revisit this matter later in Chapter 7 when I discuss tontine pricing in a world with upward or downward sloping interest rate curves. For now let's keep things simple and start with the youngest age band class

---

[18] According to Homer and Sylla (1990), the long-term rate of interest in France available on perpetuities at the time was roughly 5%.

#1, which applied to nominees who were newborns up until the age of five. Next, to properly price the French issue, I assume – and this clearly is a delicate assumption – that the maximum length of life for a typical person in this class was eighty-five years. In other words, the longest possible time the French government would be paying the first class was eighty-five years. Here is the technical question: *How much should a tontine pay out to a group with a (maximum) eighty-five-year horizon?*

Well, this now boils down to a (pure) math problem, one I alluded to in Chapter 2. Here is another way of phrasing this. For every 300 livres contributed to the tontine what is the "fair payout" rate to the annuitant pool over the next eighty-five years, so that the present value of payments at 5% system interest is exactly equal to 300 livres. Remember, in a tontine somebody will be receiving those payments until the last nominee survives (eighty-five years), so the government will be making those payments for eighty-five years.

Plugging in the interest rate of 5%, the present value of 300 livres and the time horizon of eighty-five years into the PVA formula (or any business calculator) leads to approximately 15.24 livres per year. In mortgage terms, if you borrowed 300 livres at a rate of 5%, then payments of 15.24 livres per year will pay off the entire loan in eighty-five years. Finally, expressing this as a yield by dividing the 15.4 livres into the 300 livres is equivalent to a payout rate of 5.08% per year. This is what I call the fair tontine rate assuming the eighty-five-year (maximum) horizon and assuming the 5% systemwide interest rate.

Was this the actual rate the French paid to this group? Not quite. The payout rate was 5.00%. Yes, this is very close for the first age band, but for older age bands the number was (much) higher than the same formula or approach would suggest. Look at the last column in Table 5.5 – which is what the French were offering their people – and compare with the numbers from the present value factor listed in the fourth column on the same table. The French were being too generous (relative to what a financial economist would recommend).

Take class #12, for example, which is the nominee age band from fifty-five to sixty. Assuming a maximum length of life of eighty-five years (again), the time horizon on the payments to this pool of people (the youngest of whom would be fifty-five) was thirty more years. Plugging the 5% interest, 300 livres principal, and thirty-year horizon into the main pricing formula leads to 19.52 livres, which is a fair payout rate of 6.51% to this class. Notice that the actual rate paid to this class was 10%, which is almost 3.5% higher compared with what theory would suggest. Notice that other than the first two classes, every single number in the rightmost column of Table 5.5 is higher compared with the "fair payout" rates.[19]

Could it be that I used the wrong system interest rate? Perhaps the rate should be (much) higher, so that the formula provides a larger tontine payout? If this is the case, then the 5% to ages zero to ten would be uncompetitive. Also, interest rates in France for perpetuities were in the 5% range. This is a reasonable and grounded number to use for discounting purposes. Another possibility (to explain pricing) is that the French assumed that the time horizon – which is the third critical variable in the time value of money formula – was lower than the age eighty-five that I assumed. But then again, the rate to the younger classes would have had to be higher. Also, given that there was a class of nominees above the age of sixty-five, there was an awareness that people could live to what today would be called retirement age. Another perhaps more sophisticated explanation is that the higher-than-expected payout was compensation for risk that individual participants were exposed to. After all, what is fair to the entire pool itself may not be fair to individuals within the pool. This is what economist call idiosyncratic risk and should not be compensated, really. I may be getting ahead of myself here, and I'll get back to these rather subtle issues later in the book.

The consensus among historians, though, including David Weir whom I mentioned earlier, is that the French knew they were overpaying (relative to the English) and were being generous for a reason. I'll get to his reason in a moment.

At this point it is worth repeating the comment by the economist Adam Smith, that there really is no need to be generous. According to him, people overestimate their (nominee's) longevity relative to their peers and might be inclined to accept a lower rate, compared with the fair economic rate. In that sense, the French were really paying way too much on their tontines, relative to their perpetual bonds at 5%.

Before I get to why they were being so generous, let me address a related issue.

If they weren't using the proper formula, then how exactly did the French compute the payout? Well, they used a crude rule – perhaps you can see it hiding in the last column of Table 5.5. For the first two age bands (zero to ten) they offered 1/20 = 5%. For the second two age bands (ten to twenty)

---

[19] The French created separate bands to make it "fairer" for the older band. This is why they offered the same rate to two bands. They both get the same payout, but the older band will "die out" faster and hence offer better returns to the survivors.

they offered 1/18 = 5.56%. For the third two age bands (twenty to thirty) they used 1/16 = 6.25%, and so on. There were no fancy formulas. They subtracted two years from twenty and took the reciprocal value. You might complain (especially if you are French) that it isn't fair to expect the government in 1689 to use the proper formulas, but they continued with this crude practice with most of their subsequent tontines well into the late eighteenth century.

James Riley, a noted historian, is quoted in Weir (1989, p. 100) as saying: "French financial authorities were inept in mathematics and failed to learn what Dutch and British predecessors had about the actual costs of life annuity loans." Indeed, the French continued to float (expensive and overpriced) tontines using the same crude methodology until the Revolution.

The End of the French

After the 1689 tontine, the French floated another nine popular state tontines, whereas the English floated a few tontines in Ireland and one big tontine.[20] The number of investors and nominees and the amount of funds raised was much higher in France. (I discuss the last English one in Chapter 6.)

In 1696 the French issued another tontine in which almost 10,000 shares were sold, linked to 4,000 nominees. This one had fifteen age bands, but again used the same crude methodology for determining payout rate. The French went to the market with tontines in 1733, 1734, 1744, 1745, and so on, every few years. In fact, the 1745 French tontine was astonishingly popular, with almost 30,000 shares sold to the public. And the interest rates paid to the fifteen classes (in the 1745 tontine) was 2% higher than they were for the first 1689 version. Either way tontines were extremely popular in France, much more so than in England. The (more) generous yield were likely a big part of the story.

Some argue that tontines were more popular in France compared with England because of their distinct cultural personalities. The noted actuary Alexander G. Finlaison (the grandson of John Finlaison) wrote the following in 1860, well after government tontines had past their popularity, and quoted in Weir (1981, p. 107) "They were always more popular on the continent that in this country, where benefits for the entire solace of his old age are

---

[20] See the MIT survey paper by Casey Rothschild (2003), for a discussion of the three Irish tontines that were launched in the eighteenth century, prior to the last English tontine, which was floated in the year 1789.

generally neglected by the Englishman in favor of a provision for his immediate successors."[21] It seems as if he was saying that Frenchmen thought more about themselves (and less about their children) compared with the English. That's a possible theory for why they were more popular, but remember that Alexander Finlaison was an Englishman – so he was biased.

In a more extreme version of this theory, the famous Scotsman Adam Smith in Wealth of Nations, book V, Ch. III, Pt. V – which is listed as Smith (2000) in the bibliography – offered the following explanation. He writes on page 995: "In France the seat of government not being in a great mercantile city, merchants do not make so great a proportion of the people who advance money to government. The people concerned in the finances, the farmers general [and] the receivers of taxes ... make the greater part of those who advance their money in all public exigencies." Thus, according to Adam Smith, who was writing well before the French revolution, the investors who participated in French tontines were quite different in nature, personality, and most importantly in occupation. He then goes on to write (p. 996) "Such people are commonly men of mean birth but of great wealth and frequently of great pride. They are too proud to marry their equals and women of quality disdain to marry them. They frequently resolve, therefore, to live bachelors and having neither any families of their own, not much regard for those of their relations whom they are not very fond of acknowledging." Ouch! And, if you think this is insulting to the French, Adam Smith then goes on to write (p. 995): "They desire only to live in splendor during their own time and are not unwilling that their fortune should end with themselves." He then concludes (p. 995) "To such people, who have little or no care for posterity, nothing can be more convenient than to exchange their capital for a revenue which is to last just as long [as them] and no longer". So, the French loved their tontines because they were selfish. And, while one might debate or even dismiss Adam Smith's characterization of Frenchman in the eighteenth century, even a twenty-first century (and very liberal) economist would agree that if you have no bequest motives, then tontines and/or life annuities are the ideal investment.

Personally, I suspect that it was better relative pricing – and not just weaker personalites – that was a big part of their popularity in France relative to England. In fact, large and very wealthy international investors took notice of French tontines.

---

[21] Quoted in Weir (1989).

THE SWISS ARBITRAGE THE FRENCH

Nowadays if a wealthy banker or financier contacted you to inquire if you knew of any young, healthy females you could recommend, you would likely turn away in disgust and perhaps contact the legal authorities. But in the eighteenth century in Geneva, the process of locating young and healthy females was quite popular, and not for the reasons you might suspect. These bankers wanted them as nominees for tontine annuities, hoping to arbitrage the generous pricing of the French.[22] These investors would pool together their funds and purchase a portfolio of French tontine shares – each with a different young female nominee – and they took very good care of these nominees during their life to ensure their ongoing dividends.

The French tontine mania came to a crashing end with a series of staggered blows to annuitants. The first blow was a royal edict in 1763 banning all future government tontines. They were perceived as too expensive. I suspect there should be no arguments there. Indeed, no further royal (government) tontines were issued in France after 1763. Those French people who owned one already considered themselves lucky. They continued to enjoy their dividends and payouts. But then things got worse for existing annuitants in 1770 when the Controller General of France froze tontine payments to all subscribers of all (previous) government tontines. It forcefully converted all existing tontines into straight life annuities at the same level. So if the annuitant was already receiving tontine payments of, say, 50 livres per year, then this would continue for the rest of his life. But no further raises or growth would be added. As other nominees in the same class died, their life-contingent payments would not be redistributed to survivors. Instead the money (from the deceased) was transferred to the state. The appeal of tontines was taken away retroactively. Things got even worse.

Over time (after 1770) the payment on these tontines – which were now converted to straight life annuities – fell into arrears. In other words, the government started delaying payments. In some sense one can say that they defaulted. At this point the total amount of royal French debt was so large, including tontines, life annuities, and other forms of borrowing, that servicing this debt (i.e., paying the interest alone) was consuming half of the Crown's revenues. Some have argued that the enormous debts and financial pressures are what led to the next fatal step. The final death knell for tontines arrived with the French Revolution.

---

[22] See Jennings and Trout (1982).

During the revolutionary decade starting in 1789, tontine (i.e., annuity) payments were first devalued and then debased, when they were converted from (the old) livres to the new French currency called the *assignat*. And, while this isn't the place to delve into the financial implications of the French Revolution, most annuitants ended up receiving little if anything on their tontines. No different from many other French debt holders.

According to David Weir, there were more than 30,000 French men and women who held tontine shares at the start of the French Revolution. Sadly, most of these people owned shares that were close to worthless by the end of the eighteenth century. By the time Napoleon came on the scene on the eve of the nineteenth century, the tontine and annuity certificates became nothing more than collector's items of little intrinsic financial value. Then again, the French had more than money on their minds during the violent period of the Revolution.

Why were the French so generous before the Revolution? According to Weir, French tontines (i.) paid above-market rates compared with King William's tontine and (ii.) were designed with low minimum investments precisely so that the French monarchy could forge a close link with the urban middle class who was benefiting from the tontines. In other words, the tontines were used as a type of bribe to the masses.

If this is true, then contrary to the claim made by Adam Smith, the French tontine was an expensive and onerous way for the government to borrow money and not a financial panacea. Either way, this particular method of bonding with the masses didn't quite work out as evidenced by what happened to Marie Antoinette and her husband – and a whole bunch of other royals – during the French Revolution.

In an odd twist of historical fate, just as the French were about to storm the Bastille on July 14, 1789, and begin the decade long process of the French Revolution, the English were about to launch their largest ever tontine scheme, known as the Great English Tontine of 1789. And this time the English had learned their lessons. By 1789, the English had a much better knowledge of the science of mortality. Their pricing efficiency caught up to, and surpassed, the French. Their numbers were exactly what the formula would prescribe with no extra financial gifts to the English annuitants. Adam Smith would be proud. I'll return to the 1789 tontine at the end of this chapter.

But first, considering that the French tontine was segmented by age, why did King William's tontine have constant rates for all ages? The next section provides a possible answer.

AGE DOESN'T MATTER: WHAT WERE THEY THINKING?

As I mentioned earlier, investors selected nominees in King William's tontine on whose life the annuity was contingent. They ranged in age from as young as a few days old all the way to a middle-aged fifty-year-old. Earlier I provided information about the nominees themselves, many of whom were quite famous in their own right. But now that you understand the longevity mechanics of tontines and annuities – that is, the need to select a nominee who is expected to live the longest – you might be wondering: fifty years old? What were they thinking? After all, didn't the promoters and the government understand that older nominees are more likely to die, compared with younger nominees? Why didn't the government restrict the ages or perhaps place them into different classes or categories (like Tonti himself proposed) and the French implemented?

According to P. G. M. Dickson (1967, p. 53), the attractive investment return that was implicitly being offered to investors who selected young nominees was to entice and coax the investing public into "the novel experiment of government long-term borrowing." At this early stage of the experiment the government couldn't afford to be stingy. But one still must wonder why all ages were lumped together. At the very least nominees of different ages could have been segmented, as they were in the earlier (City of London) proposals. Why should a five-year-old (nominee) benefit from the death of a thirty-five-year-old (nominee)? In Chapter 7 I argue that in the ideal tontine scheme one doesn't mix generations. But this was clearly not how King William's tontine was structured.

Now, granted, hindsight – after 320 years of actuarial science – is twenty-twenty, but even if the government wasn't "thinking" when they priced the deal, why didn't the tontine investors take advantage of the early mispricing? Why not nominate ten-year-old females as the people on whose lives the payment was contingent? Recall that this was the most likely or modal age in the nominee sample, but most nominees were older/younger.

Didn't investors realize that young girls are expected to live the longest and hence increase the chance of winning the tontine? They were certainly aware of this in Geneva a half century later. If I were participating in a tontine today, I would nominate the youngest (healthiest, of course) baby girl I could find. In the year 1693, the lowest mortality rates were at age 10.

Now, the easy answer is to throw your hands up and declare that they just weren't thinking, period. This was more than 320 years ago, and investors didn't have access to the medical, statistical, and actuarial science we have today. Perhaps they didn't really understand that death wasn't completely random and there was an age-based pattern. Then again, with people like astronomer Edmond Halley, physicist Isaac Newton, and mathematician Abraham de Moivre to consult with in London around the same time, and the large stakes involved, one desires a more satisfactory explanation for what they were thinking.[23] Perhaps a better explanation is available.

Flat Mortality Rates?

First of all, as I mentioned earlier in this chapter, in the late seventeenth century infant mortality rates were abnormally high. The first few months of life were perilous and 10% to 30% of newborn children didn't make it to their first birthdays. Today the infant mortality rate in the developed world is less than 1 in 10,000, so we take for granted that babies are likely to live longer than a ten-year-old. This was not so in 1693. It would have been risky to pick newborn infants.

How about investors who nominated twenty- and thirty-year-olds? Didn't they realize that the younger their nominee, the longer they would live, which would lead to higher income for longer? Well, here too there is a possible way to justify their (in hindsight, wrong) thinking. Perhaps they thought a twenty-year-old isn't more likely to live any longer than a thirty- or forty-year-old. Sound odd? Well, it actually resonates with some recent work on aging and a phenomenon called mortality plateauing at advanced ages. I'll get to that later. First, let me review some basic probability theory.

Imagine for a moment that the length of life obeys a fair coin toss and the chances of dying in any given decade are precisely fifty-fifty. So the chances of a newborn baby living to the age of ten are 50%, and the chances of living to the age of twenty (i.e., two heads in a row) are $0.5 \times 0.5 = 25\%$, and the chances of living to the age of thirty (i.e., three heads in a row) are $(0.5)^3 = 12.5\%$, and so on. This might sound unrealistic for a number of reasons, including the fact that even during the worst of the London plague in 1666, the survival rate for newborns to the age of fifty was probably better than $(0.5)^5 = 3.125\%$, but bear with me here for a moment. Here is how to think about this more precisely. Imagine that time is measured in decades and mortality rates are constant at exactly 50% per decade. Whether you are

---

[23] See the entertaining book by Levenson (2009), or Belenkiy (2013), for a description of some of Newton's extracurricular (outside of physics) activities at the Mint. See Bellhouse (2011) for a recent biography of de Moivre and his involvement in (an early form of) financial consulting.

Table 5.6. *How does mortality impact expected remaining length of life?*

Decade number	Ecosystem A		Ecosystem B	
	Mortality rate per decade	Expected length of life at start of decade	Mortality rate per decade	Expected length of life at start of decade
1	50%	20 years	47.7%	20.0 years
2	50%	20 years	50.1%	19.11 years
3	50%	20 years	52.7%	18.25 years
4	50%	20 years	55.4%	17.43 years
5	50%	20 years	58.2%	16.64 years
6	50%	20 years	61.2%	15.88 years
7	50%	20 years	64.3%	15.16 years

a newborn, ten years old, or forty years old, the death rate is 50%. Naturally, in such a society you are unlikely to see many eighty-year-olds.

But here is the main question. What would be the ideal age for a tontine's nominee in such an ecosystem? Would you rather nominate a newborn, a teenager, or a centenarian? (Assuming you can find any.)

If your initial gut reaction is (still) to nominate the youngest person you know, because they are likely to live the longest – then you are actually wrong. *The right answer is that it makes absolutely no difference!* Personally, if I inhabited such an ecosystem and was picking nominees for a tontine, I would pick anyone. Age would be of no relevance. No matter how old the nominee is, his or her life expectancy would be identical. In fact, nobody really ages in such a system. People die, but they don't age.

Let's go through the math. Table 5.6 compares the number of years a nominee is expected to be alive, assuming two different mortality regimes or what I call ecosystems. In the first ecosystem, the mortality rate is a constant 50% every single decade. Under a continuous mortality rate of 50% per decade, the life expectancy at birth is the inverse of the mortality rate, which is two decades or twenty years.[24] But, and this is key, if you do the exact same calculation for a nominee that is already ten years old, you get the same answer. Because the mortality rate doesn't change from decade to decade, the life expectancy remains constant with age. As long as you are

[24] Warning: The mortality rate per decade (50%) and probability of dying in any given decade (39.35%) are distinct numbers. See Appendix C.

alive, your life expectancy is a constant number of years away. There are actually a number of organisms, like lobsters, that exhibit this nonaging behavior. Sure. They get *older*, but they don't get any closer to *death*.

It might take a while for the lightbulb to go on, but eventually it will hit you. Age is meaningless (as far as death rates are concerned) when the mortality or hazard rate is constant over time.

The fourth and fifth column in the table examine the same calculation in an ecosystem in which mortality rates are not constant but actually increase over time. In ecosystem B, the mortality rate starts off in the first decade (of life) at 47.7% and then increases (by about 5% per decade) to 50.1% in the second decade and then 52.7% in the third decade, and so on. Now, I picked these numbers deliberately so that if you compute the life expectancy for a newborn, the answer is also twenty years. But in this system, once a nominee gets to the age of ten, the mortality rate has increased relative to the previous decade and the life expectancy declines – as you would expect. The ten-year-old nominee is expected to live for 19.11 more years, while the twenty-year-old nominee is expected to live 18.25 more years, and so on. Notice how small changes to the mortality rate per decade – a flat 50% compared with an increasing rate – can tip the balance from a constant life expectancy to a (slowly) shrinking one.

Here is my main point. Real human beings age, and their mortality rates do increase over time. We are unlike coin tosses for a variety of reasons, primarily because the coin is more likely to fall tails (i.e., death) the older you are. But there are many organisms that exhibit flat mortality rates as in ecosystem A; that is, their odds of dying do not change over time (and they do not age). You might be surprised to learn that lobsters do not age. Their mortality rate is the same regardless of how long they have been alive (at about 15% per year). Even more surprising – and perhaps shocking – there is a growing body of biological evidence that mortality rates at very advanced human ages (near the 100-year mark) are constant and possibly even the same for males and females. This is not quite proven science yet – and I'll discuss this again later – but the hypothesis is that if you get to the age of 105 (aka super-centenarian), the odds of dying in the next year are remarkably close to fifty-fifty.

Yes, you obviously have a very small chance of reaching 120, which is another fifteen heads in a row from age 105, but the aging process stops. I know it is hard to fathom old people not aging, but it is important to differentiate between a small chance of living a long time and aging. They are two different things.

Now, let's get back to King William's tontine in 1693. Why didn't the organizers force people to pick nominees under a certain age or within a certain range? Even more puzzling, why didn't all investors pick 10 year old females? Note that ten was the modal age. Why would someone pick a twenty-five-year-old as the nominee? Didn't they realize that the ten-year-old would live longer?

Well, one possible answer (now) is that they perhaps believed that human mortality rates were constant (like lobsters), similar to the column representing ecosystem A in the table. If, indeed, this was the case, nominees who were younger weren't any more likely to live longer than nominees who were older. Remember that this was before we learned everything we now know about aging and mortality rates. So, while they were obviously wrong, perhaps they weren't stupid.

A tontine for lobsters anyone? The last one standing gets (to be) dinner.

LESSONS LEARNED: THE GREAT TONTINE OF 1789

While King William was there to launch the *first* English tontine, the *Great* English Tontine, which was also the last national tontine, was launched under the rein of King George III in 1789 (see Figure 5.3 for an early draft). It was planned and promoted with great ambition, hoping to raise £1 million similar to the plan launched almost a century prior. This time it wasn't to finance a war against a French king. The French had their own (internal) problems in 1789 dealing with their (famous) Revolution.

The funds from the 1789 English tontine weren't earmarked for any particular war or battle. The money from this tontine was intended for general government revenue.

The plan stipulated the contribution of £100 subscription to be paid slowly over time. The investor was supposed to contribute 10 pounds on June 12, 1789, and then payments of £15 until the final payment on January 29. Recall that the 1693 tontine was paid in one lump sum, up front.

There are some other things worth noting about the 1789 (and last English) tontine. There were six distinct shares based on age, and each class had its own payout rate. The youngest (nominee) class received a payout of 4.15% and the oldest (for those above the age of sixty) received a payout of 5.6%. This was much less generous compared with the earlier terms under King William, which ranged from 10% to 7%. Interest was to be paid semiannually, at midsummer and Christmas at the Exchequer, where books

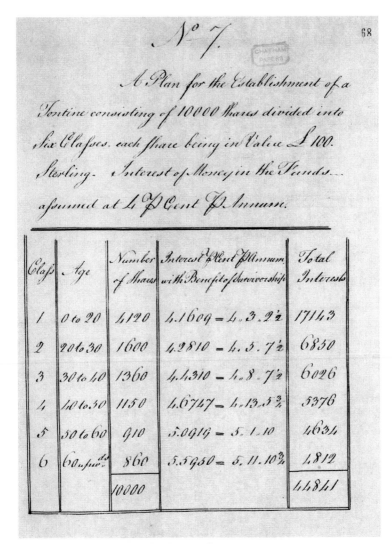

Figure 5.3. Draft of the 1789 tontine proposal.
Source and permission granted by the National Archives Imagine Library manager, Surey.

were to be kept for the tontine "in the same manner as is practiced at the bank," according to the preamble to the act which appears in the above referenced National Debt Office document (1868, p. 3) Also, this time around the government "engaged to take every method to facilitate the mode of conducting the business and to prevent frauds on the survivors," (on p. 7)

Table 5.7. *Tontine of King George III*

Class (age)	Started in 1789			Still alive in 1869	
	Subscriber shares; (nominees)	Government-appointed shares	Tontine payout rate%	Subscriber shares	Government-appointed shares
0–20	2,810; (2,435 nominees)	3,979	4.150	191 (6.79%)	269 (6.76%)
20–30	525; (441 nominees)	603	4.275	Extinct in 1864	
30–40	360; (270 nominees)	396	4.425	Extinct in 1856	
40–50	272; (187 nominees)	377	4.675	Extinct in 1845	
50–60	170; (115 nominees)	302	5.075	Extinct in 1834	
60+	82; (50 nominees)	76	5.600	Extinct in 1824?	
TOTAL	**4,219; (3,498)**	**5,733**			

The total number of shares was 10,000. Forty-eight shares were forfeited (respectively from each class: 32, 6, 4, 3, 2, 1).

Source: "A List of the surviving nominees appointed by the contributors and by the Treasury, to the Tontine of the year 1789, pursuant to an Act of Parliament ... passed in the 29th year of ... George the Third. Also a list of defaulters for the last two years." National Debt Office, May 20, 1868. England (London, 1868).

which might have been a result of some of the concerns I mentioned at the beginning of the chapter.

Another interesting feature of the 1789 tontine was that when the interest on the shares had reached £1,000 each – that is, a sufficiently large number of people had died – the tontine became an annuity. Once again, this reduced any concerns (or incentives) to murder the last few participants.

But the biggest difference between the 1693 (first) and 1789 (last) English tontines was in how the nominees were selected. The subscription for the 1789 tontine was quite weak and unenthusiastic. Only a few thousand subscribed. But the government wanted to continue the scheme as if a full 10,000 investors had subscribed. So they selected a random group of individuals to act as pseudo-nominees to fill in the missing numbers. And while these nominees were simply place fillers – they received no dividends and had no financial interest in the tontine – the government was very careful to select from among the gentry and nobility.[25]

As you can see from Table 5.7, these nominees ended up living almost the same amount of years on average as the real nominees did. One was a reasonably accurate statistical sample of the other.

STAYING ALIVE ... BY ANNUITIZING

One thing is for absolutely certain – in the best of Freakonomics tradition, being a nominee for a tontine scheme is likely to imply that you will live longer than your friends and neighbors, even if you aren't receiving the financial benefits of the tontine! This echoes Jane Austen's quote in Chapter 1 of her novel *Sense and Sensibility*: "People always live for ever when there is an annuity to be paid them."

---

[25] See Huntington (1792) for the entire list of nominees, the payout rates, and the enabling Act of Parliament.

6

Is Your Tontine a Stock or a Bond?

BUILDING FINANCIAL BRIDGES

The tontine of King William – as well as the subsequent one launched in 1789 – was debt financing, pure and simple. The tontines issued in France and the Netherlands were also debt. But recall from your Finance 101 lectures, there are other ways to finance a business, and, indeed, tontines could be used as equity financing, as well.

One of the first examples of tontine equity (i.e., not bond) financing was used to build a bridge 50 miles to the east of the City of London in the northern coast of Kent in the year 1774. For this tontine, a total of £24,000 was raised through 2,000 shares of £12 each. Dividends were paid quarterly, but the nominee had to be alive at the last day of the quarter. Of the entire amount (£24,000) raised and not used in completing the bridge, the balance was kept to repair the bridge and amend roads. Shares were canceled upon the death of a nominee. Once the 2,000 shares had been reduced by 75% to 500 (shares, nominees), the holders of the shares became proprietors of the bridge and tolls, and the shares continued as bona fide property, which was transferrable. The bridge was known as the Tontine Bridge, and the dividends came from the tolls of those who used the bridge.

THE GLASGOW TONTINE SOCIETY

Another interesting example of a tontine share structure that was used as a method of corporate financing – as opposed to government financing – was the Glasgow Tontine Society, which will soon be celebrating its 200-year anniversary. This particular scheme was launched in 1816 with a contributed capital of £20,000 shares of £25 each – a sum worth approximately thirty times as much in 2015 after inflation is accounted for – which was divided into 800 shares. This tontine was very successful with 100% of shares subscribed by 158 different investors (aka proprietors) acquiring an average of five shares each. These investors nominated a total of 442 different lives, or nominees, most of which were either their children or themselves. It seems that few nominated strangers.

The largest investor in the Glasgow Tontine Society was a Mr. Colin Blackburn Sr., who purchased a total of forty shares, representing an investment of £1,000, which is obviously not a trivial (lottery ticket) sum. Of the forty shares he acquired, fifteen units were linked to his son Colin Jr., another fifteen to his son John, and the final ten to his son Peter. We have no records indicating how long the three children lived, but this was the largest single (family) investment in the Glasgow Tontine Society. Among other notable names in 1816 was Reverend James Mylne, listed as a professor of moral philosophy at Glasgow University, who purchased five shares on his four sons and one daughter. Note that he was a professor of moral philosophy. So much for those who think tontines are amoral.

Now, to be accurate, the Glasgow Tontine Society structure was slightly different from King William's 1693 original scheme. In this scheme – which was managed by a group of seven trustees selected in a democratic manner by the 158 investors – the contributed money was used to purchase and then manage real estate property. The trustees bought various buildings and then leased them to businesses and inhabitants in downtown Glasgow. In fact, the society owned the George Inn and the Antigua Building, which are names that probably don't mean much to you unless you live in downtown Glasgow. The point here is that the rental income and revenue from these properties were distributed semiannually to the investors, provided that their nominee was still alive. And, like any other tontine, if and when a particular nominee died, the shares linked to their name were redistributed and reallocated to the survivors – a process that should be familiar by now.

But here is where it gets interesting. In contrast to King William's tontine scheme, the last remaining survivor of Glasgow's tontine society actually inherited *all* the buildings and *all* the properties. The payoff from winning – that is, having a nominee who is the last survivor – was far greater than the entire basket of dividends. The winner got everyone's principal back, which is something that was forfeited in King William's version. This seemingly minor difference is a "big deal" and raises the stakes quite substantially within the tontine.

Now, oddly enough, the detailed regulations of the Glasgow Tontine Society – a document currently stored and available in the archives of the British Library in London – placed absolutely no restrictions on the age of the nominee back in 1816. Although the regulations were very careful and extremely precise on how an investor must prove their nominee was still alive – namely, by providing a certificate from a magistrate or the minister of the parish where there nominee resided – the organizers didn't even bother to list the ages of the 442 nominees in the original document. Only the names and places of abode were listed. All we know is that in total 181 of the 442 nominees were male and 261 were female. There is no record of their ages in the year 1816 or any year after that.

I must say that it's quite odd that even in 1816 – which is more than 120 years after the launch of the 1693 tontine – the organizers of the Glasgow Tontine Society didn't appreciate the importance of placing some restriction, or for that matter even listing, the age of the tontine nominee.

The Glasgow Tontine Society was wound up and closed down in 1939. This was *124 years* after the scheme was set up in 1816, according to a notice in the *Glasgow Herald* on April 29, 1939. At this juncture you might be wondering if the last remaining nominee actually lived for 124 years. Did one of the Glasgow nominees live for 124 years? The answer is no. What happened with this particular scheme is that in 1901 – which is eighty-five years after the society was launched – there were actually four remaining nominees alive. Four of the 442 nominees survived for eighty-five years. Remember, this is 1901.

Now, think of the stakes at that point. As soon as three of the four nominees died, the remaining one would gain access to millions of pounds' worth of real estate. So instead of taking their chances, the representatives of the four shareholders folded their poker hands – so to speak. In early 1901, they entered into a new arrangement to share the properties regardless of who died next. The four survivors reached a new agreement to share the remaining property among the four shareholders, equally. Then, in 1939, the last of the assets was sold and the tontine scheme – or what remained of it – was disbanded forever.

Dealing with the last few remaining survivors in a tontine scheme can be problematic and controversial. The risk and reward trade-off becomes extreme. The survivor gets all and the losers get nothing. Recall that King William's tontine capped the payout once seven nominees remained. Other schemes have copied the same idea. But the evidence suggests that once only a handful of nominees remain they can't handle the heat, so to speak, and come to their own arrangement. The Glasgow Tontine Society is yet another good example of the importance of thinking through the last act carefully, before the tontine is launched. The winner-take-all approach is simply not a sustainable or desirable design.

Figure 6.1. One of the many tontine hotels … in Scotland.

I can personally attest to the fact that the city of Glasgow is a modern-day monument to tontine schemes. The downtown core has a street called Tontine Lane, and a large and famous structure called the Tontine Building, as well as numerous stores and shops with the word *tontine* in their name. Moreover, in addition to the tontine societies and associations discussed earlier, it is also home to a lovely hotel called, yes, the Tontine Hotel. In fact, it is one of three hotels in Scotland with the word *tontine* in its name!

Glasgow's Tontine Hotel (see Figure 6.1) is located approximately 20 miles west of the city in an area called Greenock. It was funded and constructed back in 1805 using – yes, you guessed it – a tontine scheme. A number of investors and partners got together to contribute money to build a hotel. This hotel still stands today, and it operates as a lovely bed-and-breakfast situated in Ardgowan Square, where I spent a night finishing up the manuscript to this book. As you can imagine, the last surviving partner inherited the entire hotel. Alas, the current owners (in 2014) are not related to the last remaining survivor – their family acquired the property twenty-five years ago – but the tontine spirit lives on in the hotel today.

Oh, and here is one final factoid that might generate a chuckle. The Tontine Building, which is located in downtown Glasgow on a very old and famous street called Trongate, used to have a large statue of a man riding a horse placed at the front of the building. The statue was erected in 1735 and placed at the center of the commercial district. Old pictures of the Tontine Building show this massive statue, with a man in Roman attire atop a fine horse, towering over the area. Sadly, the statue had to be moved from its eminent position in downtown Glasgow to a park a mile or so away because it was continuously vandalized by hooligans and protestors. Apparently, the rider on the horse, and the entire statue, was closely associated with a Protestant cause, in an area of Scotland that was largely Catholic. Every time Catholic passions and sentiments were aroused in Glasgow, the statue in front of the Tontine Building became the focus of protestors' ire. Oh, the man on the statue was King William III – yes, he stood for 163 years in front of the Tontine Building. This particular statue of King William – and there aren't that many in the United Kingdom – currently resides in a rather seedy area of Glasgow, in a small park inhabited mostly by vagrants and the homeless.

In fact, when I was taking a photograph in front of the statue of King William, trying carefully not to disturb the sordid characters lying on the benches in the park, one of them yelled out to me: "Long live King Billy!"

I suspect that particular Scotsman was one of the few residents of Glasgow who did not vote for independence from the UK in September 2014.

ALEXANDER HAMILTON'S DEBT PROPOSAL

In 1790, the first U.S. Secretary of the Treasury Alexander Hamilton proposed what today might be called the young nation's first *Hunger Games*. To help reduce a crushing national debt – something that evidently is not a recent phenomenon – he suggested the U.S. government replace high-interest debt with new bonds in which coupon payments would be made to a group, as opposed to individuals. The group members would share the interest payments evenly among themselves, *provided they were alive*. But once a member of the group died, his or her portion would stay in a tontine pool and be shared among the *survivors*. This process would theoretically continue until the last survivor would be entitled to the entire – potentially millions of dollars – interest payment.

This is precisely a tontine, and this obscure episode in U.S. history has become known as Hamilton's Tontine Proposal, which he claimed – in a letter to George Washington – would reduce the interest paid on U.S. debt and eventually eliminate it entirely.

Congress decided to pass on Hamilton's proposal, and Hamilton himself resigned in disgrace upon admitting an affair with a married woman, but the tontine idea never died. U.S. insurance companies began issuing tontine insurance policies to the public in the mid-nineteenth century, which became wildly popular. By the start of the twentieth century, historians have documented that half of U.S. households owned a tontine insurance policy, which *many used to support themselves throughout retirement.* The longer one actually lived, the greater their payments. This was a personal hedge against longevity, with little risk exposure for the insurance company. Sadly though, owing to shenanigans and malfeasance on the part of company executives, the influential New York State Insurance Commission banned tontine insurance in the state, and by 1910 most other states followed. Tontine (insurance) has been illegal in the United States for more than a century and most insurance executives have likely never heard of it.

THE WASHINGTON REAL ESTATE TONTINE

Another example of the equitylike (versus debtlike) tontine scheme was the so-called Washington tontine, which was spearheaded by a Mr. Benjamin Stoddert from Georgetown in late February 1805. The capital of the company was $140,000 divided into shares of $50 each. According to Article 1 of the tontine prospectus, the money was to be used to acquire "two million six hundred and thirty two thousand square feet of ground in the city of Washington." Today you probably couldn't buy a house in Washington for $140,000, but remember that at just 2% (real) interest for 210 years, the sum would have grown to approximately $70 million dollars today. Perhaps that would buy seventy houses, but not 2.6 million square feet. So, with hindsight, this investment wasn't a bad idea.

In a document written by said Benjamin Stoddert, promoting the tontine scheme, he wrote that "many of the lots now at rates of 60 to 240 dollars will command the prices given for single lots in Baltimore and other large towns for 1,000 to 15,000 dollars" (1805, p. 3). In other words, the cost of a house in downtown Washington surely must catch up to the price of housing in (much more expensive) Baltimore. This should give a chuckle to anyone who has tried to purchase a house in downtown Washington or wandered around downtown Baltimore in the early twenty-first century.

The promoter of the scheme then goes on to write in Stoddert (1805, p. 5), "If sales of the lots should be urged as fast as the constitution will permit ... it is probable that the first years interest paid will be about 3 to 4 per cent and that it will every year increase and not be short of 100 per cent per annum." In other words, every year the assets of the company would double. Stoddert (1805, p. 6) also included language about "great provisions for children" and "small deprivation now for comfortable old age." I guess there is a bit of Lorenzo de Tonti in every tontine promoter.

Like other equitylike tontines, Article 2 stated that "every subscriber may at the time of subscribing, before the 1st day of January 1806, nominate a person or persons whose life or lives the shares taken by him shall be commensurate." This is the classic separation between tontine nominee and tontine investor, which I believe created some of the problems with tontines in the past and would not be a desirable structure in the future; more on this much later. The document, which is currently stored in the British Library in London, then goes on to say that

> upon the death of any person, with whose life a share or shares shall be made commensurate, such share or shares shall thereupon be extinct, and all the interest of the owner thereof, in the property of the company dependent upon such shares, shall cease and determine, and the same shall become the property of the owners of the surviving shares.

As far as governance was concerned, the affairs of the Washington tontine were managed by five directors, who were stockholders to be chosen by ballot by stockholders at an annual meeting. Article 5 made clear that the directors are "at all times to exercise a sound discretion for the best interests of the company," which is akin to a fiduciary obligation to shareholders.

In this regard, the company was no different from the corporations of today, in which shareholders elect directors, who then hire and fire managers, and so on. Article 9 stated that all shares could be transferred in person or via power of attorney. Dividends were to be distributed semiannually on the fifteenth day of January and the fifteenth day of July.

So, the only added twist was that the shares would extinguish upon the death of a nominee. This then added mortality credits to the annual profits and dividends, money that didn't have to be distributed to the extinguished shareholders. It's interesting to wonder – although not disclosed – what happened if one of the directors of the corporation had his or her shares extinguished by a dying nominee.

As in the other equitylike tontines I have discussed, there was absolutely no limit placed on the ages of the nominees or their gender.

The final interesting feature of this particular equitylike tontine was that it included a twenty-year sunset clause. Alas, the final article (13) stipulated that on the first Monday in January of the year 1825, the Washington Tontine Company would be dissolved and the whole stock of the company would be divided among the owners – whose nominees were still alive.

NEW YORK STOCK EXCHANGE AND TONTINES

Another little-known fact is that the New York Stock Exchange (NYSE) can trace its origins and spirit to a small coffeehouse in downtown Manhattan, near present-day Wall Street, back in 1793. That coffeehouse, like the ones in London I mentioned in Chapter 5, was the place where investors (and stockjobbers) came to exchange or trade their stocks. It was filled with (coffee and) merchants and traders and even politicians.[1] The name of the coffeehouse was, yes, the Tontine Coffee House, and it had originally been funded with an equitylike tontine scheme similar to the ones used in the late eighteenth century for bridges and hotels and all sorts of business ventures.

It seems to me from reading the various prospectus and offering documents that the tontine corporate share structure wasn't motivated by hedging longevity risk. This arrangement was speculative, perhaps intending to juice up the returns from the venture and a precursor to the more extreme tontine insurance.

TONTINE INSURANCE IS BORN IN THE USA

Sometime during the fall of 1867 – when the outlaw Jesse James was at the height of his infamy robbing banks in the Midwest – the U.S. version of a tontine was born inside an insurance company in the Northeast. And, like many other innovations that were "Made in America," the transatlantic version of tontines included a unique twist that caught on like wildfire. In fact, U.S. tontines evolved into a gigantic national success that couldn't have been foreseen by even Lorenzo Tonti himself.

Recall that back in 1790, U.S. Congress had turned down Alexander Hamilton's proposal – which he made to George Washington – to pay off Revolutionary War debt with a large-scale national tontine. American politicians and elected officials didn't appreciate the tontine for a variety of reasons. But the business community saw great promise in the concept. So, while tontines in Europe were by and large a public sector (government)

[1] See the Wikipedia entry for Tontine Coffee House, http://en.wikipedia.org/wiki/Tontine _Coffee_House, last accessed on December 26, 2014

affair that were used to finance the military and their wars, the American tontine morphed into a private sector product that was actually sold as a hybrid savings plan for retirement. The nascent American insurance industry borrowed the "tontine sharing principle" and grafted the concept onto the chassis of a life insurance policy. I'll delve into the mechanics in just a bit. The source for most of the material in this section is the 1972 monograph by R. W. Cooper, as well as the 1987 article by historian R. Ransom and economist R. Sutch.

The first American insurance company to offer "Tontine Savings Fund Assurance" or "Tontine Insurance" – as these policies were marketed in the United States – was the Equitable Life Insurance Company (Equitable). The Equitable was locked in a battle for sales supremacy with rivals New York Life and Mutual Life, who were the insurance giants of the time. Equitable's launch of tontine insurance was the equivalent of Apple's iPhone launch in 2007. It was a new category of product that put them on the map and made Equitable a household name. The insurance companies who followed Equitable and offered their own tontine insurance in the late nineteenth century are the same household names you might recognize today, precursors to their corporate descendants a century later.

In fact, only a handful of American insurance companies stayed out of the tontine insurance frenzy – most prominently Connecticut Mutual Insurance Company – but even so, the tontine business reached a measure of popularity and success they had never achieved in Europe.[2]

At the peak of their American success, a total of 9 million individuals owned tontine insurance policies, which was two-thirds of all life insurance policies "on the books" in 1905, according to estimates by Ransom and Sutch (1987). They claim that this was 7.5% of total national wealth in the year. Now compare this with the scope and size of European tontines. At the height of their popularity in France – during the middle of the seventeenth century – the number of owners (only) numbered in the tens of thousands. Recall that King William's tontine in 1693 had only 600 investors. This was but a small fraction of the population of one parish in London. In contrast, by the end of the nineteenth century over half of U.S. households owned a tontine insurance policy. At the time tontine insurance was as ubiquitous and familiar to Americans as the mutual fund or mortgage is today.

I'll get to why they are virtually extinct today in just a moment. At this point, let's reflect on the irony that just as Lorenzo de Tonti's two sons ended

---

[2]   See Anonymous (1885) for a collection of articles written by executives at Connecticut Mutual Life, mostly criticizing tontine insurance.

up emigrating to America – and gaining more fame and notoriety than their dad ever did – so too did the American version of tontines outshine their European father. Needless to say, Tonti's kids weren't involved in the tontine business.

Alas, the American love affair with tontines didn't end well. Unlike Henry and Alphonse – who passed away as heroes in Arkansas and Detroit – U.S. tontine insurance died in shame and disgrace just when it was about to celebrate its fortieth birthday. The spectacular rise and dizzying fall provides a case study for how not to manage success. And it got worse. By 1907, tontine insurance was virtually banned by insurance regulators and the government in most U.S. states. Yes, banned! Which is why it is (said to be) illegal today – and you likely didn't hear of it until you picked up this book.

Here is the story of how the tontine was murdered in America.

From Hero to Zero

Tontine insurance in the U.S. had its own Lorenzo de Tonti, and his name was Henry B. Hyde. He founded the Equitable Life Insurance Company based in New York. This magnificent company was housed in – and Henry Hyde oversaw the building of – the tallest commercial building in the United States (at the time) and was the first to install elevators (in 1870). By the time Henry Hyde died in 1899 and bequeathed the company to his son – phenomenally wealthy and in the same category as J. P. Morgan – Equitable was the largest insurance company in the world. This was all due to the remarkable success of the tontine. Today one talks about hi-tech or software billionaires, but in the late nineteenth century you could describe the titans of the financial services industry as insurance billionaires.[3]

I must start by emphasizing that tontine insurance was more of a *saving* policy than a life annuity or pension product. Often I wonder if the word *tontine* was even justified in the label of this policy, but let me get to the details and let you decide.

First, tontine insurance was purchased in small installments or increments over a period of twenty years. Imagine a savings account in which you deposit a few dollars every week or every month and the policy "matures" or is terminated after twenty years of savings. Quite distinct from the European tontine, which was an *income* product, the American tontine

---

[3]   Henry Hyde joined forces with a well-known actuary by the name of Sheppard Homans, who also worked for a while at Equitable. Together they styled one of the most popular policies ever sold in the United States: tontine insurance.

was an *accumulation* policy. You had to wait twenty years before you (the policyholder) received anything. This is a testament to the patience and trust that consumers (in the nineteenth century) placed in the insurance industry and the insurance company who sold the policy.

The insurance company – within their "general" investment account – would invest the money the policyholders contributed each month. Then, at the end of the twenty-year waiting period the (very patient) policyholders could do anything they wanted with the money. They could either (i.) take the money in a lump sum of cash, (ii.) withdraw it slowly over time, or even (iii.) use the funds to purchase a conventional life annuity from the company that sold them the tontine insurance. Either way, after twenty years of waiting, the tontine phase was over. Also, there was no distinction between annuitant, nominees, and investor. There was only one participant in the American tontine, the individual who saved, waited, and reaped the reward from his or her persistence.

Now, you might be wondering at this juncture: *What in the world does this innocuous-sounding savings plan have to do with tontines or insurance?*

Well, the short answer is that the way the policy was designed, only survivors (i.e., people who were alive after twenty years) shared in the value of the savings account. If the investors (i.e., saver) died along the way, they and their beneficiaries received nothing. This is precisely the tontine element that was borrowed from the Europeans and Lorenzo de Tonti. The money (in the account) from the deceased would be distributed to the survivors. So if 10,000 people started the twenty-year countdown to maturity and only 1,000 survived for twenty years, the 1,000 would get to split the money. Heirs of the other 9,000 were out of luck.

The feature that really supercharged the investment return – and truly Americanized the tontine – was something called the "benefit of persistency." That was the secret sauce.

Remember, the well-established "benefit of survivorship" implies that you have to survive to receive the final benefit. In contrast, the "benefit of persistency" means that you only get the payout if you continue making the installment payments for the full twenty years. Recall that the tontine policy was purchased using payments spread over twenty years. So if the investor stopped contributing to the policy – even if they survived for twenty years – they would be entitled to zero, zilch, nada. They might have lived to the ripe old age of 100, but they would receive nothing. If for whatever reason they decided – or were forced because of financial reasons – to abandon their policy at some point during the saving stage, they were out of luck.

You had two forces operating in the same direction. The first was mortality, reducing the number of investors and thus increasing the potential pool for the survivors. The second force was human nature and economic circumstance. You had to hold on and keep making those payments. Investors dropped out of the tontine pool for two reasons – death and delinquency. Quite naturally, the payout to the persistent survivors was even greater.

Think of all the (poor, helpless) policyholders who were unable (for whatever reason) to hold on to the policy. They, and their heirs, were left with nothing. Now, you might think that this was a perfectly reasonable and fair way of creating a product – by adults, for adults – as long as it was clear to investors in advance. But the fact is that many "lapsers" were taken by surprise when they had to abandon their tontine insurance before it matured.

This feature of the American tontine, the total loss of the investment upon forfeiture – even if the policyholder lived a long life – is eventually what led to the policy's demise and the death of tontines in America. There were simply too many horror stories that made their way through the court system, the insurance regulators, and eventually the legislature. In fact, the few companies who didn't join the tontine insurance bandwagon in the late nineteenth century, like Connecticut Life Insurance Company (CLIC) mentioned earlier, stated as their main reason the unfairness of the deal. In fact, CLIC waged a very public and high-profile war of words with Equitable, claiming that this sort of deal wasn't suitable for Americans. The concern was that too many investors were being left with nothing.

In fact, Henry Hyde – chairman of the Equitable who pioneered the tontine insurance policy in the United States – forecasted that two-thirds to one-half of policyholders would lapse or surrender the policy before the twenty-year period was over. In the tradition of a glass being viewed as half-empty or half-full, Henry Hyde thought this was a good thing. The act of forfeiture was great for the insurance company and the policyholder, but the volume of "unhappy lapsers" was overwhelming.

Before I tell the end of the story, I'll offer an example of what the payout would have been for those who held on.

A Very Detailed Example

What follows is a detailed example of how a tontine insurance policy would have worked back in the late nineteenth century, assuming it had been purchased by a sixty-five-year-old and the "general investment" account of the insurance company was earning 4% per year. I will make some assumptions

Table 6.1. *The twenty-year life of a tontine insurance policy*

Age	# In pool	Contributions	Mortality	Lapse	Fund value
65	10,000	$500,000	0.976%	5.25%	$520,000
66	9,382	$469,124	1.079%	5.00%	$1,028,689
67	8,817	$440,862	1.191%	4.75%	$1,528,333
68	8,298	$414,918	1.316%	4.50%	$2,020,981
69	7,821	$391,033	1.453%	4.25%	$2,508,495
70	7,379	$368,974	1.605%	4.00%	$2,992,568
71	6,971	$348,531	1.772%	3.75%	$3,474,743
72	6,590	$329,517	1.956%	3.50%	$3,956,430
73	6,235	$311,763	2.160%	3.25%	$4,438,921
74	5,902	$295,115	2.384%	3.00%	$4,923,397
75	5,589	$279,436	2.632%	2.75%	$5,410,946
76	5,292	$264,599	2.905%	2.50%	$5,902,567
77	5,010	$250,491	3.205%	2.25%	$6,399,181
78	4,740	$237,007	3.536%	2.00%	$6,901,635
79	4,481	$224,053	3.901%	1.75%	$7,410,716
80	4,231	$211,546	4.302%	1.50%	$7,927,152
81	3,988	$199,408	4.744%	1.25%	$8,451,622
82	3,751	$187,574	5.229%	1.00%	$8,984,765
83	3,520	$175,988	5.763%	0.75%	$9,527,183
84	3,292	$164,602	6.350%	0.50%	$10,079,456
85	3,068	Payout per "survivor" at age eighty-five			$3,286

about death and lapse rates, but the underlying principle is identical regardless of the exact numbers. Table 6.1 illustrates the year-by-year cash flows of this hypothetical policy.

Imagine that 10,000 individuals purchased a tontine insurance policy at the age of sixty-five for a commitment or investment of $1,000 each. Recall that in the American version of the tontine, payments were not made in one lump sum. They were spread over twenty years. Assume that at the beginning of each year the investor (aka policyholder) committed to pay $50 and at the end of the twenty years he or she would receive the money in the policy. Those who survived and persisted at the age of eighty-five shared the bounty. Those who gave up or lapsed their policy at any time during the twenty-year period from the age of sixty-five to eighty-five received nothing. Note that if *everyone* persisted for twenty years and *nobody* died for the twenty years, the $50 savings per year would grow to $1,548. This is because the future value of an annuity (which begins immediately, aka due) of $50 for twenty years at 4% interest is $1,548.

You might wonder why someone might desert the tontine insurance policy during the twenty years. The answer, of course, is financial constraints. Investors might run into economic difficulties and might be forced to abandon the policy. Paying $50 per year would be impossible for the unemployed or the infirm. In fact, lapsing the policy – that is, not making the $50 annual payment anymore – might be perfectly rational for someone who is quite ill and stands little chance of living to the age of eighty-five. What is the point of paying into the pool for a few more years if you won't live to share the money inside the pool?

Let us track this hypothetical group of 10,000 investors over time. Although there are many possible paths for this diverse group, assume that (i.) the mortality and (ii.) the lapse rate followed the pattern in the fourth and fifth columns of Table 6.1. I used parameter values that are reasonable, although they don't necessarily correspond to any particular experience of real-world example. I'm trying to illustrate the concept.

In year #1 (when everyone is exactly sixty-five years old) the 10,000 members of the tontine pool each contributes $50 (at the start of the year), which grows by 4% interest (which is an assumption). By the end of the year, the tontine fund is worth $520,000. But, during the same year, ninety-eight investors died (before their sixty-sixth birthday) leaving 9,902 live policyholders at the end of the year. Then, another 520 policyholders decided to give up or abandon their policies and do not make the second-year payment due at sixty-six, leaving 9,382 members in the pool at the age of sixty-six. In the language of insurance, this is a mortality rate of 0.976% and a lapsation rate of 5.25% during the first year of the policy. This is why the second row has $469,124 in contributions (9,382 pool members contributing $50 each). This process continues year-by-year until everyone in the pool is about to turn eighty-five. At this point there are (only) 3,068 members remaining – who have not died or surrendered – who then divide the remaining $10,079,456 for a total of $3,286 per person. Recall that their total investment (not accounting for the time value of money) was $1,000 over twenty years, and it would have grown to $1,548 in a conventional savings account growing at 4% per year. But here the more-than-double value of $3,286 results in an internal rate of return (or yield) of 10.34% per year on their investment. Compare this number with the 4% interest rate that fund money earns, and you can see the gains from (persisting and) winning the tontine.

Just to be clear about this, after twenty years the tontine insurance policy matured. There was no lifetime of income or increasing payouts over time or longevity insurance or pensions. It was a twenty-year investment with an additional roulette wheel attached to the maturing value. As you might suspect, I personally believe that the relationship between the American tontine and European tontine is as tenuous as the connection between Lorenzo's tontine and the Italian *montes pietatis*, which I explained in Chapter 3.

That said, notice the increasing pattern of the mortality rate (column 4) and the declining pattern of the lapse rate (column 5) in Table 6.1. The reason for the former is (obviously) aging. The reason for the latter is rather subtle, but gets to the heart of human behavior. Namely, the closer one gets to the year of the big payout, the less inclined the investor is to abandon or surrender the policy. "Hold on for just a few more years," I'm sure the policyholders were saying to themselves as they got closer to age eighty-five. But early on the horizon is quite far and the economic incentive to persist is lower. I'm not just hypothesizing here. There is ample evidence that this is in fact how people behaved with their tontine (and other more recent) insurance policies. Without getting too technical or actuarial, the lapse rate "function" is quite dynamic.

Now the reasons I wade into the minutia and labor to differentiate between the European and American version, is that the above-described policy was attacked on various fronts – and was eventually banned in the United States. I'll get to that story in a moment. If the current ban on tontines is purely on tontine insurance policies, such as the one I just described, then perhaps true tontines with longevity insurance and a lifetime of income – as originally promoted by Lorenzo himself – aren't illegal in any way, shape, or form.

THE ARMSTRONG INVESTIGATION

By the end of the nineteenth century and the start of the twentieth, the torrent of complaints and lawsuits – from people who lapsed their policies sometime in the twenty-year period and received nothing in return – reached fever pitch and the New York state legislature convened a special committee in 1904 to investigate tontine insurance policies. The concern wasn't only the loss of value upon forfeiture. The enormous surplus that insurance companies were building up in the years prior to the tontine's maturity created a large and tempting pool of money. The money wasn't accounted for in any way, and the companies used the funds to compensate agents with enormous commissions, as well as bribing judges and politicians to stay away from scrutinizing the tontine business. The corruption was endemic and shocking. But again, this was a flaw in human nature and accounting systems – not the tontine sharing principle.

The Devil in the Life Insurance Details

Now, just to be perfectly clear, there was an additional wrinkle to the American tontine insurance policy that I haven't mentioned so far. These policies were always sold together with a conventional (twenty-year) life insurance policy. I repeat, they could not be purchased on a stand-alone basis. And, more importantly, the $50 payments (for example) over the twenty years came from the dividends on a life insurance policy. Whereas before tontines came into existence, life insurance policyholders would receive annual dividends on their insurance policy – to share in the gains that the insurance company experienced – the tontine insurance policy reinvested those gains into the tontine scheme and didn't distribute them on an annual basis. When a policyholder lapsed their tontine insurance policy, they were also lapsing their life insurance policy and had absolutely nothing to show for it all. Thousands (and possibly millions) of investors might have stopped paying premiums – for whatever reason, and then possibly died – and had nothing to show (or give their heirs) for all their efforts.

Getting back to the Armstrong investigation, the CEOs of all the major insurance companies were dragged to Albany, New York, to offer testimony on these matters, and the national media followed the proceedings with the intensity of the O. J. Simpson trial.

Would the regulators (the jury) restrict (convict) tontine insurance sales (O. J.) or would they let the celebrities off the hook?

In the end the jury came back with a guilty verdict. Of course, the executives weren't arrested or sent to the Tower of London, the Bastille, or Alcatraz. Rather, the regulators placed severe restrictions on how insurance companies could treat their policyholders, which effectively killed the tontine policy. In particular, they were forced to account for dividends on an annual basis and were forced to provide some forfeiture value to their policyholders. Within a few years no insurance company – including Equitable, who first marketed them – sold tontine savings policies for fear of running afoul of the law.

The Current State of Affairs

So, are tontines illegal in the United States today in the early twenty-first century? Well, I'm certainly not a lawyer or legal expert. But, according to law professor J. Forman, who has thought about tontines – and has written quite extensively promoting tontines for pension plans – you don't have to worry about being arrested or thrown in jail if you participate in such a scheme. I quote his professional view, which was expressed in a 2014 article coauthored with M. J. Sabin:[4]

> Although it is not free from doubt, it appears that tontine funds, tontine annuities, and tontine pensions are all legal. As already mentioned, investigations of the insurance industry in New York led to the enactment of legislation in 1906 that all but banned tontines. To be sure, the legislation did not specifically prohibit the sale of tontines; instead, it just made it difficult for companies to defer payments beyond one year.

In sum, tontine insurance policies of the nineteenth century had some severe problems associated with them, but I don't see the ban as relevant or pertinent to the resurrection of Lorenzo's dream. In fact, tontines are alive today, mostly hidden under many layers of complexity. Here are some examples.

COLLECTIVE TONTINES ON THE ISRAELI KIBBUTZ

Israel's 270 or so Kibbutzim– Hebrew for collective communities – are organized and managed according to socialist principles where pretty much everything of value is shared between and among the members.[5] The largest Kibbutz in Israel is called Ma'agan Michael with 1,400 residents and is situated on the Mediterranean shore between the city of Haifa and Tel Aviv. The smallest Kibbutz, with only ten known residents, is called Inbar and located in Galilee in northern Israel. In total, there are approximately 130,000 Israelis today living on Kibbutzim with an average of approximately 350 adult members on each Kibbutz.

Zionists from Russia, who immigrated to Israel – then called Palestine and controlled by the British Mandate – in the early twentieth century, founded the earliest Kibbutzim. The movement picked up momentum and steam after the founding of the state of Israel in 1947. In fact, they became quite fashionable and romanticized in the 1950s and 1960s when it seemed (wrongly of course, and you can blame Hollywood) that everyone in Israel lived on a Kibbutz.

Fast-forward fifty years and by the second decade of the twenty-first century the movement has waned. The number of Kibbutzim, as well as their members, peaked in the early 1990s. Today only 2.5% of the Israeli population resides on a Kibbutz, but they still adhere quite passionately to the

---

[4] Forman and Sabin (2014, p. 68). See http://ssrn.com/abstract=2393152.
[5] Source for information about Israeli Kibbutzim is http://www.jewishvirtuallibrary.org as well as http://en.wikipedia.org/wiki/Kibbutz for some of the recent statistics.

founding principles. As you might expect from a socialist utopia – although members prefer the label of "direct democracy" – residents of the Kibbutz do not own their homes, their cars, their farms, or their cows. The collective owns everything, so for the most part there is no private property. The spirit is *all for one and one for all* and in some of the more progressive Kibbutzim it is said that even spouses and lovers are shared! (Again, blame Hollywood.)

Now, this isn't the place to comment on whether such an economic system is sustainable in the long run. I mean the lack of private property and inability to reward individual effort, not the shared spouses. What is interesting and relevant to my main thesis is their unique retirement insurance arrangement.

Although members of the Kibbutz are part of the state of Israel's official Social Security program, which entitles everyone to a basic retirement income, the government income isn't quite enough to live on. So members of the Kibbutz participate in a supplemental insurance program. At a high level the way it works is as follows. Young workers contribute to a type of group insurance policy, which is invested in stocks and bonds – to the horror of Engel and Marx, I might add – and the income is distributed to the elderly *in the same Kibbutz*, when these members are no longer able to work. Think of a large mutual fund in which everyone working contributes to the fund over time, and then part of the fund is liquidated as needed to pay pensions for retirees. To the trained eye this is a type of Defined Contribution (DC) plan, with little in the way of guarantees or promises.

And, as you might have expected by now, the distribution or sharing of the income from the fund is based on the tontine principle. I'll get to the minutiae and details in a little bit, since nothing is ever simple in Israel. But, at a broad level, each retiree starts off with a base pension level (say 2,000 shekels per month), which is computed in advance assuming a certain expected pattern of mortality. Over time the payments are adjusted up or down depending on changing market conditions and – most importantly – realized mortality experience of the Kibbutz itself.

In other words, and to put it crudely, if more people than expected in the individual Kibbutz died, the monthly pension of survivors will increase (to, say, 2,100 shekels per month) and if less people than expected died, the pension is decreased (to, say, 1,900 shekels).

This volatility might not be desirable to the retiree, but that is how sharing works, I guess. I'm not quite sure how this works for the smallest Kibbutz of only ten members – perhaps they don't participate in the scheme – but my understanding is that most of the Kibbutzim in Israel have adopted this insurance plan for retirement income. I presume that there is a committee on each Kibbutz that tallies up the dead – "Is Shlomo present? Going once, going twice. We declare Shlomo dead. All in favor of Shlomo's pension going to Chaim, vote aye." – and then distribute the income to those who remain.[6]

Enter the Regulator

Here is where it gets interesting and rather surprising. A few years ago the Ministry of Finance in Israel, which oversees or regulates (everything and) this particular program, decided to take a closer look at this insurance program. In particular, the feeling amongst the technocrats within the ministry is that it is inefficient to have 270 large and small Kibbutzim with their individual insurance system segmented and separated. They proposed to merge the individual plans into one large collective – under "the bigger the better philosophy" – which might reduce costs and risks. After all, the chance of a small Kibbutz experiencing large deviations in mortality is much greater than it is for the larger ones. The argument was that a "large" retirement insurance fund for everyone would smooth out the income fluctuations, reduce the chances of large deficits accumulating, and generally be better for the system.

The insurance regulator within the ministry approached the managers of the various Kibbutzim and proposed a merger of this retirement insurance (tontine) pool. The arguments were similar to the ones I posed earlier, with some sprinkling of statistics around "bigger is better."

Well, the response from the Kibbutzim, or rather the committees who run them, was negative and downright hostile. Individually, they didn't like the idea at all. Now mind you, this wasn't a proposal to merge the actual Kibbutzim into one large Kibbutz – heaven and Marx forbid – which would be ludicrous in a place like Israel. Rather, this was simply a proposal to pool *longevity risk* and *mortality risk* among and between a much larger group. Think about it; for the smallest of Kibbutzim with less than 100 members, this would greatly reduce the fluctuation in payments.

Sounds reasonable, no? Well, as I said, all hell broke loose. When the initial protests abated, the statisticians were asked to weigh in on the matter. Neither the very large nor the very small Kibbutzim – who stand to

---

[6]   Okay, perhaps not quite, and there is some life insurance and benefits to the surviving spouse, but hopefully you get the point.

gain the most from reduced risk – liked the idea of sharing longevity risk across different Kibbutzim. Apparently it is one thing to share water, wealth, and spouses with your next-door neighbor, but completely unacceptable to share it with a rival Kibbutz a few Dunam away.

But politics and psychology aside, here is the mathematical question related to tontines. Does a large pool or collective of 125,000 retirees reduce the variability of pension payments compared to a pool of, say, 100 or 500 retirees? Translated into the language and lexicon of this book: can you manage an effective tontine with as little as fifty people? The answer – as you might expect by now – is *yes*. Small pools aren't as bad as you think. And you can thank the Law of Large Numbers. As I will explain in more detail in Chapter 7, it's amazing how small a (homogenous) pool you need to run an effective tontine. You can count on the descendants of Russian immigrants to know their Chebyshev, Markov, Kolmogorov, and Khinchin – the Russian mathematicians who refined and perfected the mathematics.

The Moral End of the Story

To date – mid-2014 – the Kibbutzim's longevity risk hasn't been merged into one large pool, and if the statisticians hired by the Kibbutzim have a say, they will probably remain small little pools for a long time to come. And on the off chance you ever visit one of these 270 collectives, there is something new and different you can ask your host as you wander around the orange groves and cow pastures. "How are you enjoying your tontine?"

Alas, in addition to yet another interesting example of tontine schemes around the world – and a unique slice of Israeli society – there is a subtler lesson that can be gleaned from the Kibbutzim. That is, moral hazard is a nonissue. Remember, if you are a retired worker of a tiny Kibbutz in the lovely Galilee Mountains and your pension depends on whether your next-door neighbor – who is also retired – survives another year, the incentive to throw him under the combine or poison his food would be too great. And the smaller the Kibbutz, the greater the incentive! In fact, the moral hazard effect might go in the exact opposite direction. You know that your tontine payment will go to a friend or a neighbor if and when you die. This is a fellow comrade who labored with you in the fields, the comrade who served with you in the same brigade (and perhaps the neighbor who shared your husband or wife!).

Here is my takeaway. Building the tontine sharing pools too large might create statistical margins of safety, reduce the risk, and increase anonymity, but there is a psychological cost, as well. Whether this phenomenon is robust to non-Kibbutzim and can be generalized – or whether this has anything to do with their objections – is debatable, but the germ of the idea has been planted.

Think about it. Would you rather share longevity risk and bonuses with a small number of members of your church, your synagogue, your neighbors, your city, your country – or the much larger and diversified world at large? I suspect the answer is that you too might prefer a smaller pool. The Law of Large Numbers is damned.

TONTINE INGREDIENT IN SWEDISH PENSIONS

The Israeli Kibbutz system is just one of many examples around the world in which the tontine sharing principle or 'tontine thinking' is currently being used in the pension and retirement system; although it might not be visible to the naked eye and certainly not called a tontine scheme. Another interesting example is the pension system in Sweden, the country who gave the world Nobel Prizes, ABBA, Ingrid Bergman, Greta Garbo, and more recently Spotify and Skype. Their 10 million (or so) inhabitants have a national pension system – run and managed by the government – which is somewhat different from Social Security in the United States or the Canadian Pension Plan in Canada.

Like many other countries, Sweden reformed its scheme in the 1990s to move away from a pure *pay-as-you-go* (PAYGO) system to a (partially) prefunded system in which individuals save up and contribute (i.e., pre-fund) their retirement accounts. In other words, your government pension is like a savings account that you can monitor and track over time. Without getting lost in the minutiae, here is a summary of how their national retirement pension works. Let's see if you can find where the tontine is hidden.

Every Swedish worker is required to contribute 7.0% of his or her annual earnings into "the system" and employers must contribute an additional 10.2% of the employee's salary into "the system," so that a total of 17.2% of earnings is credited to each employee. Note that this contribution is compulsory so Swedes can't opt out of the national plan, unlike a corporate 401(k) plan in the United States, for example, where nothing is forced.

The contributed money (i.e., the 17.2% of earning) is then invested in various funds – selected by the government and/or individuals – and the accounts "grow" over time depending on how well the economy and market does. Notice that I placed the word *grow* in quotation marks because these accounts aren't quite like mutual funds or brokerage accounts in which the underlying assets are yours. I'll return to this a bit later.

What is important is that each and every year, all Swedish citizens who participate in the pension system receive what is known as "the Orange Envelope" in the mail.[7] It is a well-publicized and widely recognized statement of their pension account balance and how it has changed over the last year. The same Orange Envelope also includes long-term projections – which is especially important for the younger cohorts – of what their pension income is forecast to be during retirement if they continue working and contributing along the same financial path.

The operations of the Swedish pension system and the minutiae are explained in the parallel Orange Report, issued by the Swedish pension authority every year around the same time.[8] Now, pay attention since here is where it gets interesting. This Orange Report says (for 2013, on p. 96), and I quote:

> The pension balances of deceased persons are credited to the survivors in the same age group in the form of inheritance gains. For persons 60 years of age or less, the inheritance gain factor is calculated as the sum of the pension balances of the deceased divided by the sum of the pension balances for the survivors in the same age group.

Did you get that? The account balance grows from year to year, partially because the *deceased* Swede's account is distributed to the *surviving* Swedes. If you are wondering, the phrase *inheritance gains* is a very polite way of saying mortality credits – which I explained in earlier chapters. Stated quite simply, those who die subsidize and increase the investment returns of those who live. In fact, in the very same Orange Report there is a picture (for 2013, on p. 97) showing the so-called inheritance gain and how it grows exponentially with age, mimicking the human force of mortality and the increasing probability of death.

Now, let me be clear. Any pension system anywhere in the world implicitly assumes some form of death rate for participants, an assumption that then flows into account growth assumptions. That is one of the many jobs of the pension actuary, to estimate and account for death rates. What is interesting and rather unique about the Swedish system is (i.) how *explicit and transparent* they have made this mechanism, and (ii.) appealing to the notion of *intergenerational fairness*, they share this risk within and between

---

[7]   This has absolutely nothing to do with William of Orange.

[8]   See http://secure.pensionsmyndigheten.se.

each individual cohort.[9] In other words, your particular account will grow – all else being equal – if and when other Swedes who were born in exactly the same year happen to die. In fact, the same Orange Report then goes on to say: "As there is some delay in information on persons dying during the year, the distribution of inheritance gains to persons aged 60 or less is made with a time lag of one year." So, as it was centuries ago, it takes time to process and report deaths!

I do not want to give the wrong impression that the Swedes have created a pension utopia brimming with simplicity and transparency. Like any other government-run bureaucracy anywhere in the world, the intricate details of the Swedish system are quite complicated and messy, ensuring the actuaries are employed for life. The Swedish system is known to pension specialists as a Notional Defined Contribution (NDC) plan, which isn't quite Defined Benefit (DB) and not quite Defined Contribution (DC). The accounts I mentioned earlier – the one every Swede sees in their annual Orange Envelope – is a "notional" account that is used for bookkeeping or accounting purposes only. There isn't some bank or fund company holding the money. To give an analogy, it's like your kids giving you the money from their paper route or Christmas presents to manage and then asking for an annual statement of what they own. You probably and immediately comingled the funds in your pocket and might have spent the money by the end of the day, but they (the kids) do have a claim against you. The Orange Envelope is the reminder.

Also, while on the details, "the system" consists of two different plans operating side by side within the government agency. One is an older system called the InkomstPension (which gets 6/7 of the contributed funds) and the other one is a newer system called the PremiumPension (which gets 1/7 of the contributed funds). Now, unless you are Swedish you probably don't care about the details here, but I must say that the plan is rather novel when compared with other Western countries.

The money in the InkomstPension is managed by four parallel investment funds, and the money in PremiumPension is managed based on (approximately 850) funds that Swedes can select individually. The inheritance gains for the (newer) PremiumPension are computed slightly differently than the (older) InkomstPension's are, based on a forward-looking expectation for mortality rates as opposed to the realized (i.e., how many

---

[9]   Another example of this in the context of retirement pensions was recently highlighted in a *New York Times* (October 11, 2014) article about the Dutch pension system, which also "rests on the idea that each generation should pay its own costs."

people actually died) method in King William's tontine. The devil really is in the details.

Here is the main point: the underlying philosophy of the Swedish pension system is precisely a tontine sharing principle for individuals in the same cohort. The Orange Report I mentioned earlier – which is made available to all Swedish citizens – includes twenty-five pages of (excruciating) detail on how the assets and accounts of the deceased are fairly and properly shared among the survivors. I must admit; I don't quite understand all the details. In comparison King William's tontine was a lot easier to explain. But then again, the total assets of the Swedish pension system are nearing 8,000 billion Swedish kronor, which dwarfs the assets of the Israeli Kibbutz system. So this is probably one of the largest tontine schemes in the world. And yet I doubt that anyone receiving the annual Orange Envelopes in the mail would be able to identify a tontine or even characterize the national pension scheme as one – but I suspect Lorenzo de Tonti would be proud and likely demand a royalty cut from the government if he were alive today.

CLASSIFICATION OF TONTINE SCHEMES

So, to wind up the *around-the-world* tontine tour I piloted in this chapter, Table 6.2 provides a systematic classification of the various scheme types observed throughout history. I have broken them down into *debt-like* and *equitylike* tontines (the two columns) and different ways in which income and capital was distributed to scheme or member participants (the four rows).

Note that in addition to the above (eight-category) classification, there were some additional (important) differences across tontine schemes. For example, most documents and schemes I encountered – except for the purely fictional ones – imposed a *lower bound* on the number of live nominees before the investments were liquidated, disbanded, and/or payments were frozen. And even if this wasn't imposed or agreed to in advance, the elected representatives of the shareholders (in the case of equity-based schemes) had the authority to implement this ex post. In other words, the remaining shareholders whose nominees were still alive could vote (by majority) to dissolve the tontine anytime they wanted, really.

Let me be clear again about the mechanics of this important safety feature. At some point in time the death of any additional nominees would have absolutely no impact on the remaining annuitants. This (obviously) reduces the moral hazard risk and (perhaps) even the taint of the tontine. Sadly, only the fictional version endures.

Table 6.2. *Classification of tontine schemes*

	Debtlike (D)	Equitylike (E)
Use of Funds	Money is *loaned* by the entire group and members are considered *creditors.*	Money is invested in an *active business* and members are *shareholders.*
Tontine Type 1A. (Lorenzo de Tonti design)	Survivors share periodic *constant interest* payments, but loan principal is forfeited.	Survivors share periodic *variable dividends,* but original share capital is forfeited.*
Tontine Type 1B. (Rare for debt, common for equity)	Survivors share periodic *constant interest* payments, and winner(s) get original principal.*	Survivors share *variable dividend* payments, and winner(s) inherit ownership of business.
Tontine Type 2. (King William's design)	Entire loan is amortized over maximum life span and survivors share *declining cash flow* stream.	Business assets are systematically liquidated and cash plus dividends are distributed to survivors.
Tontine Type 3. (Winners take all, riskiest and suboptimal)	Surviving winner(s) receive compound interest plus original principal. No periodic cash flow or income.	Dividends are reinvested (i.e., not distributed) and the winner(s) inherit ownership of an ongoing business.

* This tontine structure was never observed in practice, but it is theoretically possible.

Indeed, I will be the first to admit that whether a scheme is debtlike or equitylike, the absence of a cap is the riskiest and most (morally) distasteful type of tontine. One doesn't require much of an imagination to worry about the impact of two or three surviving nominees of a (large) tontine pool in the lawless eighteenth century, and the relevant shareholders waiting for the others to die. *Again, no tontines were structured this way.* While the absence of evidence isn't proof, I personally have not encountered any (credible) stories of tontine nominees being killed (or even disappearing or defaulting) to enhance the payments to the survivors.

For example, in King William's tontine (classified as Type 2 in the table) payments were frozen when seven nominees remained. After that, the death of a nominee (the seventh, sixth, fifth, etc.) would have no impact on remaining payments. The Treasury (or Exchequer) would keep the additional income forfeited by the death of the nominee. Some schemes were capped at 20% of the original pool size; others were frozen when income exceeded a given threshold (i.e., £1,000 per year) or after a fixed point in time, for example, twenty-five years. Eventually the mortality credits died, well before the last nominee ever did. (It is worth noting that Tonti himself didn't worry about this.)

An additional difference across schemes is that many imposed restrictions on the ages of nominees and the tontine was set up in age-banded classes. Each class might have its own distinct yield or interest rate – for example, the tontine of King George III – and in some cases the rate was the same across all band classes. This, by the way, was the original proposal by Lorenzo de Tonti, who separated nominees into age bands of approximately ten years but paid the same interest rate to all groups – which makes the tontine a worse deal at advanced ages. As I mentioned many times, the older nominees should (obviously) get more.

It is worth noting that age banding was far more common in the debt-based schemes versus the equity-based schemes (for whatever reason), which is yet another curiosity or perhaps flaw in design. For example, the Glasgow Tontine Society was an equity-based tontine scheme (classified as #1B in the table) with no limit on the age of the nominee. Likewise, the Washington Tontine, the Philadelphia Tontine, the Tontine Bridge, and so on, imposed absolutely no restrictions on the age of the nominee and were not banded into classes. The nominee was an afterthought or a minor by-product within the articles of incorporation of the tontine society.

Finally, in the realm of minutiae, some tontine schemes made payments on an annual basis, some were semiannual, and some were quarterly. In some cases the tontine shares were purchased or acquired in one lump sum (up front), and in other schemes the owner or investor could make the payments by installment over a period of a year. In addition, some tontines imposed strict conditions for *proof of life* and others were more lenient. In some sense, no two tontines were exactly the same.

To summarize, there are eight different types of tontine schemes, and some make perfect economic sense while others are pure gambles. In Chapter 7, I discuss which of these eight possible designs is the best or "optimal" from an economic perspective – and why.

7

Optimal Tontine: Hedging (Some) Longevity Risk

A RATIONAL PROBLEM WITH TONTINE'S UTILITY

Up to this point in the narrative I haven't really opined about or addressed the issue of *optimal* tontine design versus *suboptimal* design from the perspective of economic theory. Sure, I have introduced the idea of "tontine thinking" and the sharing principle, including examples of many different tontine schemes. I have discussed their historical features, focused on their payout rates, and examined whether their yield was fair, relative to prevailing interest rates and competing products. I even touched on good tontines and bad tontines from a moral or ethical viewpoint. But thus far I have stayed clear of economic theory. In this chapter I will go one level deeper – which gets a bit more technical, as well – and address the economic properties of the scheme itself and some of the rational aspects of their design. I will introduce and discuss something called Jared's *retirement tontine*, which has some similarities to the historical design but differs in some important ways.

To put this all in perspective and set the context for this chapter, think about the following questions: *How would the rational and logical Mr. Spock design a tontine scheme? And, how might it differ from the 300-year-old design of King William's tontine?*

For starters, the single biggest problem with most historical tontine schemes – whether they are equity or debt or whether they are of Type 1, Type 2, or Type 3 – can be seen in the "winner take all" picture displayed in Figure 7.1. The graph displays the range of possible payouts to the tontine annuitant/nominee – assuming they are still alive – at ages ranging from 65 to 100. This example or picture assumes that a tontine scheme with 400 members is initiated at the age of sixty-five and the (constant) payout to the entire pool is a constant 4% per year.

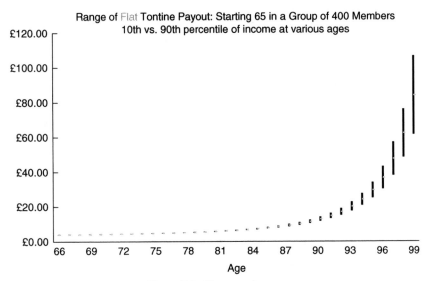

Figure 7.1. Up, up and away.

The (horizontal) x-axis displays or tracks the age of the nominee/annuitant and the (vertical) y-axis shows the payout or dividend in any given year – assuming the nominee/annuitant is alive. Remember that to build or construct this picture I have assumed that everyone in the pool is exactly the same age (sixty-five), so that in year ten everyone in the pool (who is still alive) is seventy-five, in year twenty everyone is eighty-five, and so on. This figure is a statistical projection or forecast of what the tontine payouts will be, because it is impossible to know with certainty when the other nominee or annuitant will die. The figure provides a (10% to 90%) confidence interval for payout conditional on survival.[1]

There are a few important things to notice about Figure 7.1. First and foremost the tontine payouts (conditional on survival) will grow over time. Initially, at the age of sixty-six or sixty-seven or sixty-eight, few "other" annuitants/nominees are likely to die. So there are not many mortality credits to distribute and everyone receives (approximately) 4% of their initial investment. If 400 people contribute £100 each, then the 4% interest on the £40,000, which is £1,600, is distributed to the (approximately) 400 people, which is (approximately) £4. And even if a handful of people from among the 400 happen to die in the first few years – perhaps twenty for the sake of

---

[1]   The distribution of tontine payouts is called binomial and will be discussed in more detail later on.

argument – then 1,600 divided by 380 is (only) £4.21 and indistinguishable in the figure. If everyone is still alive, they all receive £4.0, but if twenty have died, then the remaining 380 receive £4.2 in payout. It is hard for the naked eye to tell the difference.

But as the group ages and reaches seventy-five, eighty-five, and ninety-five, you can start to see a difference. First of all, people will most certainly die, so the payouts to the survivors will increase. But given the uncertainty about how many will die, there is a statistical range, which is why the graph has bars of increasing size. By the age of ninety-five we might expect only eighty survivors (from the pool of 400), which means that the expected payout is £1,600 / 80 = £20 per survivor at age ninety-five. On the other hand, perhaps a total of ninety people (from the pool of 400) will survive, in which case the realized payout would be £1,600 / 90 = £17.77 per survivor. Or maybe it is the other way around. Perhaps there are only seventy survivors, in which case the realized payout is £1,600 / 70 = £22.86 per survivor. The possible range of payouts from £17.77 to £22.86 is reflected in the length of the lines in Figure 7.1.

So, here are the two important takeaways. In the historical (Debt, Type 1a) tontine scheme, the payouts to survivors are (i.) expected to increase (obvious) and (ii.) increasingly uncertain (less obvious). Moreover, for reasons I will soon explain, Mr. Spock dislikes both of those features.

CONSUMPTION SMOOTHING OVER THE LIFECYCLE

The lifecycle model (LCM) concept is closely associated with the work of a Nobel-winning economist from MIT, Professor Franco Modigliani, in the 1950s and 1960s, although it can ultimately be traced back to the writing of Yale University's economist Irving Fisher in the 1920s. The model starts with a theory to postulate how rational people save and spend their money as they age through the lifecycle. The main practical insight of LCM is the idea that rational people will choose to spread out or *smooth their consumption* over their lifetime, in accordance with their individual preferences for consumption now versus later, and their attitudes toward all types of risk.

A practitioner of consumption smoothing will strive to even out any bumps and kinks in their income by saving/borrowing to create a stable standard of living over time. So, for example, if a consumption smoother (or LCM devotee) expects to live for two years (only) and earn $30,000 in salary income this year and $10,000 in salary income the next, they would smooth this "bumpy" income by consuming $20,000 in each year – which means saving $10,000 (a third of their income) in year one and spending 100% more than their income in year two.[2] As its name suggests, the LCM is an idealized *theory* about the rational distribution of resources over the human lifetime. Whether or not people actually optimize and behave in a manner that is consistent with the LCM is an (open and controversial) empirical question.

But whether or not real people behave according to the tenets of LCM, most economists would agree that it presents a very efficient framework for giving (normative) financial advice. For example, the Princeton-based economist Angus Deaton (2005, p. 106) wrote, in a memorial tribute to Franco Modigliani: "As far as I'm aware, no one has challenged the view that if people were capable of it they ought to plan their consumption, saving and retirement according to the principles enunciated by Modigliani and Brumberg."

How does the LCM help us in planning for spending in retirement? Within the context of retirement spending with uncertain life spans, LCM suggests that rational consumption-smoothers should balance out the *lower-probability event of living a very long time* against the *utility (or enjoyment) of consuming earlier*. In the late 1960s, the economist Menahem Yaari extended the LCM by focusing attention on the question of how it functions in the presence of longevity risk. Yaari (1965) developed a mathematical representation of the LCM that further developed the work done by Modigliani in the 1950s and insights of Fisher in the 1920s by taking longevity risk – that is the uncertainty of the length of human life – into account. Yaari described how a rational person would choose to spend his or her retirement both in the presence and absence of "actuarial notes," which can be (roughly) thought of as pensions or life annuities.

Returning to the question of how pension income shapes the (rational, consumption-smoothing) spending and consumption behavior of a retiree, one of the many insights from LCM is that the amount of preexisting pension annuity income should significantly impact the optimal spending and consumption plan of a retiree. The basic concept is this: if a retiree has more preexisting pension income, he or she can afford to

---

[2] Without getting into the mathematical details of the LCM, this brief example assumes that both the individual's subjective discount rate and market interest rates are zero, and of course that they only live and earn income for two periods (year one and year two). For more on the lifecycle model, economics, pensions and the role of annuities in pension systems around the world, see Mackenzie (2006) for example, or Warshawsky (2012) or the collection of articles in Mitchell, Piggott, and Takayama (2011). The annuity economics related literature is vast and continues to grow.

spend more from the nest egg as he or she knows that, in the event he or she lives much longer than average, into the late nineties and perhaps to centenarian territory, the pension income will still be there. Additionally, a retiree's planned consumption will also depend, the LCM tells us, on his or her specific or individual preference for consuming now versus consuming later. Taken together, we can see that advice or recommendations about withdrawal rates are meaningless without having a better understanding of (i.) the typical retiree's other income (i.e., what fraction is available as longevity insured or pension income), as well as (ii.) what we might think of as their *longevity risk aversion* (i.e., whether they are concerned about living to an advanced age), in addition to their attitudes toward other kinds of risk.

I return to the issue of "proper" or "prudent" spending rates when I describe the so-called 4% rule toward the end of Chapter 8. For now I'll focus on the economic approach.

Note that some retirees might not worry about a 5% chance of living to 100 (or, alternately, a 5% chance of losing 50% of their nest egg), while others are more risk-averse and will include these low-probability outcomes in their planning. The bottom line is that risk attitudes are relevant, as they affect consumption in retirement. This is especially important in a (real) world in which true inflation-adjusted annuities (or actuarial notes, as referred to by Yaari) are not available at reasonable prices. The LCM is a huge fan – if you want to think of it that way – of life annuities because it helps smooth consumption by eliminating (or greatly reducing) longevity risk.

OPTIMALITY: INTRODUCING JARED'S TONTINE

This brings me to the subject of optimal (or at least better) tontine design for retirees in the twenty-first century. From the discussion in the previous section regarding utility maximization, it should be clear that most retirees and rational investors would prefer a retirement income stream that does *not* grow exponentially (fast) as they age. Yes, it might be desirable to receive an income that increases by inflation every year, but not by death rates that are exponentially higher. Alas, that is the defining feature and Achilles' heel of the historical tontine: rapidly accelerating dividend *payments* over time. Even the most patient of people would not appreciate waiting to the grand old age of 100 – like Elizabeth St. John did in 1783 – to receive the annual payment of £1,081 from Her Majesty's tontine. Yes, it was a great yield on a £100 investment, but it took ninety years.

Ideally, the payment from an optimal tontine would be as close as possible to what a (constant) pension or life annuity would have provided, but without incurring the "costs" of the insurance company's conservatism. Remember the point first made by the economist Fisher about the optimality of smooth consumption.

I now arrive at the mechanics of my main product (or policy) suggestion for this book. Namely, I believe that the ideal twenty-first-century tontine scheme should be structured with declining financial *payments* over time, at a rate that would exactly offset and cancel the declining human *survival* rate with age. I call this structure Jared's tontine payout – in honor of the second-oldest person in the Bible – and I will explain why I think it is a natural way to resurrect the tontine sharing principle.[3]

First some definitions. Jared's tontine payout rate – that is, the fraction of the initial investment that should be distributed to the pool of survivors every year – is denoted by the function $d_x(i)$. Think of it as a rate, such as 10% of the initial capital in year five, or 8% in year ten, or 3% in year twenty, and so on. It is a cash flow schedule set in advance. Think of it as part of the legal prospectus for the tontine.

The time variable (i) measures the number of years that have elapsed since the scheme was initiated, and the variable (x) is the age of everyone in the tontine pool at the time it was initiated. Those are the two arguments in the formula.

As I alluded to earlier in the book, I believe that tontines – or any other retirement income system – should *not* be designed based on intergenerational subsidies. The young should not be mixing with the old. Every birth cohort should be kept separate and carry its own weight.

If, for example, people born in 1940 happen to live longer than people born in 1939 or 1941, then the financial implications (demographic dividends) should be shared or spread across individuals who were born in 1940. This is clean and transparent and appeals to a sense of fairness across generations.

On a slightly more abstract or philosophical level, I believe that having age-based grouping, rather than a completely inclusive one, is the only way to ensure that costs and benefits are pro-rated fairly across different generations. Some legal and actuarial experts have advocated (and designed) tontine-based pension systems in which anyone, of any age, can be lumped together in the same pool. Payouts (i.e., coupons or dividends) to actual

---

[3]   In work done with Tom Salisbury, we have actually used the term *natural tontine* to describe what I am here calling Jared's tontine. I will use both natural and Jared in some places.

survivors are then adjusted for the expected mortality rate of everyone else in the pool. The mathematics are elegant, but the system only works if there is perfect certainty regarding the mortality rate of any given tontine nominee. And that is never really known. I'll return to "competing" schemes in the next section.

With regard to keeping different ages apart and not mixing them into one pool, I am subscribing here, albeit counterintuitively, to a strict notion of something called "distributive justice" in the ethics and philosophy literature.[4] The concept, which broadly refers to everyone's equal share of good, first appears in Aristotle's *Nicomachean Ethics*, and is subsequently treated by theologians, jurists, and economists. This concept has also played a major role in the well-publicized debates between the philosopher John Rawls (1921–2002) and his opponents Robert Nozick (1938–2002) and Michael Sandel (b. 1953), author of the recent best-seller *What Money Can't Buy: The Moral Limits of Markets* (2012).

If we do not segment people into risk- and age-based groups, one can actually prove mathematically that one cohort will incur a disproportional, and thus unfair, cost compared with the other cohorts who are all part of the same group, *if random mortality improvements are properly accounted*. A central planner would then be forced to allocate gains and losses across generations, which would be extremely difficult to implement in a fair manner.

Taking this argument one step further (at the risk, perhaps, of going too far), I am rejecting Rawls's difference principle, which allows for lower (tontine) benefits for those who are better off in terms of longevity in order to compensate those who are worse off. Once again, keeping different age-groups separate eliminates this problem.

Anyway, philosophy and ethics aside, I promised (only) two equations in the book – the first of which was the famous Present Value Factor (PVF) introduced in Chapter 2 – and we have now arrived at the second and final one. The expression for Jared's tontine payout is:

---

[4] I am grateful and would like to acknowledge helpful comments on matters on the edge of my expertise, to Professor Jonathan Milevsky (who also happens to be my brother). He suggests the following sources (which I have not included in the References): Aristotle, *Nicomachean Ethics*, V. 2–4, 13; John Rawls, *Justice as Fairness: A Restatement* (Boston: Harvard University Press, 2001); Michael J. Sandel, *Liberalism and the Limits of Justice*, 2nd ed. (Cambridge: Cambridge University Press, 1998), 178; Robert Nozick, *Anarchy, State, and Utopia* (New York: Basic Books, 1974); Ronald Dworkin, "What Is Equality? Part 1: Equality of Resources," *Philosophy and Public Affairs* 10 (1981): 185–246; Ronald Dworkin, "What Is Equality? Part 2: Equality of Welfare," *Philosophy and Public Affairs* 10 (1981): 283–345.

$$d_x(i) = \frac{s_x(i)}{\sum_{j=1}^{\omega-x} s_x(j)(1+R)^{-j}}$$

In this formula, the function $s_x(i)$ denotes the estimated (or expected) survival rates for individual members of the tontine scheme, that is, from the initial age (x) to age $(x + i)$. The letter R denotes the assumed system interest rate (e.g., 4% or 6% or 8%), and ω denotes the maximum possible age of death for any individual member (e.g., 120 or 122). The symbol omega (ω) represents the so-called end of the mortality table and the letter j is just a summation (aka dummy) variable that counts from 1 (the lower bound) to the end of the mortality table.

Notice one variable that doesn't appear anywhere in the expression for Jared's tontine, that is the initial size of the tontine pool. It is irrelevant to the payout formula. In other words, Jared's tontine's payout rate schedule doesn't depend on how many people participate in or sign up to participate in the scheme. It only depends on the mortality estimates of the representative investor. This also means that promoters of the scheme don't have to wait and learn how many nominees/annuitants join the pool before they set the payout rate.

So much for the algebra; here are some typical numbers to help gain some financial intuition for the formula.

Detailed Example

Let's assume that a group of investors or retirees who are all sixty-five years old (and in reasonably good health) decide to set up a tontine scheme with contributions of $10,000 each. They would like to predetermine a proper payout rate schedule that satisfies Jared's tontine formula expressed above.

The first step is to hire an actuary, statistician, or demographer to establish a "survival probability function" for this group. This is a table that establishes a baseline for the fraction of sixty-five-year-olds who are expected to live for one year, five years, ten years, and so on. Here is a sample of the numbers produced by the actuary, representing the forward-looking survival probability for a homogenous group of sixty-five-year-olds. These numbers are from the Society of Actuaries (United States) for annuitants in the year 2010.

$$s_{65}(1) = 99.024\%, \ s_{65}(2) = 97.956\%, \ s_{65}(3) = 96.789\dots$$

Note that these are just the first three of the sixty numbers required, which range from $s_{65}(1)$ all the way to $s_{65}(60)$, where $\omega = 125$ is the maximum assumed length of life. Finally, for the last number required in the formula, I assume that the system interest rate is R = 4%, which is constant over the entire horizon. Think of it as the long-term bond rate in which all the capital will be invested. We now have all the ingredients to set up Jared's tontine scheme.

Plugging these numbers into the formula results in the following value for $d_{65}(1)$, which represents the first year's payout at the age of sixty-six (to survivors). Here we are. The first payment (rate) distributed to the pool is:

$$d_{65}(1) = \frac{0.99024}{(0.99024)(0.96154) + (0.97956)(0.92456) + \cdots} = 7.6739\%$$

Now, although the formula for Jared's tontine payout rate doesn't depend on the number of people who initially subscribe to the tontine, the actual dollar amount paid will obviously be a function of the contributed capital. So, in my final assumption, assuming that 1,000 people each contribute $10,000 to the tontine, the total capital in the tontine pool is $10 million.

Putting it all together according to the formula, at the end of the first year when everyone (who survived) is sixty-six years old, the pool will pay out 7.6739% of the $10 million invested capital, which is a $767,394 dividend to the survivors. Now, if in fact the actuarial forecasts proved correct – and later I'll get to what happens if they were not – then the $(0.99024)(1000) = 990$ survivors will share the $767,394 dividend for a total of $775 in the first year. Notice that this is an approximate yield of $775/10000 = 7.75\%$ on their contributed capital investment.

Now let's fast-forward to the end of year ten, for the sake of example. At the age of seventy-six – again, assuming the actuarial forecasts are correct – according to Jared's tontine formula, the value of $d_{65}(10) = 6.6019\%$. This is computed using the exact same denominator as for year one, but the numerator is now $s_{65}(10) = 85.190\%$ instead of the earlier-used $s_{65}(1) = 99.024\%$.

The interest payment to the tontine pool is 6.6019% times the original $10 million capital, which is $660,190 and much less than the first-year interest payment of $767,394. But – and this is key – the number of survivors is (only) 852, so the tontine dividend per survivor is: $660,190/852 = \$775$. Ergo, the expected dividend in year ten is identical to the dividend in year one. In fact, the tontine dividends are expected to remain exactly the same every single year. This is how Jared's tontine was constructed. It is an actuarial identity. Tontine survivors will expect a flat and constant $775 every

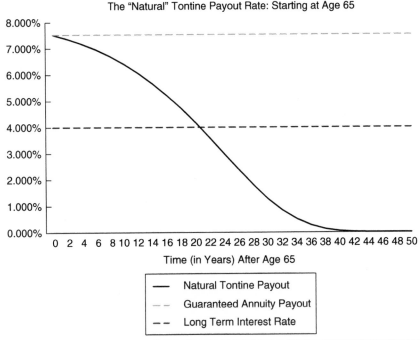

The "Natural" Tontine Payout Rate: Starting at Age 65

Time (in Years) After Age 65

——	Natural Tontine Payout
⋯⋯	Guaranteed Annuity Payout
– –	Long Term Interest Rate

Figure 7.2. Jared's tontine is more natural.

single year, forever. The declining payments will be exactly offset by the declining survival probability. The two will cancel out and you can thank the ubiquitous Law of Large Numbers, which I referred to a few times already.

Note that all of this can be done in inflation-adjusted term, as well. In other words, the payout can be adjusted every year for inflation, if, and only if, the interest rate that was used to discount cash flows and compute initial payouts was adjusted for inflation, as well.

Figure 7.2 is a picture or graphical representation of $d_{65}(i)$ for the first fifty years of the tontine. Notice how the payout rate to the pool starts off quite high and then declines smoothly and in direct proportion to survival probabilities for the same individual. The two horizontal lines at 4% and 7.75% represent the long-term (system) interest rate and the guaranteed annuity payout rate at age sixty-five, respectively. The annuity rate is a hypothetical number that represents what an insurance company who prices risk-neutrally (with no capital requirement) with no commissions and no profits would pay out in this idealized world. It is a fictitious number but a very helpful one.

Table 7.1. *Around the world: What would Jared's tontine pay?*

Country's cohort life expectancy at retirement	Long-term bond market interest rate	First-year (age 66) payout rate	Payout rate at age 80	Payout rate at age 95
A: 20 Years	5.0%	9.51%	4.72%	2.23%
B: 25 Years	3.0%	6.73%	3.84%	2.11%
C: 22 Years	4.0%	7.69%	4.07%	2.06%

Table 7.1 provides an estimate of what Jared's tontine would pay in three different (hypothetical) countries assuming long-term interest rates and longevity estimates for those countries. In fact, you can use any country's current interest rates and mortality rates to generate a similar table.[5]

In country A where the life expectancy is twenty years (and the mortality rate is assumed to be 5%) the initial tontine payout rate is 9.51%, using the above-written formula and assuming a constant mortality rate of 5%.[6] Then, as time goes on the payout rate is scheduled and predetermined to decline. By age eighty the payout rate is 4.72%, which is obtained by multiplying the 9.51% by the (fourteen-year) survival probability of 49.65% to age eighty.[7] At age ninety-five, which is twenty-nine years after the first payment is received, the payout rate to the pool is 2.23%. So, if you spend $100 on the tontine, you can expect to get $2.23 at the age of ninety-five *plus* the interest from all the people that died in the last thirty years, aka the mortality credits.

Remember that these numbers (payout rates) are worst-case scenarios. If nobody dies (in the fifteen years between ages sixty-five and eighty), you are guaranteed the payout rate listed in the table. But as people (naturally) die, their dividend is shared with the survivor. This is a tontine, after all.

Other hypothetical countries with higher life expectancy (i.e., for the people in the pool) and lower interest rates (in the bond market) would obtain or receive lower initial payouts from the tontine. They, too, would decline at a slower rate over time because the mortality rate in those countries is lower (to account for the higher life expectancy). Notice how country C has

---

[5]   See the online material for this book for an updated and detailed chart of what this table might actually look like around the world. http://www.MosheMilevsky.com

[6]   See Appendix C for more details on the annuity factor (which is the denominator in the formula) under a constant force of mortality.

[7]   This is exp (−0.05*14) = 49.65%. Recall that we are dealing with constant mortality rates over time, so the survival probability is quite simple.

a Jared tontine payout rate higher than country B (at retirement), but by age ninety-five it is lower. Remember that both interest rates and mortality rates affect these numbers at inception, but only mortality rates drive them once the scheme has been set up.

Ebola, Spanish Flu, or the Cure for Cancer?

A natural question to ask about the design or structure of Jared's tontine is: *What if the actuaries got it wrong?* What happens if ten years go by and instead of only 852 survivors (from the original 10,000) there are 900 survivors or 950 survivors? What happens then?

Recall that one of the complaints against King William's tontine is that the dividends didn't increase (i.e., too many people survived) relative to what was expected in the initial projections. Sure, the actuaries will attempt to be as accurate as possible, as opposed to being conservative or aggressive in their assumptions, because they are not guaranteeing anything. They are not benefiting from investments in the scheme – unlike the promoters of King William's tontine – so that conflict is avoided, as well.

The issue really is unexpected or statistical deviations as opposed to malice or deliberate errors on the part of the actuary who helps set up the scheme. So, getting down to it, there really are two reasons why the ex ante (expected survivors) might deviate from the ex post (realized survivors). The two different reasons reflect two types of longevity risk. One is aggregate longevity risk (often called systematic risk) and the other is individual longevity risk (aka idiosyncratic risk). If three sixty-five-year-olds enter into a tontine, there is a good chance they all survive to the end of the year and they earn no mortality credits (i.e., from the death of others). But if 3,000 people enter into a tontine, the chances are small that nobody will die. If you are one of the survivors, you will most likely earn some mortality credits. One of the other 2,999 will die during the year. The larger the pool, the smaller is the idiosyncratic risk. So big pools are comforting. You squeeze out the risk (of nobody dying).

But, there is a second risk, and that is the risk that you estimated the mortality rates incorrectly. You thought that 1% of your 3,000 pool would die in the next year – and based your tontine schedule on this rate – but in fact only 0.5% died. This is a second type of risk, which is the systematic component. That risk will be shared by the group in a tontine and larger pools won't help much.

Figure 7.3 provides a picture of this predictable variation. It is the range in which the payments will fall 80% of the time. Notice that in a natural

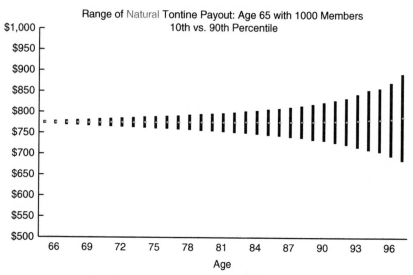

Figure 7.3. A more natural range for Jared's tontine.

tontine scheme, the range of possible income conditional on being alive looks different from the earlier picture discussed in Figure 7.1. Instead of the rapidly increasing and widening range of possibilities, the range spreads out slowly.

However, a more fundamental type of risk comes from a systemic change in population mortality patterns. A cure for cancer or the magic pill that adds five years to everyone's life expectancy will not wash out with the Law of Large Numbers, resulting in systematically lower tontine payments. On the other hand, an epidemic or catastrophe will have a structural impact on the survival rates and will permanently change the pool's dynamics. In this case, a few years might go by and a lower number of survivors will in fact translate into systematically higher tontine payments for everyone. But this is exactly the point. The pool – who all had the same initial chance to benefit from this – is sharing the risk.

In fact, this is yet another reason why different cohorts (i.e., ages) should not be mixed together into the same tontine pool, consistent with my earlier philosophical and ethical-based argument. These sorts of cures, diseases, and shocks will impact different ages at different rates. It's simply unfair to mix them together. To put it more technically, in a stochastic mortality system it is very difficult to build a tontine payout function that mixes cohorts together, is fair, and – most important – is transparent to everyone.

The Old Tontines Aren't Natural

Finally, let me compare Jared's natural tontine that I am advocating with the (old) historical variant. Think back to the description of King William's tontine in Chapter 3. In that 300-year-old version, the tontine payout function wasn't natural at all.

The payout rate was exactly 10% for the first seven years, which was from the subscription year 1693 to the year 1700. Then the payout rate was reduced by three percentage points to 7%, for the remainder of the ninety-nine years. Also, remember that in King William's tontine the payout rate didn't depend on the age of the nominee. So although the payout rate declines over time – which is closer to being natural – it didn't decline at the right rate, and certainly wasn't motivated by the probabilistic arguments I presented above.

The King Louis XIV (French) tontine I mentioned – and specifically the first one launched in 1689 – was even further from natural. Although it exhibited increasing payout rates for different nominee (initial) ages – which is actuarially sound – the payouts didn't decline over time. The French were careful not to mix their generations and cohorts. Each group of nominees subsidized and shared longevity risk within their birth cohort, which recall is one of the points I am advocating for the twenty-first century.

Using the notation I introduced above, in the French (1689 vintage) case, $d_0(i) = 5\%$, and $d_{10}(i) = 5.56\%$, and $d_{20}(i) = 6.25\%$, and so on. The tontine payout rate to the entire pool was a function of the initial age of the nominee. Then it was held constant and didn't decline over time like the tontine I am advocating.

In sum, the ideal twenty-first-century tontine borrows a very important feature from the design of King William III, which is a declining payout structure to the pool. But, like the French (as well as the second and last English state tontine from 1789), the payout rate should depend on the initial age of the nominee/annuitant (x), and the time that has elapsed since the tontine was initiated (i). Mathematically speaking, Jared's tontine payout rate is an increasing function of the age of the nominee when the tontine is set up, but a declining function of time as the tontine evolves.

Both the English and French (historical) tontine structures I discussed earlier were interesting – and perhaps even well thought out – but they were not optimal in an economic sense. The famous economist (and Scotsman) Adam Smith endorsed tontine financing based on behavioral arguments, arguing that most people think they will outlive others in their peer group. Perhaps he viewed them as winner-take-all lotteries, as opposed to insurance products that could be used to hedge personal longevity risk.

But is my plan for Jared's tontine actually optimal or just better and more logical? It is all nice and well to write down a normative expression for what the payout should be, but is there any basis in economic theory to use the $d_x(i)$ payout function? Well, here is where it gets interesting and surprising. This is beyond the mathematical scope of this book – and I refer the interested reader to the article I wrote with my research collaborator Tom Salisbury – but one can actually prove that if consumers are trying to maximize a Bernoulli (aka logarithmic) utility function, they will ask for precisely the type of function that I called Jared's tontine structure. So, yes, it is optimal. It maximizes utility. It has a strong basis in economic theory.

In fact, even if survival rates themselves are unknown (aka stochastic mortality), the optimal tontine for the same Bernoulli optimizer is (still) the tontine expressed by the $d_x(i)$ function above. Moreover, even consumers who are (much) more risk-averse than Bernoulli will not suffer too much dis-utility from Jared's tontine. All of this is explained (and proved) in much more detail in the Milevsky and Salisbury (2014) article listed in the references.

WHAT HAVE OTHERS WRITTEN? A SCHOLARLY LITERATURE REVIEW

There have been a number of other authors and writers – especially in the last decade or two – that have embraced the idea of resurrecting the tontine sharing principle or "tontine thinking," as I prefer to call it. I'm definitely not the only voice making this argument. Some of these advocates are professors (such as myself), some are journalists, and others are real-world practitioners hoping to create a new retirement income product that will sell (and make them some profits). Many of the authors have also (briefly) reviewed (selective) parts of the history of tontines. And a number of them have proposed their own (competing) annuity structures and designs that are different from the "Jared tontine payout" I introduced in the previous section.

Whether they have names like "participating annuities" or "pooled annuity funds" or "group self-annuitization," they are all motivated by one or two principles: namely, (i.) better sharing of risk and (ii.) more transparent design. A few authors have been generous to Lorenzo de Tonti and had the courtesy of giving him a polite reference, while some have ignored him altogether.

In this section I review the related academic literature and in the next I examine articles that have appeared in the popular press. But I focus exclusively on authors and writers concerned with the design and motivation of products that embed a tontine sharing principle. I can't promise to be comprehensive or exhaustive – as this is ever changing – but my objective here is to "prove" that I am not alone in this quest.[8]

Annuity Problems

It's difficult to pinpoint the exact beginning of the revival of "tontine thinking," but I would say that it started almost fifteen years ago. A forward-looking article published in 1999 under the title "Annuity Markets: Problems and Solutions" in the academic journal *The Geneva Papers on Risk and Insurance*, was written by economist David Blake. He was one of the first to hit the nail (longevity) on the head (cost). At the time, he argued that the main concern facing annuity providers – and the reasons they were not very popular among the public – was partially related to the "risk associated with mortality improvements." This is what I had called systematic (or nondiversifiable) longevity risk.

He pointed out that annuity providers could hedge some of their (usual) risks by investing in matching assets tracking their annuity liabilities, such as riskless government bonds. But there were no comparable or suitable matching assets for systematic longevity risk. Providers are unable to properly hedge longevity risk effectively. What this means is that they compensate for this type of longevity risk (to themselves) by "imposing substantial cost loadings and fees" (on the public). In other words, the consumer pays for this security or stability of income indirectly. As a solution, Blake (1999, p. 363) proposes that governments (return to) issuing longevity bonds, "with coupons declining in direct proportion to the realized mortality of a selected group of annuitants." This would help companies reduce their longevity risk and charge less for bearing the risk. In some sense, this was an early prescient piece arguing that governments should get back into the tontine business, although David Blake didn't directly say so at the time.

The Annuitized Fund (TAF)

In a 2001 article that was presented to the Staple Inn Actuarial Society (in London) called "Reinventing Annuities," actuaries M. Wadsworth, A. Findlater, and T. Boardman provide a concise historical overview of annuities in the UK – with a very brief mention of the 1693 tontine – discussing and reviewing the same problems that Blake (1999) had touched

---

[8] My apologies in advance for any omissions.

upon. They offered some practical solutions for actual product design. They start their article with a quote from Peter Drucker (the famous management consultant and professor) writing in the *Economist* in September 1999. Drucker wrote: "Providing financial protection against the new risk of not dying soon enough may well become the next century's major and most profitable financial industry." According to Wadsworth, Findlater, and Boardman (2001, p. 3), conventional annuities have many weaknesses and that "without the sharing of longevity risk, the task of achieving a satisfactory income in old age will become impossible for many."

To share longevity risk equitably they propose a new product called "The Annuitized Fund." They remind the reader that with a conventional life annuity, forfeited benefits for those who die early are distributed as benefits to others. But this mechanism is rather opaque and hard for consumers to disentangle. In the case of their proposed "Annuitized Fund" this cross subsidy would be made "explicit" and would be expressed in the form of survival or mortality credits. This sort of concept was explained in Chapter 6, in the Swedish pension system, and it makes perfect sense. In their words: "the annuitant would enjoy a lifetime tenancy of the fund, forfeiting it on death but receiving survival credits while alive" (p. 17).

Wadsworth, Findlater, and Boardman (2001, p. 3) also write : "it is likely that such sharing will have to become intra rather than inter generational (as it is now) if it is to be workable in the future." If you recall, in my earlier words, retirees and annuitants will have to share the risk of longevity improvements among themselves as opposed to with other generations.

But not everyone agrees with this view. Some scholars believe that different groups and cohorts can be mixed in an equitable and fair (although not necessarily transparent) manner. Most prominent is the work under the title of Group Self-Annuitization. The idea here is that the longevity risk is transferred from the individual to a group who absorbs and shares this risk, as opposed to a formal insurance company. It is an extension of individual self-annuitization, which is the opposite of annuitization, or buying a life annuity.

Group Self-Annuitization (GSA)

In 2005, Australian author and insurance economist J. Piggott, working with E. A. Valdez and B. Detzel, published an article in the *Journal of Risk and Insurance* under the title "The Simple Analytics of a Pooled Annuity Fund." In this article they developed a formal analysis of a type of longevity risk-pooling fund, which they christened Group Self-Annuitization (GSA).

According to the authors, the distinguishing feature of this new type of longevity insurance was that the annuitants themselves – and not the insurance company – would bear *systematic* risk, but by virtue of the Law of Large Numbers, the pool would share *idiosyncratic* risk. The closest analogy to these two different types of risk is the stock market. When you purchase a basket or index of stocks, you have eliminated the (individual) idiosyncratic risk but retain the (aggregate) systematic risk.

This shouldn't be very surprising (to readers, by now) and is a direct corollary of "tontine thinking." Their original (2005) article makes no reference to tontines, but it is clear that they are aware of this product.[9] The authors rightfully argue that their design would eliminate the need for a formal insurance company – since no shareholder capital or insurance reserves would be required – although corporations could certainly play a role in the distribution and management, which is much less capital intensive.

Technically speaking, their paper does some heavy (mathematical) lifting by deriving the payout adjustment for a "single entry group with a single annuity factor and constant expectations" (p. 498) which is similar to the "Jared tontine payout" design I suggested in the earlier part of this chapter.

The authors then go on to suggest that it is indeed possible to mix different groups and different cohorts in an equitable manner, although – in my opinion – not in a very transparent or understandable manner. They explain how payouts to survivors would be adjusted based on their (estimated) survival rates, their age, and other characteristics.

As I argued earlier, it is debatable whether it is indeed fair or desirable to mix the young and the old into one tontine pool. Piggott, Valdez, and Detzel (2005) propose adjusting annuity payouts based on the "shock" or surprise to mortality rates and the exact composition of the pool and their individual mortality expectation.

In contrast the much simpler and more transparent Jared tontine proposal would be as follows.[10] Settle on a known periodic cash flow called $X(t)$. Divide $X(t)$ by $Y(t)$ (unknown number of survivors) and thus maintain the extremely important optical clarity for the annuitant. Then again, simplicity might be in the eye of the beholder (and author). We will agree to disagree.

---

[9] In fact I have had fruitful and interesting conversations with John Piggott on various occasions regarding the optimal design of retirement annuities.

[10] Once again, please see Milevsky and Salisbury (2014) for more details.

Regardless of the differences in design, I very much agree with their conclusion that GSAs – however they are structured in the end – will have considerable appeal in countries that have adopted national defined contribution schemes and/or in which the life insurance industry is noncompetitive. Piggott, Valdez, and Detzel (2005) have gone on to write a number of follow-up papers refining their original design, which has spawned a (new) literature that has tried to improve upon the GSA or criticized its design.[11]

Alas, this is how the academic world works. The physicist Max Planck wrote "A new scientific truth does not triumph by convincing its opponents and making them see the light, but rather because its opponents eventually die, and a new generation grows up that is familiar with it." as translated in *Scientific Autobiography and Other Papers*, trans. F. Gaynor (New York, 1949), pp. 33–34 (also cited in T. S. Kuhn, *The Structure of Scientific Revolutions*). This rather famous quote is often repeated in a shorter version, "Science progresses funeral by funeral", which is quite appropriate for research on the optimal design of tontines.

Pooled Annuity Funds (PAF)

As one of those follow-up articles, "Optimal Consumption and Portfolio Choice," written by the German insurance economist M. Stamos (2008) and published in the journal *Insurance: Mathematics and Economics*, very similar arguments were made. He wrote, "A pooled annuity fund constitutes an alternative way to protect against mortality risk compared to purchasing a life annuity" (p. 58). But the crucial difference between the pooled annuity fund and the purchase of a guaranteed life annuity offered by an insurance company is that "participants of a pooled annuity fund still have to bear some mortality risk while insured annuitants bear no mortality risk at all."

Then, using Monte Carlo Simulation and utility welfare analysis (which I touched on in the early part of this chapter), Stamos (2008) derives a number of mathematical results based on some initial mathematical axioms. He shows that (i.) pooled annuity funds insure very effectively against longevity risk even if their pool size is rather small, and (ii.) only very risk-averse investors or those without access to small pools are more inclined to pay a risk premium to access private life annuity markets in order to lay off mortality risk completely. Indeed, I couldn't agree more.

Here is yet another author (and research paper) who argues that consumers should at least be given a portfolio choice of life annuities and payout

---

[11] See, for example, Valdez, Piggott, and Wang (2006).

instrument. Some would lay off or eliminate mortality risk completely (for a capital cost), and others would share the mortality risk internally. Note that some people use the term *mortality risk* and some use the term *longevity risk*, but in the context of life annuities they are usually talking about the same thing: the risk that people live longer than anticipated. Stamos (2008) makes no mention of tontines (either), but Lorenzo's spirit lives on.

Mortality-Indexed Annuities (MIA)

Continuing on the same theme, in 2011, (practicing) actuaries A. Richter and F. Weber proposed a mortality-indexed annuity (MIA) in an article published in the *North American Actuarial Journal*. They were motivated by the same concerns with aggregate or systematic mortality risk. They note that common risk management tools, such as reinsurance or hedging, are not as effective for managing the insurance and the annuity company's exposure to aggregate longevity risk, similar to the point made by Blake (1999). They then propose a new type of life annuity with "benefits contingent on actual mortality experience." In other words, they offer yet another way to design a better annuity. A similar proposal under the parallel title of longevity-indexed life annuities (instead of mortality indexed) is offered by Denuit, Haberman and Renshaw (2011). Both articles build on the same concept. Richter and Webber (2011) provide some interesting and relevant examples in which risk is shared (the way they propose) among participants from the German private health insurance market. They write: "By effectively sharing systematic longevity risk with policyholders, insurers may avoid cumulative losses (p. 212)." This is the tontine sharing principle (again) although (again) the word *tontine* doesn't appear anywhere in either of these articles.

Pooled Survival Funds (PSF)

In another advocacy piece by a consultant, but one that gives full and ample credit to Lorenzo de Tonti, the South African actuary Paul Newfield (2014) describes something he calls the Pooled Survival Fund (PSF), which is yet another name for the annuity of the future. In "The Tontine: An Improvement on the Conventional Annuity?," published in 2014 in the *Journal of Retirement*, he writes that "much of the industrialized world have long-forgotten [the tontine's] attractiveness" (p. 38). The article makes the case that a PSF, which in his view is the modern version of a tontine, can provide a superior combination of longevity insurance and income compared with traditional annuities in particular. He claims that the PSF could be readily integrated into the existing (Australian Superannuation[12]) pension system, which is an argument made by a number of U.S. academics and law professors, which I'll get to later on.

Participating Life Annuities (PLA)

Another recent article advocating the tontine sharing principle or "tontine thinking" is the paper by Portuguese economists J. M. Bravo, P. C. Real, and C. P. Silva (2009). They develop a framework (and product) in which annuitants bear some of the longevity risk themselves and (in exchange for a fee) transfer some of the risk to an insurance company. Their proposed product is slightly different from the GSA introduced above and is certainly more complicated than the Jared tontine. But their point is to offer (even) more flexibility in determining how much longevity risk a retiree is willing to take. The authors also provide some examples (or calibrate their pricing model) to Portuguese data.

So there you have it. Scholars and researchers in Australia, South Africa, Germany, and Portugal have proposed innovative tontine-like annuities. And we are not done with the international tour quite yet.

Transparent Annuities

Efficient and equitable sharing of longevity risk and reducing capital costs (and insurance fees) is an important aspect of "tontine thinking." But an equally important aspect is transparency and simplicity of design, which is often lacking in some of the above-referenced works. In fact, I would argue that transparency and simplicity are even more vital than economic efficiency is.

The importance of transparency is echoed by researchers C. Donnelly, M. Guillen, and J. P. Nielsen. They are based in Scotland, Denmark, and Spain, respectively, and have written quite a bit on the topic of optimal annuity design. See Donnelly, Guillen, and Nielsen (2013, 2014). In their most recent article (2014) published in the journal *Insurance: Mathematics and Economics*, they wrote and recognized that "the trend is to decompose

---

[12] It seems that a variant of the PSF was launched in Australia in the fall of 2014. See the October 30 article by W. Klijn at http://www.theinstoreport.com.au/articles /mercer-unveils-pooled-survival-option. This particular product was launched by Mercer, which is an actuarial consulting firm.

[retail financial] products, such that customers understand each component as well as its price" (p. 15). But, they point out, this trend has yet to be embraced by annuity providers. They then suggest a simple decomposed annuity structure that enables cost transparency and could be linked to any investment fund. That is their particular contribution.

According to Donnelly, Guillen, and Nielsen (2014), their proposed design has several attractive features not available in any of the other competing proposals. First, they claim, it works for any heterogeneous group. Second, participants can leave before death without financial penalty. And, finally, participants have complete freedom over their own investment strategies. Although they don't make reference to Lorenzo de Tonti – and the mathematical proofs are beyond the scope of this book – "tontine thinking" underlies their entire design.

Even the World Bank Steps In

In an article written by World Bank economists G. Impavido, C. Thorburn, and M. Wadsworth (2004), the authors make a statement that (by now) should be very familiar to readers. They write: "Traditional products available in most countries can require excessive minimum capital requirements.... Investment and longevity risk should be shared between providers and annuitants so that supply constraints can be relaxed." They conclude with a statement echoing many of the previously cited authors and papers. "Alternative annuity products, which imply risk sharing, could be backed by substantially lower capital investments or, equivalently, provided at substantially lower prices to consumers" (p. 29). There it is again: sharing.

Of course, this isn't the venue to debate or argue over the best possible design of an annuity that embraces the tontine sharing principle or the mathematical minutiae around proving "fairness" or that it "maximizes the most general utility function." That sort of discourse is best left in the hands of academic journals, editors, and reviewers.

My point here was to prove that I really am not alone in this quest. It isn't crazy to suppose that tontines (or some variant of them) will be resurrected in the future. And presumably there are some profits to be made, as well.

An Idea from Harvard Business School

Harvard Business School Professor J. Rotemberg is another tontine aficionado. In a (2009) white paper entitled "Can a Continuously-Liquidating Tontine (or Mutual Inheritance Fund) Succeed Where Immediate Annuities

Have Floundered?" he jumps into the "I can build a better mousetrap" arena and calls his proposal a Mutual Inheritance Fund (MIF). His product would be purchased around the age of retirement and held for life. Like life annuities the MIF would start with an up-front payment well before people receive any benefits, but it would also protect them from longevity risk. The funds that individuals would contribute to this MIF would be invested in a mutual fund and all distributions like dividends and interest would be reinvested until the contributor (i.) dies and loses the bet, or (ii.) wins and reaches some predetermined (maximum) age, for example, eighty or ninety. This is where the tontine resides; if a contributor dies before this prespecified age, his shares are liquidated and the proceeds are distributed to the other investors. Contributors or participants who are alive at the prespecified age (e.g., eighty or ninety) are also paid the value of their accumulated shares. The payout is in the form of a lump sum at discrete intervals.

The Rotemberg (2009) proposal isn't quite an instrument that generates periodic and predictable income to retirees – like the original tontine – but instead is closer to the Type 3 design I had referenced in Chapter 6. Perhaps a short enough time horizon (maximum age) could generate an income-producing asset. Is this better or worse than the other five or six proposals I mentioned above? That is hard to tell, but the main point is to illustrate the "tontine thinking" underlying the design.

I would let the market and Adam Smith's invisible hand sort out the best tontine design. After all, he was a fan, as well.

In fact, one firm– which openly embraced tontine thinking – has actually tried to create a product based on this principle.[13] This was described in "A Mutual Fund to Yield Annuity-Like Benefits," by Ralph Goldsticker (2007), who is a director at the company. The article was published as a perspectives piece in the *Financial Analysts Journal*, and it describes his proposal.

He proposes a "new" tontine-like investment vehicle as an alternative to purchased annuities. A mutual fund/tontine hybrid could provide benefits similar to those of purchased annuities but also offer many advantages. One of the things I like about this article (and the proposal) is the emphasis on the transparency. It has to be simple and easy to understand. He writes, "Full transparency is an important benefit of the tontine" (p. 67). The same theme, regarding the need for transparency and simplicity together with the value of mortality credits, is also echoed in the scholarly article by Scott, Watson and Hu (2011).

---

[13] Mellon Capital Management is based in San Francisco, and it apparently filed a patent for this concept. Mercer (in Australia) is in the process of filing its own patent for the PSF.

Fair Tontines for Pension

Finally, in a series of articles law professor J. Forman and engineer M. Sabin have grabbed the tontine by the horns, so to speak.[14] They have also advocated for a resurrection of "tontine thinking." In "A Solution to the State and Local Pension Underfunding Crisis" (2014), which appears in the *University of Pennsylvania Law Review*, they offer a comprehensive advocacy piece as well as a recipe book for pension tontines, or what they call "fair tontine annuities" (FTA), based on an idea introduced by Sabin (2010).

The two write that the tontine principle could be used to create "tontine pensions" that could be adopted by large employers to provide retirement income for their employees. Their articles go on to show how these tontine pensions would have several major advantages over most of today's pensions, annuities, and other retirement income products.

They write that "unlike traditional pensions – which are frequently underfunded, tontine pensions would always be fully funded. Second, unlike a traditional pension – where the pension plan sponsor must bear all the investment and actuarial risks, with a tontine pension, the plan sponsor bears neither of those risks" (p. ii)

Forman and Sabin (2014) go so far as to develop a model tontine pension for a typical large employer, and then use that model to estimate the benefits that would be paid to retirees.

In one hypothetical example they demonstrate that if an employer would "contribute 10% of salary to a tontine pension" for each employee each year, the benefits paid to retirees would closely resemble an actuarially fair variable annuity, but without insurance company fees and loads. In their words: "This means that tontine pensions would provide significantly higher retirement benefits than commercial annuities" (p. iii). Or, to put it differently – and in the words I used earlier – you could get the same expected income benefit at a lower up-front cost.

In Sum

The academic and scholarly literature around the "annuity of the future" continues to grow.[15] Every author has a favorite design, unique name, or

---

[14] See, Forman and Sabin (2014).
[15] See the article by McKeever (2009) for yet another legal perspective and possible alternative design for a modern tontine annuities.

mathematical technique they would like to emphasize.[16] Some emphasize fairness, others focus on the maximization of some utility function, and yet others worry about transparency and simplicity. But regardless of the exact structure – and whether he is mentioned or not – Lorenzo de Tonti would be proud to see his ideas and concepts debated in the halls of academia more than 300 years after his death. In fact, economic professor and Nobel laureate William Sharpe gave a presentation to the French Finance Association in Marseille, in May 2014 entitled; "Providing Retirement Income: TIPS, TIFs, Tranches, Tontines and Trills" in which he argued for the resurrection of Tonti's scheme, claiming they would help make retirement products cheaper and more effective.

TONTINES IN THE PRESS AND MEDIA

While most academic authors and scholars are universally upbeat about the idea of using "tontine thinking" to create the next generation of retirement income annuities, the media and press have been less enthusiastic. One constantly reads news articles claiming that tontines were banned or are illegal because of concerns with murder or other silliness. Even experienced insurance practitioners often make similar claims. As just one example, Dellinger (2006, p. 428) writes that "Tontines are generally outlawed today as contrary to public interest since they effectively create moral hazard, a situation where members have financial incentive to encourage the demise of other members ... Tontines may be more in the nature of a contest than a reasonable economic program to help participants cope with longevity risk".

But not everyone is pessimistic and even among jaded news writers Lorenzo's vision has some supporters. Here is a sampling.

In the summer of 2006, the *Financial Times* (newspaper) in conjunction with ABN Amro (investment bank) announced a competition in which they asked individuals from all walks of life to suggest the ideal or dream "financial product or service of the future." The organizers and judges reviewed 400 different submissions, and in the fall of 2006 they announced the first, second, and third place winners, with much publicity and fanfare in the *Financial Times*.

[16] See Direr (2010) or Sheshinski (2008) for alternative annuity designs that don't necessarily invoke the tontine principle but are attempts to make them more appealing to consumers. Alternatively, see Hayashi, Altonji, and Kotlikoff (1996) for a clever argument that a (large) family can serve as a self-contained annuity market, without requiring any novel annuity design.

While the person and product winning the first place aren't related to my message or King William III, the second place finish in the competition was surprising and quite relevant. His name was Philip Ralli, living in Surrey (England), and the idea that beat out 398 other submissions was a "retirement tontine." Yes. His idea was to give Britons an alternative to buying a life annuity, a process many hate and a topic I'll return to in the next chapter.

His proposal was described (quite favorably) in a *Financial Times* article published on October 9, 2006, by Robert Budden. Mr. Ralli's idea was to have investors pool their assets into an investment fund that would be managed on behalf of all investors, with the longest running survivor benefiting from superior income. This idea is rather tame and familiar. But, according to the reporter, "the judges particularly liked the transparency of the proposed scheme" (p. 1).

Now, it is unclear how or why Mr. Ralli (who is a book publisher, by the way) thought of the tontine, but the idea had been discussed in the British media for a while now. In 2004, which was two years before the competition, *Prospect Magazine* had an article suggesting a tontine as a form of longevity insurance. There the author argued, "The government should overhaul the law on tontines and permit them to be marketed in an orderly way." (p. 1)

In fact, one of the earliest media (i.e., nonacademic) pieces advocating the revival of tontines was a very brief (800-word) essay by Max Walsh in the *Sydney Morning Herald* entitled "The Tontine Way to Make Longevity Pay." It was published more than twenty years ago on April 21, 1995. The author (of the article) was discussing a book by Brian Reading on the origins of England's national debt and the role that King William's tontine played in the first attempt to borrow long-term money. The tontine was reviewed (positively) and particularly relevant for the Australian market because they had just introduced a mandatory (in 1995) superannuation system in which individuals were forced to save for retirement. The question contemplated was how this money should be invested and how it should be used to generate an income. Max Walsh's quite plausible solution was a tontine (and so it seems I was scooped by twenty years).

Other reporters, columnists, and writers – during the last twenty years – have written articles that can almost be considered equally enthusiastic. In the March 24, 2001, issue of the *Spectator* (a UK newspaper), the noted author, commentator, and financier Edward Chancellor wrote an article under the title "Live Long and Prosper." The article was likely prompted by the Prudential Insurance Company in the UK (not related to the U.S. company), and their plans to reintroduce a tontine-like annuity. Mr. Chancellor called this a "bold move" for the insurance company because "the tontine is perhaps the most discredited financial instrument in history" (wow!). But, all is not lost. He goes on to say:

> Given its checkered history, it might be concluded that the tontine should remain extinct. Yet if we leave aside moralistic objections, which smack of 19th-century righteousness, there are reasons to believe that a revival of the tontine would help address the problem of destitution in old age.

He concludes:

> In the past the greatest weakness of tontines has been inadequate regulation. Yet it is difficult to believe that this poses a serious problem today. In one sense, tontines pose less risk to members than conventional annuities since there is no contractual obligation on payout, no counter-party risk and no need for insurance-company reserves.... Tonti described his scheme as a "hidden treasure"; it is time for it to be unearthed once again.

This 2001 article by such a noted author and the insurance company's attempt to launch a tontine-like annuity generated a number of follow-up "endorsement pieces" in a variety of other newspapers. An article by Melanie Wright in the *Daily Telegraph* on March 31, 2001, called the tontine principle "ingenious."

Now, I certainly don't want to get into the actuarial minutiae here, but I must say that the Prudential (UK) annuity described above wasn't quite a tontine in the King William sense. And it actually isn't available (in 2015) anymore. Yes, Prudential (UK) today offers various annuities under the name of "income choice annuity" – which are linked to investment accounts – and "guaranteed pensions annuities," which are certainly decent products. But these are not (my vision of) Jared's tontines.

What exactly happened between 2001 and 2015 is unclear. Perhaps Prudential (UK) found little demand for tontines and Adam Smith's invisible hand rendered a negative verdict.

In 2007 there was again a flurry of activity and discussion in the media around the subject of tontines. A highly visible (front-page) article by *Financial Times* authors Joanna Chung and Gillian Tett (February 24, 2007) had a mouthful of a title and subtitle: "Death and the Salesmen: As People Live Longer, Pension Funds Struggle to Keep Up, Which Is Where a New, Highly Profitable Market Will Come In – One That Bets On Matters of Life and Death." The (almost 4,000-word) article focused on longevity bonds and the work of (the earlier-mentioned professor) David Blake, but the authors also started their article with the story of King William's tontine. They wrote, "The very first time that the British state issued a bond, back in the 17th century to fund a war against France, it did so doing a longevity gamble" (2007, 26).

While Chung and Tett allude to the "incentive to murder," they (too) claim that "historians have not found any tangible cases of this happening" (2007, 26). And as I pointed out in Chapter 4, the real shenanigans were very low death rates as opposed to excessive mortality. They claim that "tontines proved disastrous for government finance" (perhaps life annuities, but not tontines) and that "the tontine schemes became so costly that the government abandoned it" (it wasn't really about cost). While one can debate how and why tontines have become extinct, Chung and Tett (2007) clearly weren't as encouraging as Chancellor (2001). But they both seem to agree on the society's cost of incurring longevity risk and that tontines might be able to help.

A *Forbes* article less than a month later, on March 12, 2007, was even less flattering of the tontine concept. In "Last Retiree Standing: Here's an Investment Vehicle You Could Kill For," Ashlea Ebeling reported on the recent (in 2007) patent filling by Mellon Financial for a hybrid-tontine (which I discussed above in the academic article by Goldsticker). The last line in the Forbes article is "the biggest hurdle will be changing state laws that ban tontines ... and getting past the laugh factor." Yes, another lukewarm endorsement. A similar theme was echoed in an article in the *Daily Telegraph* on March 31, 2007, by Richard Barry. He accepted the premise that "a tontine can provide a neat and affordable solution to the problem" but worried about whether it was legal.

When in June 2007 another financial institution, Schroders, discussed the possible reintroduction of tontine, the chief investment officer had to preempt concerns about legality and incentives to murder by saying, "I am not talking about a return to the days of cups laced with arsenic," according to a story in *Money Marketing* magazine on June 28, 2007. Another noted (American) industry expert and author Kerry Pechter wrote a piece in *Annuity Market News* entitled "Possible Tontine Revival Raises Worries." His first sentence perpetuated the myth: "Tontines are banned.... because they're considered an incentive to homicide."

In Sum

It is virtually impossible to manufacture, launch, and promote a "new" financial product without winning some influential members of the press and media on your side. Getting the public to understand how a tontine works and why it makes sense (without laughing) is a critical barrier to overcome.

All in all, I counted more than thirty popular articles written by a diverse group of authors during the last two decades. While none of them were outright against them, and many of them were appreciative of "tontine thinking" – all of them made reference to the public relation "issues" in reviving tontines.

We have an uphill battle in rehabilitating the "most discredited financial instrument in history." But one company seems to have managed to avoid the public relations problem – and has had much success with tontine thinking – by cleverly avoiding the odious word itself.

TIAA-CREF: POSSIBLY THE BIGGEST TONTINE IN THE WORLD

In downtown New York City there is a collection of buildings on Third Avenue housing a company that few people other than teachers, university professors, and hospital workers have heard of. The company is called TIAA-CREF, which is an awkward abbreviation for the much more cumbersome Teachers Insurance and Annuity Association & College Retirement Equity Fund.[17] TIAA-CREF is essentially a large pension fund, which pays more annuities to retirees than any other (non-state owned) company in the world. Every year it sends payments totaling over a billion U.S. dollars to retirees, which at first glance is no different from many other pension funds and insurance companies around the word. But, where TIAA-CREF differs from other retirement titans is as follows. TIAA-CREF has the ability to revise these payments (up or down) based on realized and experienced mortality rates as their actuaries see fit. The company has the discretion to react to changes in longevity patterns in general and the experience of their annuitants in particular. Also, given their unique ownership structure, they have no shareholders – arguing for higher returns on equity – to placate.

In a sense, very little is guaranteed. Annuitants in TIAA-CREF are part of a large co-operative pool, very similar to the Kibbutz I mentioned earlier. If these annuitants end up living longer than planned or expected, TIAA-CREF can protect itself and future generations by reducing income from one year to the next. It calls this a participating annuity and again is

---

[17] Disclosure: I spent two summers visiting TIAA-CREF. The first was as a student actuarial trainee in 1989 and the second was as a visiting fellow in 2001.

one of the very few companies in the United States to offer them. Also, this company has the highest of credit rating from the agencies such as Moodys and Standard and Poors, precisely because they take so little risk on their corporate balance sheet. To me, this is tontine thinking in practice. Of course, TIAA-CREF would never call it a tontine, but similar to the Swedish pension system, the dividend payout philosophy is clearly influenced by "tontine thinking."[18]

And, while the formula the company uses to adjust payouts from time to time isn't anywhere near as simple as Jared's tontine – and the mortality credits are not nearly as transparent, and I'm putting this midly – TIAA-CREF is as close as you can currently get to historical tontines in the United States.

This unique company has been around for almost a century, originally founded – in 1918 to create pensions for retiring teachers – by the great Scottish American industrialist and philanthropist Andrew Carnegie. There it is again. Tontines, retirement, and Scotland, all in the same sentence. Coincidence?

---

[18] See Biggs (1969) and Duncan (1952) for some additional information about the (early) technical design of TIAA-CREF annuities.

8

Conclusion: Tontines for
the Twenty-First Century

DON'T PROMISE MORE THAN YOU CAN DELIVER

If you want a hassle-free PhD, then retired London School of Economics (LSE) Professor Ragnar Norberg isn't someone you want on your thesis examination committee. In fact, if you are a newly minted academic presenting scientific results at a research seminar, then you probably don't want him in the audience either. Professor Norberg is an old-school Scandinavian actuary in the famed tradition of Filip Lundberg (1876–1965), Harald Cramér (1893–1985), and Thorvald N. Thiele (1838–1910). During his distinguished career he has been a director of the Laboratory for Actuarial Mathematics in Copenhagen, has written more than 100 technical research articles and is the associate editor of many leading scholarly journals in the field. More importantly he doesn't suffer fools lightly and – most delightful and refreshing – he tells it like it is.[1]

Professor Norberg was invited to speak at a conference in Toronto soon after the financial crises of 2008, when risk management failures, economic catastrophes, and financial meltdowns were fresh and pressing on everyone's mind. Intellectually speaking, anything and everything was "on the table." Financial markets were under attack. Naturally, given his expertise in the field of insurance and actuarial science, he was asked by the organizers to address some of the real-world problems experienced by insurance companies. Household names such as Manulife in Canada, AIG in the United States, and Equitable in the UK (a decade earlier) had been close to the

---

[1] I know Professor Norberg quite well and now consider him a good friend. But more than twenty years ago as I was finishing-up my graduate studies I presented some results from my doctoral thesis at a Dutch insurance conference at which Professor Norberg was presiding. Needless to say, I learned an important lesson in humility that morning in Amsterdam.

brink as a result of bad risk management – and the audience was eager to hear his views on lessons to be learned from the crisis. Remember, these companies had made financial promises to their policyholders – for example, to pay them a high level of income for life – and were at risk of defaulting on those promises owing to poor risk management.

Although Professor Norberg's talk was replete with the mathematics of stochastic processes, he made a remarkable and very eloquent statement that has resonated and stuck with me ever since.[2] In fact, it is what inspired me to think differently about the role of insurance companies and even pension funds in providing retirement income. He said (and I quote): "Insurance companies and pension funds guaranteed too much. They should promise only what they can keep." They should stick to the business of sharing, pooling, and transferring risk, only.

Now think about this for a moment. Here was one of the most widely published actuaries of our era, a scholar who had taught and trained some of the best insurance actuaries who now work for the biggest insurance companies in the world. Effectively he was saying that these same companies should completely change the way they run their business. Instead of creating more effective hedges via more complex mathematical models, or designing better derivative securities or offering more complex financial options – Professor Norberg was arguing for less. In fact, he was arguing for none at all: *no guarantees*. The proper way to run a company is to *spread* risk across a group, *share* it within the group, *absorb* it within the group. This is precisely "tontine thinking."

This might be a good time to remind the reader that a classical tontine – and most definitely Jared's tontine – guarantees very little. Figure 8.1 is a visualization of this concept. It compares the longevity risk faced by a company issuing life annuities versus tontines. In a conventional life annuity – which is the graphic in the middle – the insurance company is exposed to longevity risk from day one. If a few more people than expected survive, then they "are on the hook" for the extra payments. The company has made guarantees and they must stand by them. But with the tontine scheme – which is the graphic on either side – the risk is shared by the pool itself. The company guarantees nothing. They are merely custodians and managers.

Now, Professor Norberg made his remarks to a group of academics and scholars in the field of insurance mathematics and not to executives or regulators, which is why you didn't read about this in the *Wall Street Journal*.

---

[2] As I was preparing this manuscript, I asked him to confirm these remarks again.

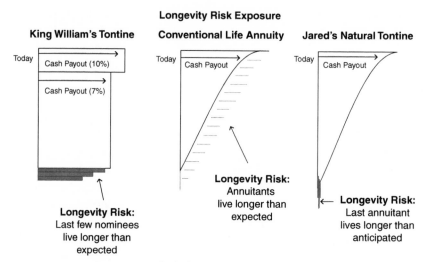

Figure 8.1. Which design might a regulator prefer?

But I reckon it was the absentee's loss. To quote the Danish philosopher Søren Kierkegaard, in his book *Works of Love* [published in 1847, translated by Howard and Edna Hong in 1998, published by Princeton university press] "a '*no*' does not hide anything, but a '*yes*' very easily becomes an illusion, a self-deception."

Yes, it is human nature for individuals to seek long-term promises, guarantees, and security – and it is the hubris of clever insurance company executives who believe they can offer these policies – but we live in a world that can't afford to make such pledges. This is precisely why the tontine concept is so powerful; nothing is guaranteed. All demographic risk is shared.

Professor Norberg isn't the only noted scholar to make a plea for simplicity and more transparency or someone who believes we should "just say no" to more promises. Other scholars agree with him wholeheartedly. Interestingly, though, Professor Norberg wasn't the first esteemed actuary to issue warnings about life insurance and annuity promises and pricing. In fact, the Britain's first national actuary made similar points almost two centuries ago – after examining the records of King William's tontine.

John Finlaison

In mid-1840, John Finlaison – whom I mentioned earlier – wrote an urgent letter to the Chancellor of the Exchequer, imploring the government to change the way they price and sell life annuities to the public. John

Finlaison was no commoner exercising his democratic right to complain about prices and yields. Rather, his official position was Actuary of the National Debt from the years 1822 to 1851. Arguably he was the world's first full-time (industry) actuary who then went on to launch the British Institute of Actuaries, where his son and then grandson (Alexander, also mentioned earlier) served in the same roles. In fact, wandering around downtown London, you will find entire buildings named in the Finlaison family's honor.

In contrast to most people who might complain that the prices of goods and services purchased by retirees were too high, Finlaison's concern was that prices were too *low*. The government was guaranteeing too much and not charging enough, that is, not managing their risk correctly. Sounds familiar?

In handwritten letters to members of Parliament, he presented convincing data that British retirees and pensioners were living much longer than what was assumed in the government's pricing schedule.[3] This then meant that payments were made for longer, costing the government more than they had budgeted. Again, they guaranteed too much.

Finlaison expressed great concern that pricing wasn't sustainable and urged them to lower the payouts and raise the fees. At the very least, he argued, males and females should be paying different prices for annuities. Prior to his work in 1829, nobody thought to differentiate pricing (of annuities, let alone tontines) by gender.

To boil this all down to its financial essence, according to Finlaison's calculations on the eve of the Victorian era, Her Majesty's government was selling life annuities worth £175 in present values term, for a mere £100 up-front cost, which was a good deal for retirees – but not for the entity standing behind the promise.

Forgetting History, Doomed to Repeat It

You would think that the government, pension and insurance industry would learn to reduce mispricing errors and better manage their risks by now. Indeed, the last two centuries are littered with similar examples, whether they have to do with life annuities, life insurance, long-term care, or other forms of insurance. Alas, the long-festering battles over the underfunding of state pension plans are yet another good example of mispricing.

---

[3]   Finlaison's letters and supporting actuarial data are labeled reference item T1/3744 and were available at the British National Archives in London.

Table 8.1. *Variable annuity guarantees: Now vs. then*

	Now (2015)	Then (2005)
Lifetime Income Rate	4%–5%	7%–8%
Guaranteed Return	1%–2%	5%–6%
Step-Up Frequency	Monthly	Daily
Choice of Investments	Very Restricted	Anything Goes
Insurance Fees	80–120 basis points	20–40 basis points
# of Comp. Offering	8–10	20–25

Source: Author compilation.

They all come down to the same thing: bad assumptions leading to expensive and unmanageable guarantees.

Lo and behold, now history has been repeating itself with variable annuities. This time around it isn't *human longevity* that's causing problems. Rather, it is *human rationality* that is rupturing the pricing models.

VARIABLE ANNUITY UPHEAVALS OF 2008

About twenty blocks away from my office in downtown Toronto is a huge testament or monument to one of the greatest financial disasters in the twenty-first century. No, it isn't a shrine for the millions of mortgage holders who lost their houses during the Great Recession,[4] and it certainly isn't a statue of disgraced financial adviser and criminal Bernie Madoff. In fact, it really isn't a monument at all. I'm referring to the headquarters of a great insurance company called Manulife Financial, and the disaster I'm referring to goes under the awkward name of Guaranteed Living Withdrawal Benefits – aka GLWBs. These GLWBs nearly brought the company – and perhaps the entire industry – to the point of insolvency. The main problem? Guaranteeing a lifetime of income … via the stock market. The stock market isn't a place for guarantees.

Can We Have Your Variable Annuity (VA) Back?

Let me back up a wee bit and ask you to ponder this. When the company that manufactured your car contacts you out of the blue and asks to "buy it back," or when the tailor who made your suit suddenly offers to replace

---

[4] In fact, the global financial crises of 2007–2008 was rather mild for Canadian consumers and homeowners. Their property values didn't decline (as of yet).

it with a better one – are they doing it out of the goodness of their hearts? Rather, they likely made some sort of mistake in the design, and possibly a fatal one.

Variable Annuity (VA) policies in the United States are investment funds with various guarantees or promises associated with them. North American insurance companies have spent a good part of the last few years trying to buy themselves out of those promises. Namely, offering to buy back the VA policies that they sold a few years earlier. And I don't think it's because they want to display the certificates in a museum or an archive. They made some fatal pricing mistakes – and now must suffer the consequences by setting aside large cash reserves to back those guarantees – and they want a redo.

As a recent report by Moody's Investor's Services – which was profiled with much fanfare in the *Wall Street Journal* (June 26, 2014) – indicated, most insurance companies assumed that policyholders and customers were (to put it bluntly) *idiots*. They assumed individuals would lapse or surrender their VA policies at the worst possible time (for the owner). They assumed you would cancel the home insurance coverage just as the hurricane was arriving or cancel the life insurance just before the priest was about to administer last rites.

Well, you don't have to be Mr. Spock to realize that *assumption* isn't a very reliable or sound word. Perhaps when the sun is shining and life is good people give up their insurance, but not in bad times and certainly not in the era of annuity analytics.

VAs with rich guaranteed living and death benefits allowed policyholders to participate in the upside of the market and generate a princely income that far exceeded what was available from other comparable instruments. So as long as they didn't listen to the media nonsense about the "evils of annuities," many effectively arbitraged the insurance companies.[5]

Now, in their defense, perhaps the insurance company executives had been exposed to disproportionate amounts of behavioral finance theory peddled by psychologists with scant regard for mathematical finance and the market value of put options. Recall that according to this non-Vulcan view of the world, consumers are highly irrational, susceptible to systematic errors in judgment, emotional, fickle, and easily manipulated. If that was true – and

---

[5] Fair disclosure: I include myself in this category. I purchased a (severely underpriced) variable annuity (VA) "guarantee" from an insurance company (in 2009) that promised me a yield of 5% inflation-adjusted income for life. The underlying assets are invested in the (riskiest) small-cap fund I could find. In other words, I get market upside potential plus a put-option on a life annuity. So far this company has yet to "offer" to buy it back. I'm still waiting.

the client was Homer Simpson – they would surely lapse or exchange the policy well before it would come back to haunt the manufacturer.

But, according to Moody's, the wake-up call is in the data. Whether it is by good intuition or by greater numerical shrewdness, clients and their advisers are getting smarter about utilizing guarantees. They are learning to keep their coverage, optimize their policies, and maximize their value. Of course, not all of them are behaving this way – and lucky for the insurance company. There is still plenty of irrationality to go around (observe your teenage kids, for example), but there is less of it relative to what the insurance companies assumed. This has caused much grief and hence the buyback offers.

If a product offers you a guaranteed 5%, 6%, or 7% income for the rest of your life, it becomes more valuable when interest rates are lower, human longevity is higher, and markets are more volatile. The exact relationship and models linking these variables are subjects for PhD dissertations, but the underlying intuition is ironclad. So, run the numbers and don't walk away from a good deal.

And even if all the math makes your head spin and your eyes water, perhaps a shortcut is to call up your local insurance rep and ask them: "What are you, your psychologists, and your actuaries hoping (praying?) I will do?" If you get a coherent answer out of them, needless to say, you should do the opposite.

Variable annuities at the turn of the twenty-first century were very complex derivatives with multiple embedded options – most of whom were mispriced. They shared little in common with King William's tontines or the annuities that promised a lifetime of secure income.

THE WORD *ANNUITY* IS MEANINGLESS TODAY

My point here is that the word *annuity* itself is becoming meaningless. It can represent a simple life annuity, a complicated VA, an indexed annuity, a savings plan, and even pure longevity insurance,[6] which begins payment (and income) at very advanced ages. Some annuities are horrendously overpriced and some are ridiculously cheap, like the ones I described above. Some are illiquid and irreversible, and others are no different from (expensive) mutual funds. The word really is meaningless.

---

[6] See the survey article by Webb (2010) on the current state of longevity insurance (in the United States) and the declining amount of true insurance in (what are now called) annuities.

There is a sense that consumers don't like or appreciate annuities, but if you consider Social Security and government pensions as one type of annuity – which is how they should be viewed – they are among the most popular programs in history.

Some have termed this the "annuity puzzle" in that so few people voluntarily purchase life annuities. But even the notion of a puzzle is debated. There are many examples of retirees who embrace these products and annuitization via pensions at retirement.[7] Following are some examples of the heterogeneity and difference of opinion in different countries.

WHY DO BRITONS HATE THEIR ANNUITIES?

It is rather odd. For the country that gave the world King William's tontine and now claims the throne of the biggest annuity market in the world, Britons really hate annuities. The vitriol against UK annuities and their insurance promoters has increased in recent years, and one of the major newspapers recently referred to annuities as the most hated financial product in Britain.[8] After years of complaints and concerns, in March 2014 the government finally did something about it. With a few lines in the budget of Chancellor George Osborne, the annuity market was killed off, or at least mortally wounded. Here is what happened, why it happened, and what led up to it.

For decades every British citizen was required to convert their tax-sheltered savings account into a life annuity at the point of retirement, which was sold by an insurance company. Remember that governments got out of the business centuries ago. This requirement or rule was never popular and was slowly watered down over the years. Retirees could spend a limited portion of their pension pot (with no adverse tax implications) as they pleased, but they were forced to "annuitize" the remaining funds in the account by the age of seventy-five. So, every year approximately 420,000 (unhappy?) people purchased annuities worth £14bn, which made the UK the largest annuity market in the world.

The government thinking behind "compulsory annuitization," as it was called, was that if Britons were allowed to spend their entire pension pot as they pleased, they would do exactly that – spend it all. Forced annuitization was there to protect consumers. Yes, this is rather paternalistic and

---

[7] As pointed out by economists Benartzi, Previtero, and Thaler (2011), the evidence of a true aversion to annuities is inconclusive and dependent on context as well as framing.

[8] Patrick Collinson and Harriet Meyer in the *Guardian*, March 19, 2014.

condescending, but the alternative of poor and cashless retirees wasn't any better. Remember that the UK doesn't have a large Social Security or government pension system like the United States or Canada, for example. The pension pot of money really does have to last and support you for the rest of your life. So by seventy-five the expectation was that you gather up the eggs and head to the nearest insurance company and get yourself some longevity insurance with the money that had been sheltered from tax. If the government gave you a tax break, then it was entitled to dictate how you spent it. And, in the 1980s and 1990s when interest rates were high and longevity estimates were low, these annuity rates didn't seem that bad.

But as interest rates plummeted in the last decade – and the life expectancy assumptions about "who buys annuities" increased – the payout rates available on these life annuities headed in one very clear and rapid direction, downward.[9] This actuarial fact should come as no surprise or great shock to those who waded through the technicalities of Chapter 7. Whereas in 2000 British retirees could get a life annuity that paid approximately 9% for life – that is, every 100 pounds in the pot would generate 9 pounds for life – by 2013 the payout rates in the UK had dropped to 5%. Retirees blamed the insurance companies for offering them low rates and the government for forcing them to accept those rates. The public furor only got worse when housing prices soared, giving the (misguided) impression that using the pension pot to buy another house would be the best use for the funds. London housing prices have increased by 18% (yes, eighteen) per year in the last few years, according to the *Economist*.[10]

Consumer advocates and the major newspapers started an organized and systematic campaign to abolish mandatory annuitization. Of course, it's quite difficult to wage war against globally depressed interest rates and demographic patterns, so the target chosen was the greedy insurance companies who were supposedly making abnormal and outrageous profits. Things really got nasty.

Here is a direct quote from the *Telegraph* – which is one of the largest and widely read newspapers in the UK – from March 8, 2013, which was a few days before the government caved in.

The inflammatory headline started with: "Pensioners Being Ripped Off by Profit Margins on Annuities." The article then went on to say:

---

[9] See Finkelstein and Poterba (2002) for more in adverse selection effects in the British annuity market and whether or not prices are "fair" relative to consumers' expectations of their own mortality rates.

[10] "The *Economist* Explains Why London's House Prices Are Soaring," May 14, 2014.

> A *Telegraph* investigation has raised concerns about the profits that insurance companies and other firms are making on annuities. Only one annuities provider, Standard Life, has disclosed its margins on annuities, revealing that it pockets almost 20p of every pound a customer pays for an annuity. Other firms refuse to reveal their margins, and experts warn that the industry is concealing large profits … These huge margins are outrageous.

Other magazines and dailies ran personal stories of retirees who after being forced to purchase annuities, lived only a few years, and then died, leaving their heirs with absolutely nothing. There were other stories of retirees whose life annuity income wasn't enough to cover their expenses and regretted having been "forced" to give their money to insurance companies. To make things worse, some insurance companies were actually offering some pretty lousy rates on life annuities – assuming that consumers were too lazy to shop around. As I said earlier, they became the most hated financial instrument in Britain.

After relentless badgering by the *Telegraph* and consumer advocates, David Cameron's coalition government of the Conservative Party and Liberal Democrats threw in the towel. Chancellor George Osborne said on March 19, during his 2014 budget speech: "Let me be clear: No one will have to buy an annuity … People who have worked hard and saved hard all their lives, and done the right thing, should be trusted with their own finances."[11]

Like King William's tontine more than 300 years ago, anyone could participate but nobody would be forced. Annuitization was 100% optional. Perhaps this is fair, but after sixty years as the largest annuity market in the world, the change was a shocker.

This news was unexpected by both insurance experts and the market in general. In fact, the stock market prices of the major UK annuity providers – whose profits would obviously suffer – took a huge hit on that day. The biggest insurance companies, like Legal & General, Aviva, Prudential, Standard Life, and Resolution, saw their market prices drop by more than 10%. Remember, these companies sell much more than just life annuities. They sell life insurance and health and investment products. Still, a hit to (only) their life annuity sales was bad enough news to cause a major dent in their market value. Another lesser-known company called Partnership Assurance, which had recently been listed on the London Stock Exchange (LSE) in June 2013 at a valuation of £1.8bn, and only sold life annuities, saw

---

[11] The text of his entire speech is available at https://www.gov.uk/government/speeches/chancellor-george-osbornes-budget-2014-speech

its stock price fall by 55% from 320 to 120 pence, on the day of the budget announcement. Annuities are a big business in the UK – or should I say were a big business. The future is unclear. Will people still see the value of longevity insurance within annuities? That is certainly what insurance companies assured their panicked shareholders when their stock melted down. I'm a bit more skeptical.

Oddly, during the same exact week of the "annuity market massacre," the stock price of Carnival Corporation, which is the world's largest cruise ship operator – jointly listed on the New York and the London Stock Exchanges – increased by 5%. It was quite a good week for bookings, as well. One can speculate that the pot of money that wasn't going to purchase annuities would now be allocated to retirement travel and leisure. This was great news for Carnival's shareholders, who might also be pensioners living on a life annuity.

Here is my main point. As I have alluded to many times in this book, perhaps one possible solution to the problem of retirees who dislike – or even hate – life annuities is to make sure they understand what it is they give up and lose from their prejudice against annuities.

Bundling yields and payouts together and quoting them as one big percentage – for example, 5% for life or 9% for life – obscures how much of this income comes from pooling and sharing longevity risk and how much can be blamed on the Bank of England and low interest rates. In fact, most consumers – without expertise in finance and mathematics – have a difficult time with percentages, which is something I'll return to in a later section on the so-called 4% rule. This is why I'm a fan of the Swedish pension system – or at least how it is presented – where they separate the so-called inheritance gains from the investment gains in their retirement scheme.

In contrast to a conventional life annuity – which confuses many and antagonizes others – a properly designed tontine scheme avoids some of the optical problems. For every single dollar, pound, or euro that retirees are willing to forgo and bequeath to members of the pool, they earn a continuous stream of "other people's money" while they are still alive. How much they choose to allocate to such a scheme will depend on their preferences and desire to trade off financial legacy for income sustainability. I covered all of this in Chapter 7.

Indeed, the aversion to annuitization is not universal, and, when properly positioned and explained, it can be quite popular. The evidence of this can be found at the base of the Andes Mountains in far-flung Chile.

WHY DO CHILEANS LOVE THEIR ANNUITIES?

In contrast to the recent situation in the UK, Chile is on the other side of the (planet and) spectrum. To an academic economist exquisite Chile is somewhat of a utopia. I'm not referring to the Andes Mountains or Atacama Desert, although they are remarkable. Rather, I'm referring to its government's approach to economic policy. Like a number of other South American countries, many of Chile's cabinet ministers and even elected politicians earned graduate degrees and doctorates in economics, having been trained in the best universities. In fact, none other than the great Milton Friedman himself helped design the plumbing of their economic system in the early 1980s. Even today, public and political discourse is replete with phrases usually reserved for graduate courses on microeconomics.

Chile's retirement system was redesigned from scratch a mere twenty-five years ago, in the post-Allende epoch. Remarkably, Chileans have no universal government-run pension program, like Social Security in the United States. Rather, every Chilean citizen saves and invests for his or her own retirement. What is even more perplexing is that when they reach retirement age – and transition to the de-accumulation phase, withdrawing money from their individual accounts – they do something few retirees do anywhere else in the world. Most of them voluntarily annuitize. To put it bluntly, they walk into their neighborhood insurance company with their accumulated nest egg and say: "Please give me an income for life."

So, this is the *desafío de la renta vitalicia* (annuity puzzle, very loosely translated) that took me to Santiago. Why do so many Chileans buy life annuities? Is it something they put in all those pisco sours?

Some Background

Chile mandates that all employees in the workforce must contribute at least 10% of their pretax salary into an individual account Defined Contribution (DC) plan, managed through the payroll system. Within these accounts they are allowed to allocate wealth between a limited set of diversified (low-cost) mutual funds, all of which are managed by the private sector. These individual accounts are held by custodians and are completely independent from the employer. With such an arm's-length approach, portability, ownership, and even employer bankruptcy risk shouldn't be a concern. The closest analogy I could find in North America would be replacing

Social Security with one big 401(k) plan, in which every single worker is obligated – and not merely nudged – to contribute.

The value of the account grows with time and age, but obviously varies depending on the particular funds selected, asset allocation, and so forth. Like everyone else, the 2008–2009 global financial crisis adversely affected their account values – especially those participants who allocated to equities – but the Chilean economy has grown at a very impressive pace of late. And like so many *home-biased investors* all over the world, the majority of these individual accounts are allocated to stocks and bonds in … you guessed it, Chile. Unlike the Greeks, Spaniards, and Portuguese, for example, this bias didn't bite them.

The Chilean Pension Model, as it is called, has been exported to a number of other Latin American countries in the region – much to the Chileans' pride and delight. Similar models have been implemented in much larger countries such as Mexico, Peru, Columbia, and even Argentina (until the government in Buenos Aires absconded with the money a few years ago).

While this relatively young model isn't immune to the mind-numbing rules and exclusions that afflict all government-administered plans anywhere else on planet Earth, their retirees have two basic options: They can either (i.) continue to invest their account in a variety of stock and bond funds while withdrawing money from the account, aka self-annuitization, or (ii.) use the accumulated funds to purchase a life annuity. Technically, a third option could be any combination of (i.) and (ii.).

But, as I mentioned earlier, approximately 65% of Chileans in this system get to retirement, sit down with a financial adviser – which is mandated, by the way – and provide very simple instructions. "Please buy me a life annuity with all of it."

Now, lest you suspect I am talking about small sums in a small country, each year more than 20,000 life annuity contracts are voluntarily issued in Chile. This is the *second-highest number in the world* after the grand-annuity-daddy of them all, the UK, which I mentioned earlier. Remember, that Chile has a population of 17 million people and their insurance companies issue more life annuity policies than the United States, Japan, or Germany. It is no surprise that many international insurance companies have been setting up shop in Santiago, as more and more Chileans reach retirement.

This 65% rate of annuitization is quite puzzling, when contrasted with a 5% rate (at best) in the United States. In fact, some regulators are getting concerned that more than 85% of insurance industry reserves are linked to *life annuity* liabilities, while the other 15% is in *life insurance* liabilities. Most companies don't use reinsurance, which means that this lopsidedness exposes the industry to a unique type of longevity risk. What if Chileans live longer than projected by the actuaries? And, to be honest, after having spent a week in charming Santiago, I wouldn't be surprised if their tranquil lifestyle produces a disproportionate number of centenarians.

Some Want More

Without getting too caught up in the political minutiae, not all regulators were unhappy or concerned with the high levels of annuitization, and commensurate low level of stock-and-bond-based retirement income plans, especially given the sound actuarial economics of mortality credits. In their defense, insurance industry representatives claimed to be properly updating their mortality assumptions and carefully monitoring their balance sheet and risk exposure.

In fact, one cabinet-level minister contended that stock-and-bond-based income plans should be entirely abolished for lower-income retirees. Her words to me were: "This group within society should not have their limited retirement income exposed to the vagaries of the stock and bond market, especially considering they have no more human capital remaining to extract."

So, besides enthusiastic ministers and regulators, here are some reasons I offer for why life annuities are so popular in Chile.

Neutral Commissions. When *independent* retirement advisers – those who stand between the retiree and their decision – offer guidance, it is commission-neutral, unlike how things work on this side of the equator. In other words, the compensation to the independent Chilean retirement adviser isn't affected by whether they suggest a life annuity, a mutual fund, or any combination. (Alas, when the Chilean retirement adviser is an employee of a mutual fund company, the annuitization rate is lower. Surprise!)

Better Illustrations. All retirees are shown (mandated, regulated) illustrations that suggest a volatile and possibly declining income stream *if* they go with the systematic withdrawal plan (SWiP), *and if* long-term investment assumptions are not met. In other words, they have a better understanding of the risk.

Inflation Protection. All life annuities sold in Chile are indexed to inflation, or more precisely to *unidades de fomento* (UF) as opposed to nominal pesos. So, there is no inflation risk to the annuitant, thus making it a more secure source of real lifetime income. In the United States most life annuities are nominal, and the few real ones are really expensive too.

They Are Pensionless. Remember that for most Chileans this individual account is all the retirement money they have. There is no other DB corporate or government pension plan, which would backstop their retirement spending. They have no other form of longevity insurance other than the life annuity.

Perceived Safety. The Chilean government explicitly backs or guarantees insurance company payments (up to a limit) in the event of insolvency or bankruptcy. This is different from the U.S. system, which has developed a mutual arrangement between companies and is overseen by the individual states. Perhaps the annuity they buy in the private market actually feels like Social Security, familiar in North America.

Of course, none of this explains the *all-or-nothing* attitude that prevails with most of these accounts. My view is that a proper retirement product allocation should include a mix of the two. Why not annuitize 40%, 60%, or 80% and then SWiP the rest? Or annuitize slowly. Why are so many annuitizing *all of their* retirement account?

My main point is as follows, even in a society or country in which annuities are widely accepted (and have reasonably good reputations) there should be concerns for the longevity risk posed by the industry.

So how does one do a better job of explaining this to consumers? I think financial advisers, financial planners, stockbrokers, and insurance agents have a huge role to play in this education initiative. But they are not all one big homogenous group of intermediaries.

THE INVESTMENT TRIBE, THE INSURANCE CLAN, AND THE 4% RULE

Today, within the financial-planning profession very broadly defined, there are two distinct approaches or philosophies of retirement income generation; that is, the process of converting a lump sum of retirement *savings* into a lifetime of *income*. And both have deep flaws, which (I believe) properly designed tontines might be able to overcome. Let me elaborate on the two camps before I delve into their problems.

One can imagine the two groups as distinct tribes or clans. The first group is rather large in size and consists of very passionate and upbeat followers who were trained in the art of life insurance marketing and sales. They spent their younger years honing the skills necessary for successfully selling all forms of life, health, and disability insurance. They are comfortable and well versed in the language of personal risk and family hazards. All of them know people – and have experienced clients – who died suddenly. They truly understand at a visceral level the importance of protecting a family against unexpected financial shocks. They almost relish having these rather unpleasant conversations with clients, and they know how to have them tactfully and with grace. I'll call them the "insurance clan," since they are cliquey, tend to stick together, and also have very effective government lobbying organizations.

The second group is just as committed as the insurance clan is – perhaps slightly smaller on a global scale – but they have not been immersed in the world of mortality, health, and longevity risk. They grew up imbibing the waters of capital markets, stocks, bonds, and security selection. They wait breathlessly for central bankers, treasury secretaries, and hedge fund managers to opine on world events. I would dare say, at the risk of antagonizing the insurance clan, that this second group tends to be more cerebral and intellectual. A sizable percentage of their members have advanced economics, finance, and business degrees. I'll call them the "investment tribe" given the core beliefs they share, which can often border on religious dogma. In fact, the ultraorthodox members of this tribe believe that markets are extremely efficient and that clients should have investments that are (mostly) indexed as opposed to actively managed.

Members of both the insurance clan and investment tribe are eagerly anticipating your retirement so they can help manage your nest egg – for a fee or a commission, of course. Those from the insurance clan use language peppered with references to actuarial jargon and whole-life-participating insurance. The best of the insurance clan simply tell stories about real people, their goals, and their dreams. In contrast, the investment tribe will lead their discussions with assumptions about expected investment returns and forward-looking guidance. It is rather easy to detect which of the two tribes a so-called financial adviser emanates from.

Now, yes, there are a growing number of people who (claim) to belong to both tribes and can pass themselves off rather convincingly in both societies, but these are the exception and not the rule. It is a good trend to observe – that is, these growing dualists – but they started life in the insurance clan or the investment tribe.

Regardless of clan or tribe, all financial advisers want to do good for their clients – but they all have their biases – which is why I think that both could benefit from some "tontine thinking."

Annuities

As you might expect, the insurance tribe is well aware of the benefits that life annuities can provide. They have worked with insurance companies who manufacture insurance product for most of their professional life. They understand the value of risk pooling and diversification. To them – and I do hesitate to say this – the biggest problem with life annuities is that their commissions aren't as juicy or lucrative as whole life insurance or some other disability risk policy. The problem with the insurance clan and their embrace of annuities is that they focus on the name first and what the product actually does second. As I argued earlier, the word *annuity* really has become rather meaningless today. Many annuities are expensive bond funds and others are mutual funds with a thin veneer of insurance. Most importantly, the insurance companies charge a pretty penny for the protection they offer.

The investment tribe tends to shun insurance solutions in general and annuities in particular and takes a rather different approach to generating income in retirement. They have embraced something called the 4% rule, which is another way of saying: "I can bake a better annuity at home."

The 4% rule very generally states that, at retirement, one should continue to invest in a (perhaps more conservative) portfolio of stocks and bonds, and then – to be safe – withdraw 4% per year, which "research has shown" is the prudent drawdown rate.[12] Now, there are many different variations of the 4% rule, which is often the problem with this approach. But to its credit the 4% rule has achieved much publicity (in the media and press), and there are countless articles and financial institutions advocating a variant of 4%. For better or for worse, the retirement income conversation now starts with the "4 percent rule".

Mathematically speaking, if you invest $100 in a portfolio that earns exactly 5% interest every single year and you withdraw (at the end of the year) $4 plus inflation of (assumed) 2% every single year, the portfolio will be able to sustain forty-five of these withdrawals. To be clear, at the end of year one you withdraw $4.08 and then at the end of year two it is $4.16, each year increasing by 2% to combat price inflation. Under this (deterministic) scenario, the longevity of your portfolio is exactly forty-five years, which should be more than enough, even for centenarians.

---

[12] See the original paper by Bengen (1990) as well as the various "retirement spending" theories cited in Zwecker (2010), Milevsky (2012) or Pfau (2012), as well as Finke, Pfau and Blanchett (2013). This is yet another vast and growing literature.

Table 8.2. *The many different interpretations of the 4% rule*

Start with $100,000	What should I withdraw next year, if inflation over 12 months is 2% and …		
Variants of Strategy	Portfolio Falls 20%.	Portfolio Grows by 5% as Expected.	Portfolio Soars 30%.
"The Original Intent"	Spend $4,080.	Spend $4,080.	Spend $4,080.
"Forget about Inflation"	Spend $4,000.	Spend $4,000.	Spend $4,000.
"4% of Account Balance"	Spend 4% of 80% of $100,000 = $3,200.	Spend 4% of $105,000 = $4,200.	Spend 4% of 130% of $100,000 = $5,200.
"Take It One Year at a Time"	Adjust. Cut Back. Spend Less.	Spend $4,080 as Planned.	Enjoy Life and Spend More.

Of course, in the real world (today) it is almost impossible to find an investment that will provide (and guarantee) a constant 5% every single year for forty-five years. This is where the 4% rule comes in. It "assures" you – or perhaps the word *hope* is better – that if you maintain a balanced portfolio that is *expected* to grow at 5% per year and you limit your withdrawals to the same $4 plus inflation, the portfolio should last with "reasonable confidence" for thirty years.[13]

This is not the place to debate the merits of the 4% rule, but my point here is that even if one sticks to the literal implementation of the strategy – which few people do – it is not a very good way to manage retirement finances. If you want to maintain a constant (inflation adjusted) standard of living, why not buy a life annuity? What if you retire early and/or live longer than thirty years? What if markets earn less than 5% (compounded annually) for long periods of time? How do you adjust?

These are all legitimate questions – I believe – but the bigger problem that I have seen (anecdotally) is that everyone has their own interpretation of the 4% rule. Table 8.2 offers a subset of the different interpretations I have seen. Some assume the 4% is of the portfolio value, others take the liberty of ignoring inflation, and others abandon the rule during times of stress and turbulence.

---

[13] For the quants here, this would be the geometric mean (gm) and not the arithmetic mean (AM), which would be higher.

My Point

Now, regardless of how exactly one interprets this rule, which has been embraced by the investment tribe – or how exactly it is modified for the twenty-first century – by definition it tends to focus on (i.) spending rates and (ii.) capital markets, but not enough on the role that longevity insurance and annuities might play in the optimal portfolio. Indeed, one of the additional psychological benefits of a properly defined tontine annuity is that it reduces the confusion and misunderstanding around an affordable spending rate. At the end of the year (or perhaps at the end of the month) everyone gets a payment, which is framed as a suggested spending rate. The psychological debate over how much to withdraw is mitigated. The tontine dividend becomes the post-retirement salary. Yes, it might vary or fluctuate somewhat depending on the deaths of other members, but nothing in life is really guaranteed (for free).

THE FUTURE OF RETIREMENT INCOME ... A TONTINE?

We are coming to the end and some self-reflection is apt. What have I tried to achieve here?

By *familiarizing* the reader with the history, characters, and overall economic rationale for tontine (i.e., *pooling and sharing*) schemes – and King William's tontine of 1693 in particular – I am hoping the reader will acknowledge their social value. King William's tontine showed you the mortality credits, explicitly.

Naturally, this book really wasn't just about telling interesting tales. The point was to make you comfortable with the idea, to generate familiarity, to provoke the "Ah, yes, I read about those ... quite interesting." At the very least, the next time you hear the phrase *tontine scheme* and *retirement savings* in the same sentence you won't shudder with revulsion or, worse, ignorance.

In some sense, I am hoping that readers will help advocate – implicitly or explicitly – the acceptance of tontines as useful and valuable products worthy of reintroduction into society after almost a century of wandering in the wilderness.

Yes, there have been some spectacular failures and critical problems with tontines during the last three centuries – from mispricing and fraud to apathy and revulsion – but I believe that Lorenzo de Tonti's original insight was a valid one. As Tonti (1654, p. 14) put it so succinctly in his proposal to King Louis the XIV of France, "A tontine ... will oblige those whose interest it is to prolong the life of the old to treat them with respect and care because of the advantages they will find and hope to see." This might seem terribly cynical and self-serving to anyone but an economist, but remember that incentives really do matter.

Now obviously, writing in the 1650s, Lorenzo couldn't make reference to the sharing of systematic mortality risk, reduction of capital charges, and the surprisingly quick benefits of the Law of Large Numbers – all of which were centuries away from being formulated. Indeed, Lorenzo's most compelling argument was a sociological one: to help finance the care of old people. And there certainly will be many of them in the future.

Alas, even if you believe that your children or your neighbor's and village's children have a moral obligation to care for you when you are old, I can assure you – and as most people who have been in that situation of providing care for the elderly can attest – many people would be willing to give up their assets (when they die) if they could earn more cash while they are still alive. There is a growing "die broke" movement in the United States (and around the world) and tontine investments are the ideal die-broker.

Yes, of course, there is a role for government programs like Social Security and pensions to provide a basic, minimal level of income for those in the lower 40% of the wealth distribution, but it is the other 60% that concern me. For them, to put it bluntly, I believe tontines and annuities should be a (bigger) part of the retirement income cocktail.

Don't get me wrong here. I am not saying that everyone should join a tontine scheme or that you should have most of your precious "nest egg" in a tontine scheme or that tontine schemes will eliminate pension deficits, solve the retirement crisis – that is, people aren't saving enough for retirement – and bring about world peace.

My point is limited and my reach is modest. Namely, I think that tontine annuities should be added to the "approved and endorsed" menu of financial and insurance products that are available to de-accumulate wealth at retirement. Yes, you should also have money invested in stocks and bonds and cash and real estate, long-term care policies, and perhaps even some conventional annuities – if the insurance company doesn't charge too much for the guarantee.

Tontine annuities have an important role to play in the final act of the human lifecycle, *even if the word* tontine *is nowhere to be seen in the product description.* Let's infuse retirement income product design with "tontine thinking."

So, how do you know if the product you are considering is the twenty-first-century incarnation of Lorenzo's scheme? Here are my criteria or blueprints for a modern-day tontine annuity. Remember, I'm not focusing on (public or private) pension design, the choice between DC or DB systems and the problem of underfunded plans. I am concerned with the proper design of private arrangements between consenting adults to help share and pool their assets as they age – without putting the public purse at risk.

Item #1: The Right Group. The ideal tontine association or *society* – and that is what this really is, a society – would consist of a group of a few hundred people close in age and comparable in health who contribute a relatively modest sum and similar amount of *capital* into an investment pool. The nominee would have to be the annuitant. The two roles should not be split and shares should not be tradable, unlike King William's version. The nominee = the annuitant = the investor. Ideally these *members* would form or create this modern-day tontine society a decade or two before their retirement years, perhaps during the early fifties. And while it is conceivable that this society could be formed with groups at older ages, starting early would allow for the so-called magic of compound interest to accumulate and – more significantly – help reduce anti-selection problems. Recall from Chapter 5 that anti-selection is the problem – or perhaps better described as phenomenon – in which individuals who benefit the most from the insurance protection are the ones that actually purchase the insurance policy. For life and health insurance, for example, this would be sicker people who sign up for coverage, and for tontine annuities this would be members who are healthier and expect to live longer. There is nothing wrong with being healthy and anti-selecting into a tontine pool, but for the sake of fairness it is important to ensure that like are pooled with like. Although one might observe heterogeneity or dispersion of health status at all ages, the earlier in life members are segmented into these tontine pools, the less of an issue this problem would be. And what about all those in poor health? Should they be deprived of the benefits and privileges of participating in tontine schemes? The answer, of course, is that they would arrange their own tontine scheme with members of similar health status. The key in item #1 is to group like with like. Male with males, females with females, old with old, young with young, and so on. I don't believe that mixing different groups, cohorts, and populations with different mortality rates and survival probabilities is the way to construct the optimal retirement income tontine. That said, I do acknowledge that there are ways and algorithms that can adjust payouts and credits by each individual's estimated mortality rate, but it leads to transparency and fairness problems. King

William's tontine allowed any *investor* to select any *nominee* of any age and then direct the cash flow to any *annuitant*. If I were king, this would not be allowed.

Item #2: Investments. The tontine's invested capital – that is, the money that was contributed by scheme members – would be managed by a fiduciary for a modest fee. I mean a fraction of a percentage per year. This is the accumulation (i.e., saving or growth) phase of the tontine and works as follows. A trustee invests contributed money in a few generic funds, such as stock (index) funds, or bond (index) funds, or a cash fund. Members would decide how much of their capital they would like allocated to each of the eligible tontine mutual funds. For example, a fifty-year-old member might *contribute* $10,000 of capital to a tontine scheme. The member could allocate the capital so that 60% is in stock-based tontine fund and 40% is in bond-based tontine fund. And, for the next ten or perhaps twenty years at most – with an exact *maturity date* agreed upon by the tontine members in advance – all investment gains, dividends, and interest would be reallocated to the same tontine, so that the 60/40 allocation is maintained over time. Alternatively, the tontine members might agree in advance to a declining (aka glide-path) reduction in exposure to stocks over the fifteen or twenty years. All members wouldn't have to invest in the same investments or the same tontine. This is no different from any other mutual fund. The key, of course, is that being a tontine scheme the money would belong to the surviving members – only. If and when a member of the tontine society passes away, or if they died prior to the maturity date, they would lose their entire capital and their money would be distributed to everyone in their cohort. So, if Joe had $6,000 in the "stock" tontine and $4,000 in the "bond" tontine, and he died, $10,000 would be evenly distributed to everyone else in the pool. If there were ten other people in the pool when Joe died, each would get $1,000 "inheritance gain" to allocate and invest as they please. Joe's wife, kids, and heirs would get – nothing. The total loss of the money is why nobody in their right mind would allocate all, or even most, of their retirement savings to such a scheme. Each member would decide for themselves the optimal allocation to tontines, as well as the optimal financial risk exposure. So, quite distinct from King William's tontine, which was designed as a payout vehicle only, the ideal saving tontine would allow for a robust mix of investments for ten to fifteen years *before* it converts into an income tontine. Perhaps I can call it a deferred income Jared tontine?

Item #3: Formulas. A decade or two after the tontine society had been created, the trustee would begin distributing or returning the pool of money to the surviving members. The exact *payout formula* or mechanism for distributing the capital and all the gains would be agreed upon in advance when the scheme was initiated and the members joined. As I argued in Chapter 7, an optimal formula would distribute a relatively large sum to the members initially – when many members are still expected to be alive – but the same formula would dictate that over time the dollar amount distributed would decline as the number of surviving members is expected to decline, as well. The optimal tontine does not reward the last few survivors with all the money or a large fraction of the income. The objective is to have a pay-out or cash flow that is relatively constant *per member* over time, regardless of whether or not the exact specification of the Jared tontine I described is adopted. So, for example, the payout formula might specify that 10% of the value of the tontine pool is distributed in the first year after the maturity date. If the pool is worth $10,000,000 and there are 100 survivors, then the survivors as a group would extract 10% of 10,000,000, which is an even million dollars. The million would be split among the 100 survivors for an income of $10,000 in the first year of the tontine scheme's payout phase. In the next year, 9% of the pool would be distributed, then perhaps 8% of the pool the next year, and so on. I'm not advocating a 10%, 9%, 8% rule or suggesting this is optimal. As I discussed in Chapter 7, the optimal tontine payout formula is subtle and sensitive to various demographic factors – but this would all be determined in advance. The key is that the total amount of money to be distributed to the group in aggregate would decline. But remember that the number of survivors is declining, as well. I would antici-pate the actual payments to the surviving scheme members are expected to be rather stable, although there are obviously no guarantees.

Remember that if you want guarantees, you should purchase a conven-tional life annuity from an insurance company – and pay the price of the promise. The key in item #3 is the clear, transparent, and preapproved rule for distributing the tontine scheme's assets after the maturity date. It has to be crystal clear to participants in advance how the money will be distrib-uted. Leaving any sort of discretion for a board of directors or investment trustees to adapt to market circumstances may sound prudent and reason-able but is likely to create more problems than solutions. Once again, the payout formula of the pool's assets should be ironclad and set in advance. So, if and when retired tontine scheme members complain that their div-idends aren't as large as they anticipated, they will have only one group to blame; namely, themselves for not dying fast enough. Recall that for King William's tontine the payout formula was very clear from the begin-ning, namely, 10% of the contributed capital would be distributed in the first seven years (of the payout phase) and this would decline to 7% of the contributed capital after seven years. The mortality credits (i.e., inheritance gains) must be explicit. If the annuitant gets a dividend for 15% – he or she will know that X% was interest yield and Y% was mortality credits, even though X itself might decline over time as Y continues to grow.

In a rather prescient statement quoted in Walford (1871) regarding the payout structure of King William's tontine and the concerns over fraud, he writes: "Why was it enacted by Parliament that the original interest at ten percent should be reduced to seven percent after the first seven years? Because the Parliament wisely foresaw that a great many nominees would be infants in hopes of being the last survivors and that according to the course of nature most part of them would be swept away in seven years time, so that the increase of interest by their death would make a compensation for the lowering of it from ten to seven. If this is not the true reason, let anybody tell me other" (p. 115).

Item #4: Transparent Optics. One of the many problems with conventional payout annuities in the twenty-first century is the inability of consumers – with limited financial literacy or sophistication – to appreciate the value of mortality credits and role of longevity insurance in protecting their retirement. They don't see how the death of other participants directly impacts (and increases) their payout and returns. They view the insurance company as keeping the money when they die, or they consider the guaranteed payouts too low, or they simply don't trust the insurance company. These are behavioral explanations to the so-called annuity puzzle. And, while the mathematical design of a tontine is important, how this is explained to existing members and potential members is even more vital. Recall from Chapter 6 that tontine insurance at the beginning of the twentieth century in the United States suffered from a public relations disaster when policyholders realized that their investment returns weren't as high as they had expected. Of course, this was also due to fraud on the part of insurance company managers who paid themselves (as well as judges and politicians) excessively and "bad formulas" for adjusting payouts. But clear communication and ongoing monitoring over time would have gone a long way toward alleviating the problem with tontine insurance. In the name of clarity and transparency, I would recommend that every year, during both the *accumulation* phase (prematurity) and the *de-accumulation* phase (postmaturity) members receive *statements* that show how much their capital has earned from investment returns and other people's dying. I know this might sound morbid and distasteful to some, but transparency is essential. To paraphrase Cuba Gooding Jr. in the movie *Jerry Maguire, show me the mortality credits!* This is particularly important in the de-accumulation phase. A statement would show the entire million dollar fund earning (for example) $100,000 in investment gains and then another $200,000 from the death of tontine members. At older ages the amount gained from deaths would increase (exponentially) and the mortality credits would come alive on the statements. Annuitants in King William's tontine knew exactly *why* they were getting *what* they were getting. The same concept applies to the Swedish pension system. The inheritance gains, as they are called, are cold and crystal clear.

Item#5: Windup Leftover. There is, of course, one final (nuisance) matter and that is what happens to the capital in the tontine when there are a small handful of members left and especially when the final member of the scheme dies. There are elements that are a bit untidy. Even the best of actuaries can't predict when the last survivor of a 250-member tontine scheme will die. Sure, he or she could provide an expectation or probability, but there are no certainties in life or death. This uncertainty would generate quite a bit of volatility of income toward the end of the pool's life. Some might view this as the Achilles' heel of the tontine scheme. If there is only $1,000 in the pool when the last survivor is 120 years of age, and they end up living another five years, their standard of living (i.e., income) will take a large hit. The maximum expected life expectancy directly impacts the payout formula. That is something one lucky person will indeed have to contend with. And, what to do about the leftovers? My recommendation would be to stipulate a charity (Alzheimer's Research?) that will get money. I doubt anyone would object (since they are dead by then).

In sum, these are my five items or suggestions for the design of optimal tontines: (i.) a few hundred people in homogenous pools in which the member is the nominee; (ii.) freedom to take financial risk and earn the equity risk premium while you are waiting; (iii.) a very clear payout function at the maturity retirement date; plus (iv.) effective member communication; and, finally, (v.) a windup beneficiary. These are all the lessons for the twenty-first century that one can learn from King William's tontine of 1693.

It remains to be seen *if and when* such a tontine annuity – Jared or not – will become available on a mass scale, or who will sponsor the tontine and whether regulators and government will stand in the way. Who knows, perhaps in the absence of private market enthusiasm, the federal government itself will step forward and sponsor the next generation of tontine schemes. In fact, two noted academics Professor Henry Hu and Professor Terrance Odean recently proposed in a *New York Times* editorial that the U.S. government should sell federally issued inflation-adjusted life annuities to the public. See Hu and Odean (2011) for details on how their scheme would work. Under their proposal, the federal government would be making (yet more) long-term promises that in my opinion will be hard to quantify or guarantee. To put it politely, the Federal and State governments have a lousy record in acknowledging the true value of liabilities generated by long-dated longevity-linked promises (i.e., social security and state pensions).

As an alternative, why not offer tontines? I can assure you that I will be the first to sign up. I will probably not live to be Methuselah, but I certainly might be a Jared.

LONGEVITY RISK SHARING: EX ANTE VS. EX POST

When I was growing up – and I suspect the same is true for most older readers – I was taught from a young age that you shouldn't spend money you don't have or "eat it" before you have actually "earned it." Even if you have been promised or guaranteed the funds, it isn't smart to spend it all before it has actually been received. Okay, yes, perhaps you can take out a so-called advance or borrow against some of it, but don't consume it *all* until it's safely in your wallet. That is common financial sense, although not necessarily practiced by the millions of consumers in the twenty-first century who live entirely on credit.

Well, the exact same good principle applies in the very grown-up arena of longevity risk sharing. One of the main arguments in this book – to put it bluntly – is that the only way for individuals in society to afford the retirement they dream of is for them to embrace the idea that the dead (retirees) should subsidize the living (retirees). Longevity risk should be shared. I encourage baby boomers and their children to enter into a longevity-sharing pact with others in their cohort so that the assets and wealth of the deceased can be used to enhance the returns of the living. You can extend the longevity of your money and your portfolio if you embrace tontine thinking.

But – and this is key – it is highly prudent to wait until these retirees are actually deceased before their money is spent on the living. That is the problem with guaranteed pensions and life annuities as they are sold today. The companies are relying on actuarial forecasts of how long people are going to live on average – spending the expected gains today – and hoping that their estimates prove correct. They are expecting the many who die before their life expectancy to bequeath a million dollars and are allocating those gains to everyone else, today. They are also assuming some people will lapse their annuities and are spending those funds, as well. In my opinion they are committing the same sin of pre-spending the money before they have actually received it. I say wait. Don't bank on it quite yet.

This in essence is the difference between a conventional life annuity and a tontine scheme. In the life annuity the payments are guaranteed (and constant) for life because the insurance company is *spreading the money* they think *they will receive from everyone who dies early*, over the entire group of retirees they are pooling. This might help "smooth" the ups and downs over time, but it obscures the value of the mortality credits.

In contrast I would argue that mortality credits – that is, the money bequeathed to the pool by the deceased – should only be spent after they have been received, which is called *ex post*. The vendors of a life annuity spend these mortality credits ex ante (in advance) and then hope that the ex post realizations match the ex ante assumptions. That's risky.

Now, of course, insurance actuaries have been doing this for centuries, and the reader might wonder who am I to question how they run their business? After all, doesn't the Law of Large Numbers guarantee that things will work out for them as long as they have a large enough pool?

Yes. The Law of Large Numbers provides an ironclad mathematical guarantee that as long as the company sells enough independent life annuities, and those odds are well known in advance, then the ex post will match the ex ante. But this mathematical law *only* applies if all of these deaths are independent and unrelated events. In other words, it is based on the subtle assumption that the annuitant receiving $1,000 per month in New York City is completely unrelated to the annuitant receiving $1,000 per month in Chicago, and so on.

But if these mortality rates are actually dependent or correlated with each other, the Law of Large Numbers breaks down. Selling more annuity policies makes things worse (for the company) and exposes them to greater risk.

Now why – you might ask – might these complete strangers affect each other? Well, for starters, if and when we manage to cure cancer, eliminate diabetes, and kill Alzheimer's, life expectancy will increase for everyone. And, suddenly, lives that you thought were independent of each other become very dependent. By "dependent on each other," I mean that if *one* member of a (random) pair happens to live longer than expected, there is a greater chance that the *second* member of that pair will live longer than average, as well. This breaks the statistical independence and increases the overall liability risk.[14] In the language of statistics, the standard deviation

---

[14] The mathematics can get quite dicey, but I actually "proved" this in a paper with Jenny Young and David Promislow. See Milevsky, Young, and Promislow (2006).

per policy will not go to zero when the insurance company sells more policies. Bigger is worse. This is precisely why I believe that we should wait to spend the "mortality credits" or gains from death until they actually occur.

Now, a modern insurance company (or their government regulators) will argue that they haven't ignored or forgotten these risks and that companies have set aside reserve (and capital) to protect against unexpected financial losses from unexpected health gains. But do you think that this capital the shareholders invest in the company is free? Are they doing this as a public service? No, they expect a return on their capital, on the order of 10% to 15%, and don't forget the commissions to the insurance agents and brokers which can be extra.

This 10% to 15% return on capital that shareholders expected to earn filters through the multiple layers of management in the company and when compounded with commissions and other expenses translates into a product that becomes opaque and unappealing to most retirees. You want proof? Look at the stunningly low rate of voluntary annuitization around the world. In fact, look at what the UK did with mandatory annuitization.

Everyone loves guarantees, whether it be for the price of a house, a car, or a lifetime of income. But if the cost of this guarantee gets too high – and on the order of 10% to 20% relative to its expected discounted value – then many rational people might say, "No, thanks. I'll take my tontine chances."

Here is the financial bottom line: I estimate that investing in a properly designed tontine scheme will reduce the (expected) cost of your retirement income by approximately 10% to 20%. And, to quote the great John Bogle, these "costs" really matter. So I ask, where is the Vanguard of retirement income for the middle class masses?

At the very least – even if you think that the guaranteed annuity is worth the cost – it's time we give people a chance to choose, just like King William's scheme did more than 320 years ago.

Would you like a tontine or a life annuity … or a mixture of the two? That is the dilemma (that should be) faced by soon-to-be retirees who are trying to figure out how to finance their golden years.

It is time to embrace tontine thinking.

What Did William Really Know?

It's reasonable to ask in this last section, how much King William III (equestrian statue in the below figure) really knew about the tontine launched by the English Parliament in the early part of 1693. How involved was he? Would the king of England know of such a scheme?

The Dutch King William III (1650–1702) is one of the least-known and even less appreciated English monarchs. Everyone knows about all the Georges in the seventeenth and eighteenth centuries, as well as King Henry VIII in the sixteenth century, but not much about King William III. Even the first Norman king of England (back in the eleventh century), William the Conqueror, is a better-known "historical William" and more recognized in the twenty-first century.

Although King William III reigned for almost fifteen years, and during a most critical period of English history, his name recognition is really nowhere near the Jameses, Charleses, and Georgeses. One of the leading historians of the period, Tony Claydon (2002), wrote the following in the summary to his biography: "The British never really took to William III. In his lifetime he was unpopular for his lack of sociability, for his preference for old friends from the Netherlands over Britons and for the endless drain of resources to maintain his wars" (p. 188). The expert or consensus view about King William III is that he had only two activities or preoccupations that were worthy of his time. The first was waging a lifetime war against King Louis XIV and the second was pursuing and haranguing English Parliament to get the resources for his war. Basically, he had one thing on his mind and that was to *keep the money flowing*.

And yet, it was precisely that drain on resources and war effort that forced Parliament to get extraordinarily creative in securing funds for their war-hungry monarch. The creativity led to the creation of the first

The king and I.

long-term national debt, the first English tontine scheme, the Bank of England, and so on.

It's really difficult to believe that William III was doing anything but following financial matters very closely. He certainly was in town during the parliamentary proceedings (in the fall and winter) since his military campaigns took place mostly in the summer. He had to give royal assent to acts and bills before they became the law of the land, and anything to do with war financing was a personal fixation of his. The 1693 experiment in long-term financing truly was King William's tontine.

King William III's connection to his tontine is more than just coincidental in time and place. As I mentioned in Chapter 3, the best-known promoter of tontines, Lorenzo de Tonti, was imprisoned by Louis XIV – William's lifetime enemy – in the French Bastille for the last decade of his life.

William's tutor as a teenager, John de Witt, was quite likely the first person (on the European continent and possibly the western world) to write about the valuation of life annuities and work out the relationship between mortality rates and annuity payouts. King William III has been quoted as saying that the greatest educational influence during his time in the Netherlands – when he was a mere William of Orange – was John de Witt. His personal tutor as a teenager and lasting mentor was the first European actuary. Coincidence?

The earliest successful tontine scheme had been launched in the Netherlands, in Kampen (circa 1670), which is not far from where William grew up. William's favorite nephew, the Duke of Gloucester, who was named William Henry in his uncle's honor – and would have inherited his uncle's crown had he not died prematurely – was the most famous nominee of the 1693 tontine. Oh, and of the (only) two or three statues of King William III in Britain, the largest was placed in downtown Glasgow, Scotland, right in front of the Tontine Building, near Tontine Lane, which of course was funded by a tontine scheme.

In my mind, King William III will be forever linked with financial innovation, long-term borrowing, the first government-issued life annuities, and, of course, tontines.

Long live – all tontine nominees and – King Billy!

APPENDIX A

The List of Nominees

This list (except for the rightmost column) is compiled and transcribed from a summary of the (original) Heyrick (1694) document, which is stored in the archives of the British Library and confirmed against the updated Heyrick (1695) list. The 1695 document is part of the collection of the Institute and Faculty of Actuaries (which is also the cover image of the book). The number of years lived, in which (only) a lower bound is provided is based on the King (1730) surviving nominee list and the Anonymous (1749) surviving nominee list, which are both available in the British Library. The nominees listed with an exact number of years lived is based on (i.) the assumption that their deaths were recorded in chronological order in the final page of the King (1730) list, and (ii.) the number of nominees who died in every year is based on the JHC (1803) document.

Presumably, Finlaison (1829) himself had access to the exact death dates of all the nominees on this list, since he compiled one of the earliest English mortality (and life expectancy) tables based on this tontine. Alas, I haven't been able to locate the Finlaison "list," but I would love to get my hands on it.

Nominee (shares)	Name (alphabetical)	Place or parish of residence	1693 Age	Years lived
1	Samuel Acton	Cheshire	39	55
2	Elizabeth Adams	Salop	2	> 39
3	Henry Adderly	London	8	27
4	Samuel Adenbrook	Huntingdonshire	9	> 65
5	Bythia Adlam	Surrey	3	> 40
6	Phillipis Agas	Middlesex	8	19
7	Anthony Allen	Hertfordshire	8	> 64
8	Daniel Allen	Hertfordshire	5	16
9	Henry Allen	Hertfordshire	2	> 58
10	James Allen	Hertfordshire	11	34
11	John Allen	Hertfordshire	6	> 62
12	Thomas Allen	Hertfordshire	10	> 66
13	Moyso Amirault	Netherlands	10	> 66
14	Richard Arnold	Surrey	21	50
15	John Ash	Wiltshire	9	29
16	Samuel Ash	Wiltshire	6	15
17	William Ash	Wiltshire	7	> 44
18	Alice Ashley	Bedfordshire	9	19
19	Sarah Ashley	Bedfordshire	8	> 64
20	Sarah Atkinson	Westminster	16	24
21	Elizabeth Austen	Kent	5	> 61
22	John Austen	Kent	3	> 59
23	Mary Austen	London	15	18
24	Mary Austen	Essex	13	41
25	Robert Austen	Essex	5	38
26	Margaret Ayescough	Lincolnshire	2	28
27	Mary Ayescough	Lincolnshire	25	48
28	Isabel Ayscough	Lincolnshire	3	> 59
29	Andrew Baker	Worcestershire	4	> 60
30	Ann Baker	Buckinghamshire	6	> 43
31	Samuel Baker	Buckinghamshire	3	> 59
32	John Baker	Middlesex	14	45
33	Joseph Baker	Middlesex	8	> 64
34	Judith Baker	Southwark	13	> 69
35	Henry Baldwin	London	13	20
36	Samuel Baldwin	London	18	> 55
37	Thomas Ball	Italy	22	> 78
38	William Ball	Devonshire	24	43
39	Dorothy Bambrigg	Derby	15	32
40	Henry Bannage	Netherlands	6	8
41	George Bard	Derby	12	27
42	Benjamin Barnardiston	Suffolk	6	34
43	Samuel Barnardiston	Suffolk	9	29

Nominee (shares)	Name (alphabetical)	Place or parish of residence	1693 Age	Years lived
44	Nicholas Barneby	Hertfordshire	12	21
45	Abigall Bass	Suffolk	10	> 66
46	Richard Bayley	Middlesex	9	> 65
47	William Bayley	Middlesex	9	20
48	Samuel Bedford	Lincolnshire	9	35
49	Ann Beke	Buckinghamshire	8	> 64
50	Elizabeth Beke	Buckinghamshire	7	9
51	Mary Beke	Buckinghamshire	6	> 62
52	Thomas Belchamber	Cambridge	21	53
53	Mary Bellafis	Yorkshire	12	15
54	Robert Bennion	Wiltshire	13	24
55	Dorothy Benson	Yorkshire	18	24
56	Elizabeth Benson	Yorkshire	19	27
57	Robert Benson	Yorkshire	17	> 54
58	Jane Benson	Middlesex	13	> 50
59	Martha Benson	Middlesex	14	> 51
60	Susanna Benson	Middlesex	12	47
61	William Benson	Middlesex	11	> 67
62	Catherine Benson	London	2	25
63	Mary Berkeley	Surrey	14	40
64	Eleonara Bertie	Buckinghamshire	3	22
65	Henry Bigg	Wiltshire	2	> 39
66	William Bigg	Wiltshire	5	29
67	Isaac Bigott	Berkshire	12	24
68	Elizabeth Billers	London	10	> 66
69	Martha Billers	London	6	37
70	George Blackall	Middlesex	9	24
71	Abraham Blackmore	London	16	> 53
72	Humfry Blackmore	London	23	35
73 (2)	Anthony Blagrave	Berkshire	12	> 49
74	Esther Blagrave	Berkshire	11	> 48
75	John Blakey	Yorkshire	15	50
76	John Blencowe	Northamptonshire	17	> 54
77	Thomas Blencowe	Northamptonshire	12	> 68
78	William Blencowe	Northamptonshire	11	29
79	Frances Blow	London	11	43
80	Selina Blow	London	8	> 64
81	Tyrrill Blow	London	12	30
82	Benjamin Boddington	London	1	> 57
83	Isaac Boddington	London	13	> 50
84	James Boddington	London	7	25
85	John Boddington	London	17	20
86	Sarah Boddington	London	3	> 40

(continued)

Nominee (shares)	Name (alphabetical)	Place or parish of residence	1693 Age	Years lived
87	William Bonest	London	16	> 53
88 (2)	Mary Booth	Middlesex	41	> 78
89	Elizabeth Bostock	Nottinghamshire	19	> 56
90	John Boughey	Stafford	6	29
91	Elizabeth Brabant	Hertfordshire	3	37
92	Charles Brawne	Somersetshire	1	32
93	Samuel Brewster	Middlesex	23	49
94	Alexander Briggs	London	34	35
95	Ann Briggs	Norfolk	10	> 66
96	Elizabeth Briggs	Norfolk	5	13
97	Mary Briggs	Norfolk	9	> 65
98	John Briggs	Sussex	5	38
99	William Briggs	Sussex	4	22
100	Edward Bromfield	Middlesex	13	31
101	Thomas Bromfield	Middlesex	9	39
102	William Bromfield	Middlesex	12	> 49
103	Adam Browne	Kent	23	39
104	Charles Browne	London	13	16
105	John Browne	Bedfordshire	3	27
106	Lucy Browne	Bedfordshire	5	> 61
107	John Browne	Yorkshire	30	> 67
108 (2)	Sarah Browne	Netherlands	5	9
109	John Brownlow	Surrey	3	> 59
110	James Bruce	London	9	29
111	Elizabeth Buck	Cambridge	14	> 51
112	Rebecca Buck	Cambridge	12	> 49
113	Isabell Budd	London	15	> 52
114	Sarah Budd	London	37	66
115	Moses Alvares Bueno	Netherlands	4	> 60
116	Edward Bulstrode	Buckinghamshire	14	> 51
117	John Bulstrode	London	10	> 47
118	Lucy Burgoyne	Bedfordshire	9	> 46
119	Burgundy	France	11	26
120	Ann Burleigh	Norwich	10	30
121	Elizabeth Burnham	Middlesex	40	49
122	Elizabeth Burton	Middlesex	3	> 40
123	William Burton	Westminster	1	> 57
124	William Burton	Westminster	27	56
125	Thomas Busbridge	Sussex	8	17
126	Katherine Byrom	Lancashire	5	24
127	Angelice Calendrini	Geneva	1	20
128	Cecilia Cann	Somersetshire	7	> 44
129	Elizabeth Cann	Somersetshire	12	> 68

Nominee (shares)	Name (alphabetical)	Place or parish of residence	1693 Age	Years lived
130	Margaret Cann	Somersetshire	6	13
131	Elizabeth Capper	Surrey	11	45
132	Mary Capper	Surrey	16	29
133	William Carew	Cornwall	3	> 40
134	Robert Carpenter	Middlesex	3	> 40
135	William Carr	Middlesex	18	37
136	Robert Carswell	Dorsetshireshire	12	> 49
137	Thomas Cartwright	Middlesex	22	> 59
138	Ann Casebart	Middlesex	19	36
139	Daniel Causton	Middlesex	8	> 45
140	Charity Causton	Middlesex	28	59
141	John Causton	Middlesex	3	> 59
142	Martha Causton	Middlesex	9	> 46
143	Thomas Causton	Spain	1	> 56
144	James Causton	Spain	5	20
145 (2)	John Chamberlein	Westminster	26	59
146	Sheldon Chambers	London	10	42
147	Elizabeth Champion	Middlesex	9	> 46
148 (2)	Lambart Chandeler	Surrey	47	77
149	Elizabeth Chandler	Sussex	9	> 65
150	Elizabeth Chaplin	London	14	> 70
151	Ann Chaplin	London	16	28
152	Sarah Chaplin	London	12	> 49
153	Charlotte Mary Chardin	Middlesex	10	> 47
154	John Chardin	Middlesex	6	> 62
155	Sarah Chase	London	7	> 63
156	Ann Cheret	Middlesex	16	> 53
157	Diana Cheret	Middlesex	11	> 48
158	William Henry Cheret	Middlesex	4	33
159	Benjamin Child	Berkshire	8	> 64
160	Mary Child	Berkshire	6	> 62
161	Lydia Child	Berkshire	3	29
162	Samuel Child	London	1	> 56
163	James Child	London	8	23
164	Thomas Child	London	6	20
165	William Child	London	3	14
166	Mary Childe	Gloucestershire	30	56
167	Edward Clarke	Middlesex	8	> 45
168	Ann Clarke	Middlesex	11	27
169	Joseph Clarke	Surrey	13	> 69
170	James Clarke	Surrey	17	46
171	Lydia Clarke	Surrey	15	> 71
172	Edward Clarke	Lincolnshire	9	> 46

(continued)

Nominee (shares)	Name (alphabetical)	Place or parish of residence	1693 Age	Years lived
173	Mary Clarke	Surrey	4	6
174	Elizabeth Clarke	London	8	> 45
175	Godfrey Clarke	Derby	16	> 53
176 (2)	Joseph Clarke	London	11	15
177	John Clarke	London	4	36
178	Margaret Felicia Clutterbook	Middlesex	20	> 57
179	Teresa Victoria Clutterbook	Middlesex	26	29
180	John Coape	Derby	5	> 42
181	William Coape	Derby	2	> 58
182	Richard Cobb	Berkshire	10	> 47
183	John Cocks	Wiltshire	5	25
184	Charles Coker	Southampton	5	> 61
185	John Coker	Southampton	1	29
186	Grace Cole	Isle of Wight	7	> 63
187	Jane Cole	Isle of Wight	3	> 59
188	Richard Cole	Isle of Wight	10	16
189	Barbara Collins	Kent	11	19
190 (2)	Reynold Colthorp	Hampshire	4	20
191	Spencer Compton	Northamptonshire	18	> 55
192	John Comyns	Essex	8	> 45
193	Sutton John Coney	Rutland	13	> 69
194	Elizabeth Cook	London	4	> 60
195	Drainer Cook	London	8	17
196	Robert Cook	Gloucestershire	30	58
197	Dennis Cooke	Gloucestershire	5	> 61
198	George Cooke	Yorkshire	6	> 62
199	William Cooke	Gloucestershire	11	24
200	Daniel Coolidge	Cambridge	21	55
201	Thomas Cooper	Nottinghamshire	18	> 55
202	William Cornelius	London	16	50
203	Elizabeth Cornish	London	4	> 60
204 (2)	John Cornwallis	Whitehall	14	18
205	John Cowley	Northumberland	8	> 64
206	Elizabeth Cowley	Essex	18	24
207	Sarah Cowley	Essex	20	31
208 (2)	Thomas Crabb	London	3	> 40
209	James Cranmer	Surrey	9	> 65
210	Thomas Cranmer	Surrey	6	> 62
211	Walgrave Crew	Middlesex	20	21
212 (2)	Anthony Crofts	Suffolk	9	37
213	William Crofts	Suffolk	11	12
214 (2)	John Croke	London	18	35

Nominee (shares)	Name (alphabetical)	Place or parish of residence	1693 Age	Years lived
215	Samuel Crompton	Derby	14	> 70
216	John Cross	Hertfordshire	3	29
217	Samuel Cross	Devonshire	19	52
218	Nathaniel Cullen	Kent	21	23
219	Ann Dalton	Westminster	3	> 59
220	Ann Dalton	Westminster	30	58
221	Mary Dalton	Westminster	10	45
222	Daniel Danvers	London	18	> 74
223	Arthur Darlington	Chester	33	47
224	James Darrel	London	13	> 50
225	John Darrel	London	6	11
226	Marmaduke Darrel	London	10	17
227	John Dawling	Surrey	26	50
228	Thomas Dawnay	Yorkshire	6	15
229 (2)	Mark de Fonseca	Brussels	22	> 78
230	Peter de la Bat	Netherlands	2	> 58
231	Phillip James de la Combe	Netherlands	21	34
232	Peter de la Fontaine	Netherlands	24	47
233	Benjamin de Meherene de la Consiellere	London	9	32
234	Rachel de Mesquita	Netherlands	15	47
235	Anna Gabriele de Mirande	Netherlands	15	25
236	Margaret de Mirmand	Cleeves	14	45
237 (2)	Mary de Mousan	Netherlands	34	> 71
238	Magdelane Geantille de Rossieres	Westminster	11	> 67
239	Peter Richard de Vendargues	Geneva	11	> 48
240 (2)	Frances de Vignoles	Westminster	6	24
241 (2)	Louise de Vignoles	Westminster	8	22
242	Reynier de Yongh	Middlesex	2	> 39
243	Esther Deacon	Middlesex	10	> 66
244	Elizabeth Deacon	Middlesex	14	49
245	Mary Deacon	Middlesex	9	> 46
246	Thomas Death	London	14	> 51
247	Alexander Deffilholl Camas	Cleeves	8	25
248	Giles Dent	Middlesex	10	33
249	Ann Louise des Glereaux	Cleeves	7	> 44
250	Paul A. Thevenni des Glereaux	Cleeves	5	> 42
251	Edward Desbouverie	London	5	> 42

(*continued*)

Nominee (shares)	Name (alphabetical)	Place or parish of residence	1693 Age	Years lived
252 (2)	William Desbouverie	London	3	15
253	Theophilus Dillingham	London	17	> 73
254	Henry Dobson	Hampshire	3	> 59
255	John Dodd	London	1	22
256	Ann Dolben	London	6	> 43
257	Elizabeth Dolben	London	7	> 63
258	John Dolben	London	2	20
259	Katherine Dolben	London	9	39
260	William Dolben	London	4	19
261	James Dorville	London	19	33
262	John Dowley	London	23	> 60
263	Prew Downing	Middlesex	4	> 60
264	Thomas Drafgate	London	8	> 45
265 (2)	Helena Du Moulin	Netherlands	49	69
266 (3)	Richard Ducane	London	12	> 49
267	Jane Dummer	London	4	> 41
268	Mary Dummer	London	12	21
269	Sarah Dummer	London	10	17
270	Susanna Dummer	London	8	19
271	John Duncomb	Middlesex	13	> 69
272	William Duncomb	Middlesex	3	> 59
273	John Louis Dupan	Geneva	4	> 60
274	James Dupan	Geneva	3	4
275	Ann Mary Dupeyron	Netherlands	8	> 64
276	James Dupeyron	Netherlands	1	> 56
277	Cornelia Dupeyron	Netherlands	4	8
278	John Dupeyron	Netherlands	10	> 66
279	Judith Dupeyron	Netherlands	12	47
280	John Lewis Duponcet	Netherlands	18	> 55
281	Mary Duris	Westminster	16	> 72
282	Jacob Dutry	London	14	32
283	William Dutry	Netherlands	21	34
284	Bernard Eales	London	11	> 67
285	Benjamin Eales	London	3	31
286	Ellinor Earle	Somersetshire	2	33
287	Anna Maria Eaton	Middlesex	2	> 58
288	Josiah Eaton	Middlesex	9	22
289	Hannah Edden	London	7	> 44
290	Rebecca Ekins	Northamptonshire	9	> 65
291	Martha Elking	London	8	33
292	Elizabeth Emmerton	London	2	> 39
293	William Emmerton	London	3	11
294	George England	Norfolk	13	44

Nominee (shares)	Name (alphabetical)	Place or parish of residence	1693 Age	Years lived
295	Samuel Estup	Worcestershire	6	> 62
296	Anthony Etterick	Middlesex	30	> 67
297	William Etterick	Durham	32	> 69
298	James Everard	Southampton	16	31
299	Robert Eyre	Southampton	1	1
300	Roger Fairbrother	Southampton	4	30
301	Edward Fairchild	Devonshire	28	> 65
302	George Fairchild	Devonshire	21	56
303	Henry Fane	Devonshire	8	21
304	John Farewell	Westminster	8	21
305	Anthony Farringdon	Middlesex	9	> 65
306	Francis Faure	Geneva	17	> 54
307	John Louis Faure	Geneva	1	> 56
308	James Faure	Geneva	3	> 59
309	Nicholas Fenn	Middlesex	14	49
310	Dorothy Fillingham	Nottinghamshire	6	> 62
311	Essex Finch	London	9	> 65
312	William Finch	London	10	39
313	John Fisher	London	13	33
314	Mary Fitzhugh	London	1	23
315	Peter Fletcher	Kent	23	42
316	Susanna Fletcher	Cumberland	20	35
317 (5)	Paul Foley	Hertfordshire	5	> 42
318	Martin Folkes	Middlesex	3	> 59
319	James Foster	Wiltshire	5	> 61
320	Thomas Fothergill	Yorkshire	4	> 41
321	Elizabeth Foyle	Southampton	12	20
322	John Franken	Netherlands	17	34
323	John Frederick	London	15	> 71
324	Charles Frederick	London	8	21
325	Leonora Frederick	London	6	> 43
326	Mary Frederick	London	11	> 48
327	Thomas Frederick	London	12	> 49
328	Daniel Fromantell	Norfolk	15	> 52
329	Samuel Fromantell	Norfolk	9	22
330	John Fulford	Devonshire	1	1
331	Elizabeth Fuller	Sussex	36	55
332	Richard Fuller	Norfolk	7	42
333	Elizabeth Fulwood	Lincolnshire	16	42
334	Catherine Gainsborough	Hampshire	27	40
335 (2)	James Gambier	Middlesex	1	> 39
336	Leonard Gammon	Middlesex	2	25
337	Mariana Gassard	Geneva	22	32

(*continued*)

Nominee (shares)	Name (alphabetical)	Place or parish of residence	1693 Age	Years lived
338	Elizabeth Gatchell	Somersetshire	20	36
339	Charles Gendrault	Middlesex	3	5
340	Elizabeth Gibbon	London	12	> 68
341	James Gibbon	Middlesex	2	> 39
342	William Glegg	Chester	5	> 61
343	William J.H., Duke of Gloucester	Middlesex	4	11
344	Ann Good	Surrey	22	> 78
345	Barnham Good	Surrey	23	> 60
346	Francis Good	Surrey	17	> 54
347	Philadelphia Good	Surrey	24	> 80
348	Abigall Goodwin	Middlesex	28	56
349	Elizabeth Gore	Kent	15	35
350	Mary Gosfright	London	9	> 46
351	Thomas Gould	Exon	4	> 60
352	Elizabeth Gould	Exon	24	32
353	George Gould	Exon	31	34
354	James Gould	Exon	24	31
355	Mary Graham	Yorkshire	10	> 66
356	David Gray	London	30	37
357	John Green	Middlesex	15	> 52
358	Johanna Green	Middlesex	14	30
359	Mary Green	Westminster	21	> 58
360	Robert Green	Middlesex	12	33
361	Strangewales Green	Middlesex	9	22
362	Thomas Green	Westminster	9	> 46
363	Mary Gregg	London	3	> 40
364	Barabara Gregory	Nottinghamshire	14	> 51
365	Jane Gregory	Nottinghamshire	11	> 67
366	Mary Gregory	Nottinghamshire	10	> 66
367	Richard Gregory	Westminster	19	25
368	Theophilus Gregory	Nottinghamshire	13	41
369	Thomas Grove	Suffolk	9	30
370	William Grove	Suffolk	7	33
371	James Guillot	London	10	> 66
372	Elizabeth Hale	Hertfordshire	11	> 67
373	Bernard Hale	Hertfordshire	15	44
374	Edward Hall	Middlesex	10	22
375	Hannah Halsey	Westminster	23	34
376	Richard Halsey	Suffolk	15	> 52
377	Frances Halsted	London	8	> 45
378	Ann Halsted	London	5	35
379	Robert Ham	Devonshire	4	> 41

Nominee (shares)	Name (alphabetical)	Place or parish of residence	1693 Age	Years lived
380	John Hamilton	Yorkshire	3	24
381 (2)	James Hara	Westminster	4	> 60
382 (2)	Mary Hara	Westminster	10	> 66
383	William Anthony Hardy	Netherlands	3	17
384 (2)	Charles Harel	Middlesex	20	> 57
385	James Harfell	Southampton	6	24
386	William Harker	Yorkshire	13	> 50
387	John Harris	Devonshire	1	> 38
388	John Harris	Southton	12	> 68
389	John Harris	London	15	32
390	Mary Harris	London	11	25
391	Richard Harris	Southton	3	21
392	Thomas Harris	Southton	6	36
393	James Harrison	Middlesex	18	> 55
394	Jane Harvey	Northamptonshire	9	> 46
395	Ann Hawley	Somersetshire	4	> 60
396	Edward Hawley	Somersetshire	7	> 44
397	Henry Hawley	Somersetshire	8	> 64
398	Chales Hawley	Somersetshire	5	21
399	Whitfield Hayter	London	27	57
400	Ann Heard	Westminster	22	> 59
401	Ann Heathcott	London	10	> 47
402	Frances Heathcott	London	8	> 45
403	John Heathcott	London	4	> 60
404	Ferdinand Sigismond Heiden	Germany	10	> 47
405	John Hellier	Westminster	13	44
406	Alice Herne	London	2	> 58
407	Sarah Herne	London	9	> 46
408	William Herne	London	5	> 42
409	Charles Herne	London	4	37
410	Elizabeth Herne	London	14	49
411	Frederick Herne	London	19	38
412	John Herne	London	10	22
413	Joseph Herne	London	13	43
414	Mary Herne	London	8	28
415	Nicholas Herne	London	6	21
416	Carr Hervey	Suffolk	2	30
417	Elizabeth Hervey	Suffolk	1	2
418	Isabella Carr Hervey	Suffolk	4	27
419	Dorothy Heydon	Somersetshire	10	> 47
420	Martha Heydon	Norfolk	12	> 68
421	Ann Hickman	Lincolnshire	2	> 58

(*continued*)

Nominee (shares)	Name (alphabetical)	Place or parish of residence	1693 Age	Years lived
422	Stephen Hickman	Lincolnshire	4	13
423	Willoughby Hickman	Lincolnshire	6	19
424	Timothy Hickman	London	18	24
425	Peter Hicks	London	6	33
426	Anna Hide	Middlesex	4	> 60
427	John Hide	Middlesex	1	> 57
428	Ann Hieron	Derby	10	> 47
429	Richard Hill	Westminster	35	64
430	Mary Hoare	London	7	> 63
431	Henry Hoare	London	16	46
432	James Hoare	London	6	22
433	John Hoare	London	11	38
434	Richard Hoare	London	20	40
435	Thomas Hoare	London	9	28
436	Robert Hodgson	Surrey	21	31
437	William Hodgson	London	12	17
438	Amy Holebrook	Isle of Wight	6	> 62
439	Anna Holebrook	Isle of Wight	4	> 60
440	Grace Holebrook	Isle of Wight	8	> 64
441	Ann Holebrook	Isle of Wight	13	41
442	Mary Holebrook	Isle of Wight	10	> 66
443	Richard Holebrook	Isle of Wight	1	> 38
444 (2)	Richard Holland	Middlesex	5	> 42
445	Jane Holland	Middlesex	2	14
446 (2)	John Hollis	London	25	> 62
447	Thomas Hollis	Kent	8	> 45
448	Susanna Houghton	London	11	25
449	Mathew Howard	Middlesex	10	> 47
450	Annabella Howard	Westminster	20	49
451	Hannah Howard	Middlesex	4	11
452	Samuel Howard	Middlesex	2	19
453	Sarah Howard	Middlesex	6	17
454 (2)	Thomas Howard	Surrey	5	8
455	Thomas Hudson	London	2	15
456	Susanna Hunt	Rutland	25	> 81
457	Michael Hunt	Middlesex	14	40
458	William Hussey	Lincolnshire	18	24
459	George Hutchinson	London	12	> 49
460	Richard Hutchinson	London	13	42
461	Nathaniel Iles	London	12	47
462	Henry Ingram	Yorkshire	2	> 58
463	Edward Machell Ingram	Yorkshire	7	33
464	John Ingram	Yorkshire	0	21

Nominee (shares)	Name (alphabetical)	Place or parish of residence	1693 Age	Years lived
465	Rich. Ingram	Sussex	6	33
466	Joshua Ironmonger	Hertfordshire	8	12
467	Matthew Ironmonger	Hertfordshire	13	19
468	Susanna Isaac	Devonshire	6	> 62
469	John Ives	Norfolk	8	> 64
470	Joseph Jackson	Norfolk	11	> 67
471	Joseph Jackson	Gloucestershire	2	> 58
472	Mary Jackson	London	15	> 71
473	Richard Jackson	Essex	5	> 61
474	John Jekyl	Westminster	19	> 56
475	Richard Jekyl	Westminster	13	> 50
476	Thomas Jekyl	Westminster	14	> 70
477	Tryphena Jekyl	Westminster	15	> 71
478	George Jennings	Westminster	5	> 42
479	Stephen Jermin	London	6	36
480	Gasbard Jobbard	Geneva	35	> 72
481	Ann Johnson	Buckinghamshire	20	> 76
482	Martha Johnson	Lincolnshire	5	> 61
483	Spinckes Johnson	Lincolnshire	4	> 41
484	Chales Johnson	Middlesex	15	42
485	Edward Johnson	Suffolk	30	52
486	Esther Johnson	Surrey	12	44
487	William Johnson	Cornwall	6	16
488	Catherine Jones	London	10	> 47
489	Hester Kendrick	London	10	> 66
490	Sarah Kent	Oxon	12	33
491 (2)	John Kerby	Netherlands	24	> 80
492 (2)	William Kerby	Netherlands	22	37
493	Peter King	Devonshire	24	> 61
494	Jane Kingdon	Middlesex	10	> 66
495	John Knight	Middlesex	9	> 46
496	Mariana La Mande	Geneva	7	> 63
497	Alexander La Mande	Geneva	11	17
498	Elizabeth Lacey	London	13	19
499	Lancelot Lake	Kent	3	16
500	Henry Lamb	London	0	> 37
501	Miles Lamb	Middlesex	15	> 52
502	John Lamb	London	10	26
503	William Lamb	London	5	26
504	Jane Lamb	Middlesex	14	23
505	William Lamb	Middlesex	17	49
506	John Lamb	London	12	35
507	Obadiah Lane	Stafford	5	23

(*continued*)

Nominee (shares)	Name (alphabetical)	Place or parish of residence	1693 Age	Years lived
508	Thomas Lane	London	6	18
509	Frances Langton	Lincolnshire	7	37
510	William Lascoe	London	28	40
511 (5)	Wilfred Lawson	Cumberland	27	43
512	John Lawton	Stafford	4	> 41
513	Catherine Lee	London	1	> 37
514	Henry Lee	London	8	> 45
515	Elizabeth Lee	Middlesex	9	> 46
516	George Lee	London	4	7
517	Godfrey Lee	London	10	45
518	Mary Lee	London	11	35
519	Magdalen Henrietta Lefebure	Netherlands	2	4
520	Ann Leighton	Oxford	9	21
521	Robert Leighton	Oxford	3	25
522	Benjamin Lethieulier	London	6	> 62
523	Christopher Lethieulier	London	17	> 54
524	Mary Lethieulier	London	11	> 67
525	Abraham Levy	Netherlands	7	> 63
526	Jacob de Abraham Levy	Netherlands	22	> 59
527	Jeve Llewelling	Salop	11	37
528	Ann Lloyd	Litchfield	10	> 47
529	Elizabeth Lloyd	Middlesex	2	> 58
530	William Lloyd	Litchfield	20	40
531	Francis Lloyd	Carmarthen	3	32
532	Charles Lombard	Middlesex	14	27
533	Mary Long	Essex	24	48
534	Isabell Lott	Yorkshire	6	> 62
535	Barbara Love	London	4	> 60
536	Joseph Low	Middlesex	8	> 64
537	Mary Low	Nottinghamshire	11	> 48
538	Caleb Lowdham	Exon	21	> 58
539	Caleb Lowdham	Exon	46	66
540	Robert Lowther	Yorkshire	18	> 74
541	Lancelot Lowther	Cumberland	14	> 70
542	Gerard Lowther	Yorkshire	14	21
543	John James Lulin	Geneva	1	> 57
544	John Anthony Lulin	Geneva	9	10
545	Magdalen Lulin	Geneva	8	9
546	Jane Lutener	Kent	14	> 70
547	Francis Luttrell	Middlesex	10	> 66
548	Elizabeth Lyddall	London	2	> 39
549	Ann Lyde	Middlesex	3	36

Nominee (shares)	Name (alphabetical)	Place or parish of residence	1693 Age	Years lived
550 (3)	Elizabeth Lynford	London	26	> 63
551	Barbara Lyster	Westminster	13	> 50
552	Frances Lyster	Westminster	18	> 74
553	Catherine Lyster	Yorkshire	3	> 40
554	John Lyster	Yorkshire	10	> 66
555	Barbara Lyster	Westminster	19	23
556	Jacob Machado	Netherlands	7	> 63
557	Jehudith Machado	Netherlands	15	> 71
558	Mariana Machado	Netherlands	5	> 42
559	Abigall Machado	Netherlands	9	29
560	Sarah Machado	Netherlands	11	33
561	Benjamin Mackerell	Norwich	8	> 45
562	Gilbert Malcher	London	7	> 63
563	Dorcas Malcher	London	4	9
564	Mary Malyn	Nottinghamshire	13	> 50
565	Henry Mandey	Middlesex	11	> 67
566	Benjamin Mandey	Middlesex	10	41
567	Edward Manning	Kent	1	23
568	Robert Mapletoft	Kent	9	31
569	Jane Markland	Southampton	12	> 49
570	Leonard Marr	Essex	15	29
571	Margaret Marshal	Middlesex	9	> 46
572	Ann Marsham	Hertfordshire	6	10
573 (2)	Elizabeth Marsham	Hertfordshire	9	31
574	Ferdinando Marsham	Hertfordshire	5	9
575	Margaretta Marsham	Hertfordshire	8	38
576	Robert Marsham	Hertfordshire	7	40
577	Elizabeth Martin	Devonshire	7	> 63
578	Thomas Martin	Devonshire	4	> 41
579	Gartred Martin	Devonshire	15	49
580	John Martin	Devonshire	8	37
581	Nicholas Martin	Devonshire	11	35
582	John Martin	Middlesex	31	65
583 (2)	Tuchin Martin	Middlesex	24	38
584	Henry Marwood	Lincolnshire	11	> 48
585	Thomas Marwood	Lincolnshire	4	> 60
586	Joan Masters	Southwark	51	72
587	Mary Mathew	Exon	3	> 40
588	Burdetta Mathew	Exon	2	13
589	John Mathew	Exon	1	8
590	Ann Maynard	Middlesex	6	> 62
591	Thomas Maynard	Middlesex	7	> 44
592	Sarah Mellish	Yorkshire	21	47

(*continued*)

Nominee (shares)	Name (alphabetical)	Place or parish of residence	1693 Age	Years lived
593	Ann Mercer	London	10	25
594	George Mercer	London	6	38
595	Thomas Mercer	London	21	44
596	Clara Mertins	Westminster	7	> 44
597	John Henry Mertins	Westminster	1	> 57
598	Carolina Hester Mertins	Westminster	4	8
599	Edward Mertins	Westminster	5	21
600	John Methwin	Wiltshire	5	28
601	Ann Middleton	Sussex	3	> 59
602	Mary Middylton	Denbigh	5	> 42
603	Charles Miller	Middlesex	6	> 43
604	Ann Moody	Middlesex	19	54
605	Thomas Moore	London	13	> 69
606	Henry Mordant	London	23	40
607	Annabella Moreton	Dublin	6	> 62
608	Richard Moreton	Dublin	10	> 47
609	Honour Moreton	London	7	18
610	Charles Morley	Southampton	1	> 57
611	George Morley	Southampton	8	> 64
612	Frances Morley	Southampton	6	27
613	Jane Morrice	Kent	18	33
614	Edward Mountague	Northamptonshire	7	> 44
615	George Mountague	Northamptonshire	9	> 46
616	Magdalen Moure	Netherlands	20	> 57
617	Theobald Munns	Westminster	2	> 39
618	Elizabeth Murray	Westminster	8	> 64
619	Richard Musgrave	Somersetshire	8	> 45
620	Alice Mynn	London	27	53
621	Ann Nesbett	London	1	> 38
622	Phillip Nesbett	London	5	> 42
623	Elizabeth Nevile	Westminster	2	> 58
624	Mary Nevile	Westminster	12	> 68
625	John Nevile	Nottinghamshire	42	62
626	Mary Newdigate	Warwick	17	> 54
627	Frances Newdigate	Warwick	16	40
628	Elizabeth Newnham	Hertfordshire	6	> 62
629	Theodocia Newnham	Hertfordshire	9	32
630	Henry Newport	Salop	10	> 47
631	Richard Newport	Salop	8	30
632	William Newsham	Warwick	6	> 43
633	Catherine Newsham	Southampton	2	5
634	William Newsham	Warwick	30	52
635	Michael Newton	Westminster	1	> 38

Nominee (shares)	Name (alphabetical)	Place or parish of residence	1693 Age	Years lived
636	Carey Newton	Westminster	13	27
637	John Newton	Leicester	20	20
638	Thomas Niccholls	Salop	9	> 46
639	Thomas Niccoll	Northamptonshire	4	> 60
640	William Nicholas	London	25	> 81
641	Elizabeth Noell	Gainsborough	4	> 41
642	Rachell Noell	Gainsborough	3	18
643 (2)	Elizabeth Norborough	Kent	11	31
644 (2)	James Norborough	Kent	7	24
645 (2)	John Norborough	Kent	8	20
646	Mary Norris	Middlesex	15	> 52
647	Jane Nowes	London	5	> 42
648	Richard Oakely	London	9	17
649	Samuel Oakely	London	12	23
650	Thomas Oldfield	Nottinghamshire	19	28
651	Henry Oliver	Devonshire	12	17
652	Braithwate Ottway	Middlesex	24	> 80
653	James Oxenden	London	2	5
654	Ann Packer	Westminster	14	> 51
655	Isabella Packer	Westminster	17	> 73
656	Robert Packer	Berkshire	15	> 52
657	Phillip Packer	Westminster	16	34
658	Dorothy Pagett	Middlesex	17	> 73
659	Dorcas Pagett	Middlesex	19	36
660	Benjamin Palmer	Middlesex	11	15
661	Henry Palmer	Middlesex	4	38
662	Elizabeth Parker	Somersetshire	28	49
663	Dormer Parkhurst	Northamptonshire	5	> 61
664	Charles Moline Parsons	Middlesex	0	1
665	George Paske	Hertfordshire	10	> 66
666	James Paske	Hertfordshire	7	> 44
667 (2)	Symon Patrick	Ely	12	30
668	Frances Pauckhurst	Sussex	16	> 72
669	William Pawlett	Westminster	9	> 46
670	Francis Pearson	Yorkshire	7	> 63
671	Abigail Pease	Netherlands	11	> 67
672	George Pease	Netherlands	10	> 47
673	Joseph Pease	Netherlands	5	> 61
674	William Pease	Netherlands	7	> 44
675	Ann Pease	Netherlands	3	32
676	Stephen Peloquin	Somersetshire	38	70
677	James Penrice	London	9	33
678	Richard Percivall	Flint	5	> 42

(*continued*)

Nominee (shares)	Name (alphabetical)	Place or parish of residence	1693 Age	Years lived
679	Fiennes Percivall	Flint	6	22
680	John Peters	Middlesex	2	> 58
681	Dorothy Pettit	Middlesex	9	> 46
682	Mary Pettit	London	5	> 61
683	Hellen Phillipponneau	Germany	13	> 50
684	John Phillips	Middlesex	26	> 63
685	Thomas Phillips	Carmarthen	8	> 64
686	Elizabeth Pierrepont	Salop	7	12
687	Granado Pigot	Cambridge	3	> 59
688	Rebecca Pigot	Cambridge	12	> 68
689	John Pine	Devonshire	11	> 67
690	Malachy Pine	Devonshire	10	33
691	William Pine	Devonshire	8	26
692 (2)	Stephen Piper	Westminster	36	66
693	Gervas Pirrepont	Salop	45	66
694	Martha Pitt	London	5	> 42
695	Christopher Pitt	Middlesex	6	7
696	Robert Pitt	Middlesex	8	34
697	George Play	Devonshire	24	25
698	Joseph Plestow	London	13	28
699	Mark Stuart Pleydell	Berkshire	1	> 57
700	Catherine Pleydell	Wiltshire	30	52
701	Charles Pleydell	Wiltshire	5	9
702	Hugh Pluckenet	Westminster	6	> 43
703	Brook Pluckenet	Westminster	8	43
704	Elizabeth Pluckenet	Westminster	12	45
705	James Plumb	London	8	26
706	Fitz. William Plumptree	Nottinghamshire	7	> 63
707	Henry Plumptree	Nottinghamshire	13	> 50
708	John Plumptree	Nottinghamshire	14	> 70
709	Charles Polhill	Kent	14	> 70
710	David Polhill	Kent	19	> 75
711	Henry Polhill	Kent	16	> 72
712	Edward Pordage	Middlesex	5	> 61
713	Margaret Porter	Nottinghamshire	14	> 70
714	Thomas Porter	Suffolk	8	19
715	Elizabeth Poulden	London	14	31
716	Richard Poulden	London	12	21
717	Elizabeth Poulden	Essex	7	36
718	John Poulden	Essex	8	24
719	Mary Poulden	Essex	11	42
720	Mary Preistman	Middlesex	4	6
721	Frances Proby	Huntingdonshire	2	37

Nominee (shares)	Name (alphabetical)	Place or parish of residence	1693 Age	Years lived
722	Ann Proctor	London	23	37
723	Samuel Proctor	London	2	31
724	Edward Pryor	Southampton	5	> 42
725	Mary Pryor	Middlesex	28	51
726	George Pye	Surrey	8	> 45
727	Elizabeth Pyle	Southampton	1	> 56
728	Edward Radcliffe	Hertfordshire	6	> 62
729	Ralph Radcliffe	Hertfordshire	10	> 47
730	Deborah Randolph	Kent	26	> 63
731 (2)	Jonathan Rashleigh	Cornwall	2	> 58
732 (2)	Phillip Rashleigh	Cornwall	4	> 41
733	James Rashleigh	Hertfordshire	5	6
734 (2)	Sarah Rashleigh	Cornwall	5	38
735	Thomas Rawlins	Middlesex	22	47
736	Daniel Rawlinson	London	5	22
737	Mary Rawlinson	London	30	58
738	Thomas Rawlinson	London	12	46
739	John Raymond	Essex	4	37
740	Elizabeth Read	Essex	6	> 43
741 (2)	Samuel Read	Middlesex	10	> 47
742	Kelly Read	Essex	2	18
743	Honoria Read	Middlesex	5	8
744	John Read	Middlesex	2	27
745	Thomas Read	Middlesex	7	8
746	Mary Read	Huntingdonshire	5	39
747	John Reading	London	15	28
748	Mary Reading	London	12	38
749	Thomas Reason	Middlesex	9	> 46
750	John Reeve	London	10	11
751	Samuel Reeve	London	6	26
752	Robert Revell	Derby	24	47
753	Jacob Reynardson	Middlesex	40	62
754	Christopher Moyser Rich	Middlesex	0	> 56
755	John Rich	Middlesex	1	> 57
756 (3)	Daniel Richards	Devonshire	36	48
757	Thomas Richardson	Middlesex	13	20
758	Alice Richers	London	1	> 56
759 (2)	Diana Richers	London	5	6
760	Elizabeth Roberts	Middlesex	9	> 65
761	Martha Robinson	London	12	> 68
762	Amy Robinson	London	9	30
763	Elihu Robinson	London	6	33
764	Samuel Robinson	London	9	22

(*continued*)

Nominee (shares)	Name (alphabetical)	Place or parish of residence	1693 Age	Years lived
765	Elizabeth Roe	Southampton	8	36
766	James Rogers	London	4	> 41
767	Elizabeth Rooth	Westminster	4	30
768	Churchill Rose	Dorchester	3	> 59
769	Ann Rose	Devonshire	12	30
770	Sarah Rose	Devonshire	15	15
771	Francis Rose	London	12	21
772	John Row	Devonshire	12	26
773	Hannah Rowland	Devonshire	15	43
774	Charles Rowley	Westminster	14	21
775	Thomas Rowney	Oxford	0	> 56
776	Dorothy Rudyerd	Berkshire	1	> 57
777	Ruperta (Prince Rupert's daug.)	Russell Street	19	> 56
778	Darby Russell	Stafford	4	24
779	Wryothesly Russell	Bedfordshire	12	25
780	Mary Sadlier	Hertfordshire	22	30
781	John Saintlo	Westminster	6	> 62
782	Mary Sandford	Westmorland	18	> 74
783	Michael Sansom	London	10	28
784	George Sayer	Middlesex	3	> 40
785	Sarah Sayer	Westminster	22	> 59
786	Charlotte Schmettau	Germany	3	> 59
787	Hervey Seale	London	7	> 44
788	Alice Sealy	Somersetshire	23	> 79
789	John Sealy	Somersetshire	14	> 70
790	Elizabeth Seaman	Yorkshire	15	41
791	Robert Seddon	Derby	32	> 69
792	Gualterus Senserfe	Netherlands	7	> 63
793	James Senserfe	Netherlands	36	> 73
794	Henry Shackleton	Yorkshire	11	> 67
795	Annabella Shackleton	Yorkshire	12	47
796	Elizabeth Sharpe	London	11	> 48
797	Elizabeth Sherbrook	London	4	> 41
798	Henry Sherbrooke	Nottinghamshire	11	> 67
799	Gabriel Sherlow	Surrey	17	40
800	Dorothy Shetterdine	Hertfordshire	11	> 67
801	Elizabeth Shetterdine	Hertfordshire	15	> 71
802	Meliora Shetterdine	Hertfordshire	18	23
803	Louise C. Shewrin and Heiden	Germany	21	> 77
804	Thomas Short	Middlesex	1	> 37
805	John Short	Middlesex	3	18

Nominee (shares)	Name (alphabetical)	Place or parish of residence	1693 Age	Years lived
806	Catharine Shorter	Middlesex	9	> 46
807	Elizabeth Shovell	White-Chappell	1	> 56
808	Samuel Skinner	London	10	> 66
809	Mary Skinner	London	2	9
810	Elizabeth Slaughter	London	14	21
811	Frances Slaughter	London	12	26
812	John Slaughter	London	10	22
813	Jane Slee	Norfolk	4	> 41
814	Andrew Slee	Norfolk	8	9
815	John Slowman	London	7	28
816	Mary Smith	London	14	> 70
817	Theodore Smith	Westminster	7	> 63
818	Catherine Smith	London	11	25
819	John Smith	London	16	38
820	Jonathon Smith	London	34	65
821 (2)	Nathaniel Smith	Surrey	13	43
822	Rebecca Smith	Middlesex	8	15
823	James Snell	London	4	18
824	John South	London	3	> 59
825	Catherine Spencer	Westminster	23	29
826	John Spencer	Hertfordshire	15	50
827	Judith Spicer	Exon	7	> 44
828	Lucia Spicer	Middlesex	30	> 67
829	Elizabeth Squibb	Middlesex	10	> 47
830	Philidelphia Squibb	Middlesex	9	> 65
831	William Squibb	Middlesex	13	32
832	Jane Squire	Yorkshire	7	> 44
833	Priscilla Squire	Yorkshire	8	> 45
834	Elizabeth St John	London	10	100
835	John Stacey	London	41	> 78
836	Jane Staple	Westminster	2	> 58
837	Rebecca Staunton	London	3	> 59
838	John Steer	Surrey	2	> 58
839	John Garnett Stephens	Kent	1	> 39
840	Anthony Steventon	Kent	10	> 47
841	Jane Steventon	Kent	7	25
842	John Steventon	Kent	12	42
843	Peter Storer	London	9	> 65
844	John Storer	London	10	44
845	Simeon Stuart	Southampton	8	> 64
846	Mary Studd	Essex	12	> 68
847	Thomas Sutton	Middlesex	16	> 72
848	Robert Sutton	Middlesex	10	37

(continued)

Nominee (shares)	Name (alphabetical)	Place or parish of residence	1693 Age	Years lived
849	John Symonds	Surrey	4	> 60
850	Nathaniel Symonds	Surrey	5	> 61
851	Elizabeth Symonds	London	2	27
852	Audry Symons	Devonshire	27	> 64
853	Ann Tash	Surrey	35	> 72
854	Elizabeth Tash	Surrey	1	28
855 (4)	Hatton Tash	Surrey	5	36
856	Thomazin Tash	Surrey	3	28
857	Hubert Tassell	Norfolk	3	> 59
858	William Tatham	Surrey	14	18
859	Joseph Taylor	London	13	34
860	Elizabeth Taylor	Surrey	11	> 67
861	Anna Taylor	Essex	12	> 68
862	Rebecca Taylor	Essex	14	> 70
863 (2)	Ann Tempest	London	4	> 41
864 (2)	Charles Tempest	London	1	> 38
865 (2)	Elizabeth Tempest	London	6	> 43
866 (2)	Thomas Tempest	London	3	> 40
867 (2)	William Tempest	London	11	> 67
868 (2)	Mary Tempest	London	22	> 78
869 (2)	John Tempest	London	0	32
870 (2)	Mary Tempest	London	9	19
871 (2)	Robert Tempest	London	7	24
872	Dorothy Temple	Surrey	5	> 61
873	Elizabeth Temple	Surrey	6	> 62
874	Arthur Temple	Buckinghamshire	12	21
875	Henry Temple	Buckinghamshire	13	23
876	Purbeck Temple	Buckinghamshire	17	23
877	Fisher Tench	Essex	20	> 57
878	Margaret Thompson	London	1	29
879	Margaret Thrale	London	13	> 69
880	Sarah Thrale	London	10	44
881	Jonathan Tilden	London	15	25
882	Mary Tilden	London	16	33
883	Alice Tipping	Middlesex	18	41
884	Leonard Tipping	Middlesex	20	23
885	Gabriel Tohourdin	London	14	> 51
886	Elizabeth Tooley	London	10	> 47
887	Richard Topham	Berkshire	22	> 59
888	Alice Toplady	London	16	> 72
889	Timothy Topping	Wiltshire	5	> 42
890	Thomas Topping	Wiltshire	7	26
891	Jane Tothall	Middlesex	2	> 39

Nominee (shares)	Name (alphabetical)	Place or parish of residence	1693 Age	Years lived
892	Christiana Tothall	Middlesex	15	28
893	William Tothall	Middlesex	0	19
894	Ann Tovey	Middlesex	4	12
895	Elizabeth Traffles	Winchester	6	> 43
896	Martha Maria Traffles	Winchester	1	> 38
897	Mary Traffles	Winchester	5	> 61
898	George Treby	Middlesex	7	> 44
899	Charlotte Trelawney	Exon	5	> 42
900	Elizabeth Trelawney	Devonshire	1	> 38
901	Mary Trelawney	Devonshire	5	> 61
902	Ann Trelawney	Devonshire	4	13
903	Theodocia Trent	Middlesex	30	> 67
904	John Trent	Middlesex	4	25
905	Hester Trotman	Wiltshire	11	38
906	Nathaniel Trotman	Wiltshire	10	45
907	Margaret Truman	Nottinghamshire	7	40
908	John Tryons	Northton	7	> 63
909	Samuel Turner	London	23	45
910	John Turrall	Berkshire	14	> 51
911	William Umfrevill	Middlesex	40	51
912	Elizabeth M. Van Keerbergen	Netherlands	6	> 62
913	John Van Leate	Middlesex	1	32
914	Catherine Vanzoelen	Somersetshire	5	28
915	William Henry Vanzoelen	Somersetshire	4	31
916	John Vaughan	Carmarthen	27	56
917	Stephen Venables	London	2	> 39
918	Thomas Venables	London	4	> 60
919 (2)	Ann Margaret Vernatti	Middlesex	8	> 64
920 (2)	Constantine Vernatti	Middlesex	14	21
921	Ann Vince	Middlesex	21	> 58
922	Mary Vince	Middlesex	12	> 68
923	Walter Vincent	Cornwall	9	12
924	John Wade	Gloucestershire	10	43
925	Clement Wakelin	London	7	> 44
926	Sarah Walbank	Oxon	36	45
927	John Walcot	Lincolnshire	16	22
928 (2)	Grace Waldo	Middlesex	11	43
929	Mary Walker	London	4	> 41
930	William Walker	London	13	27
931	Mary Waller	London	4	22
932	Richard Waller	London	3	18

(continued)

Nominee (shares)	Name (alphabetical)	Place or parish of residence	1693 Age	Years lived
933	Elizabeth Wallis	Oxford	3	> 40
934	John Wallis	Oxford	9	> 65
935	Mary Wallis	Oxford	5	> 61
936	John Wallop	Southampton	3	> 59
937	Edward Ward	Essex	11	> 48
938	Sarah Ward	Essex	3	> 59
939	Thomas Ward	Essex	10	> 47
940	Thomas Ward	London	2	> 39
941	Mary Warre	Middlesex	2	> 39
942	Richard Warre	Middlesex	0	> 56
943	Thomas Warton	Surrey	5	> 61
944	Thomas Watson	Oxford	6	> 62
945	Ann Weavor	London	11	> 67
946	Arthur Weavor	London	12	> 68
947	Thomas Weavor	London	9	> 65
948	John Werden	Westminster	10	> 66
949	Thomas Western	London	1	> 39
950	Elizabeth Wheeler	London	4	39
951	Thomas Whistler	London	7	27
952	Henry Whitaker	Dorsetshire	6	> 43
953	Walter Whitaker	Dorsetshire	3	> 59
954	Anna Maria White	London	9	> 46
955	Peter White	London	13	> 69
956	John White	Southampton	5	> 61
957	Mary White	Southampton	3	> 59
958	Susanna Whittel	Yorkshire	15	37
959	Grace Whynyard	Westminster	13	> 50
960	John Whynyard	Westminster	12	> 68
961	Charles Whynyard	Westminster	6	16
962	Margaret Whynyard	Westminster	9	38
963	Jermin Wich	Westminster	22	42
964	John Wickens	Hertfordshire	5	> 61
965	Nicholas Wickens	Hertfordshire	3	> 40
966	Dorothy Wigfall	London	13	> 69
967	Elizabeth Wigfall	London	16	> 53
968	Daniel Wigfall	London	10	26
969	Henry Wigfall	London	11	33
970	John Wigfall	London	14	32
971	Mary Wigfall	London	8	40
972	Rebecca Wigfall	London	2	13
973	Temperance Wigfall	London	5	28
974	Thomas Wigfall	London	9	21
975	Samuel Wildey	Middlesex	13	> 69

Nominee (shares)	Name (alphabetical)	Place or parish of residence	1693 Age	Years lived
976	Joseph Wildigoss	France	29	> 66
977	Elizabeth Wilkes	Middlesex	12	33
978	Mary Willis	Cambridge	19	> 75
979	Ann Wilson	London	4	> 60
980	Elizabeth Wilson	London	19	> 56
981	William Wilson	London	8	36
982	John Christopher Winckler	Germany	6	17
983	Rachel Wingate	Bedfordshire	3	> 40
984	John Winter	Southampton	10	> 47
985	Robert Winter	Southampton	8	> 64
986	William Winter	Southampton	3	21
987	Robert Wintle	Gloucestershire	11	> 67
988	Eusebius Wither	Middlesex	14	> 70
989	Mary Wittewrong	Hertfordshire	4	33
990	Samuel Wittewrong	Hertfordshire	9	21
991	Timothy Wittewrong	Hertfordshire	8	29
992	Elizabeth Wittewrong	Hertfordshire	18	> 55
993	Ellen Wittewrong	Hertfordshire	10	> 66
994	James Wittewrong	Buckinghamshire	11	> 48
995	Thomas Wittewrong	Buckinghamshire	13	24
996	Mary Woods	London	13	> 69
997	John Wordsworth	Yorkshire	1	28
998	Stuart Worsley	Southampton	14	29
999	Thomas Worsley	Yorkshire	7	> 63
1000	Jane Wowen	Worcestershire	11	> 67
1001	Thomas Wren	Hertfordshire	8	35
1002	Jane Wright	Salop	18	48
1003	Nathan Wright	Essex	7	> 44
1004	Nicholas Wyse	Exeter	11	32
1005	Lea Ximenes	Netherlands	5	> 42
1006	Manuel Ximenes	Netherlands	3	> 40
1007	Gratia Ximenes	Netherlands	13	44
1008	Rachel Ximenes	Netherlands	7	> 44
1009	Esther Ximenes	Netherlands	2	2
1010	Edmond Yarbrough	Yorkshire	5	> 61
1011	Thomas Yeate	Dorchester	8	31
1012	George Yeate	Dorchester	14	> 51
1013	Arthur Zouch	Middlesex	21	> 77

The Gompertz-Makeham Law of Mortality

In a number of earlier chapters I made reference to the Gompertz-Makeham (or just plain Gompertz) Law of Mortality. In particular, I used this law of mortality in Chapter 7 when I introduced and described Jared's tontine pay-out rate and in Chapter 2 when I discussed the probability density function of the "present value" of the tontine versus annuity cash-flow payout. Well, in this appendix I offer a brief explanation of this well-known law, as well as the analytic representation I used plus a bit of information about the person after whom it is named. For those interested the technical details, see Milevsky (2012), which is a popular book covering the most important equations in the field of retirement income planning.

For starters, age-dependent mortality rates for adults – for example, those displayed in Table 5.3 but continued to older ages – seem rather arbitrary at first, but there is actually an underlying pattern to them. In particular, for people between the ages of twenty and ninety – mortality rates not only increase consistently every year with age, they actually increase by approximately 9% every year.

In mathematical symbols, if the starting mortality or death rate per year was q percent at age y, (for example, $q = 2\%$ at age fifty) then it is $q(1 + z)$ percent in year $(y + 1)$ and then $q(1 + z)^2$ percent in year $(y + 2)$, and then $q(1 + z)^3$ percent in year $(y + 3)$, and so on, where z is approximately 9%. Human adult mortality rates – regardless of what particular group of humans or population you select and whether it is in the seventeenth or nineteenth or twenty-first century – are an exponentially increasing function of age with a (growth rate) parameter of 9%.

What this also means (mathematically) is that if you take the logarithms of these annual mortality rates denoted by q, they can be approximated quite nicely by a straight line and determined by a slope and an intercept. Now, there are some exceptions to this rule (such as the infants we discussed in Chapter 5, teenagers and young adults who just learned how to drive in the twenty-first century and very old adults like Jared from the Preface), but generally speaking the 9% is a rather good approximation for "modeling" purposes and something that underlies the calculations in Chapter 7.

Of course, this "9% more-deaths-per-year rule" is not something I just stumbled on or a fluke of the data. This fundamental biological observation was first made by the British demographer and actuary Gompertz (1779–1865), and is today known as the Gompertz "Law of Mortality" in his honor. His groundbreaking research on human mortality modeling was partially based on tontine and annuity mortality rates and published in the year 1825 in *Philosophical Transaction of the Royal Society*, almost a century after the early empirical work of John Finlaison, who examined survival rates for the 1693 and 1789 tontine. As I mentioned previously, King William's tontine was more than just a financial and insurance product. It became an important source of demographic and actuarial data.

This "9% per year" observation is more than simply actuarial trivia in that it offers a powerful and reasonable analytic tool to compute survival probabilities to any age, *as a function of just two basic parameters*. A few years after Gompertz discovered (or formulated) his law, another actuary by the name of William Makeham proposed an additional variation to account for random (non-age-dependent) deaths, which then became known as the Gompertz-Makeham Law of Mortality.

And while the actuarial and statistical theory is more than is required for this book, the concise formula for the survival probability – from any age, to any age – under this Law of Mortality can be written as $\ln[s_x(t)] = -\mu t + (1 - e^{(t/b)})e^{(x-m)/b}$. In this expression, the time variable t denotes the survival period, the variable x denotes the current age of the individual, and the three parameters (μ, m, b) denote the (i.) random accidental death rate, (ii.) the modal value of life in years, and (iii.) the dispersion coefficient in years. Taking the exponent of the left-hand side of the mathematical expression, and thus "undoing" the logarithms, one obtains the survival probability itself.

Here is an example. Assume that you are currently fifty years old and would like to estimate the probability you will live (at least) to the age of ninety, which is forty more years. Recall that this sort of number would be required to compute Jared's tontine payout rate, for instance. According to the limited version of the Gompertz Law of Mortality – that is without the Makeham constant – the survival probability depends on just two parameters; the modal (m) value of life at birth, measured in years, and the dispersion (b) value of life also measured in years.

These two numbers can loosely be thought of as the mean and standard deviation of your remaining future lifetime, which is obviously a random variable in the formal sense. More precisely, the modal value of life is the age at which you are most likely to die, but is actually a few years higher than the fifty-fifty (median life span) point. This is due to the skewness of the remaining lifetime distribution. Ok, technicalities aside, if – for example – the modal value is $m = 80$ years and the dispersion value is $b = 11$ years, the survival probability from the age of fifty to age ninety is 8.9%, which can also be expressed as a 91.1% probability of dying prior to age ninety.

In contrast, under a higher modal value of $m = 92$ years instead of the lower $m = 80$, the survival probability from the age of fifty to age ninety increases to 44.4%. Note how the extra twelve years of expected lifespan (in the modal sense) will add 35.5 percentage points to the survival probability. If you "believe" that your modal value of life is in fact $m = 92$ years, then the probability of surviving to age ninety-five (from age fifty) is 27.5% and the probability of surviving to age 100 and becoming a centenarian is 12.9%, which is obviously quite optimistic.

As you can plainly see, changing the modal value (m) by just a few years can have a dramatic effect on the probabilities. For those readers familiar with modern portfolio theory, this is analogous to using the lognormal distribution to approximate long-term although not daily, weekly, or monthly portfolio returns. The model isn't perfect, but it's a reasonable good start and justified by theory. The analytics are well understood, but the parameters are debatable. The good news is that the "fit" for mortality models such as the Gompertz-Makeham Law is that they tend to fit adult ages around retirement remarkably well. Indeed, the fit is much better than the lognormal distribution to historical stock returns. And, while I don't want to get caught up in the actuarial minutiae and demographic details, the Gompertz Law of Mortality has withstood the test of time as a good approximation. I am a big fan and use it often.

Interestingly, while the law was popularized by William Makeham (who added his own constant in front of the exponential term), Benjamin Gompertz himself realized the importance of accidents and other non-age-related factors. He wrote (1825, 517): "It is possible that death may be the consequence of two generally co-existing causes. The one [is] chance, without previous disposition to death or deterioration. The other [is] a deterioration, or an increased inability to withstand destruction." On a historical note, the seventy-page paper Benjamin Gompertz wrote and presented to the Royal Society of London in 1825 – the same society at which Edmond Halley presented his work on annuity pricing in 1693 – doesn't include the analytic expression for the survival probability I displayed above. He described the above equation in words and logarithms as opposed to algebraic symbols.

With an actual equation for the mortality and survival rates, companies could then do a much better job of computing premiums, setting reserves, and managing risk. This was many years ahead of the crude and approximate work done to price the annuities in the late seventeenth century by Edmond Halley or Abraham De Moivre.

See the U.S-based study by Gavrilov and Gavrilova (2011), for a discussion and evidence around the goodness-of-fit of the Gompertz model to actual mortality and longevity data even at very advanced ages. Benjamin Gompertz may have died in 1865, but his model lives-on in the twenty-first century.

Benjamin Gompertz was hired as the chief [and possibly the first] actuary at one of the largest insurance companies in England, the Alliance Assurance Company, and was a full member of the London Stock Exchange, while retaining an active involvement in the Astronomical Society. Here is yet another example of an astronomer and member of the Royal Society who contributed to actuarial finance and insurance matters. Perhaps an undergraduate degree in physics and astronomy should be the required pre-requisite for a career in the actuarial and insurance industry?

14% for One, 12% for Two, or 10% for Three?

Recall from Chapter 4 that one year after King William's tontine was launched, the government Exchequer in England offered a robust collections of annuities for sale in 1694, but at payouts and yields that were independent of the age of the annuitant. No matter how old or how young you were, the payout rate and income you received was the same.

The first annuity available paid 14% for a single life. In exchange for £100 (which was the minimal purchase price) the annuitant would receive £14 for life. Another option was a double-life annuity yielding 12%, which allowed the investors to protect themselves by nominating two lives, perhaps a husband and a wife. A third life annuity option paid a 10% yield, and allowed for three annuitants in the contract. In other words, as long as any one of three named annuitants (husband, wife, and child?) was alive, the government continued making the relevant payment of £10 per £100. If you are wondering, there was no quadruple life annuity sold. The value of N, so to speak, stopped at 3.

However, a final (fourth) annuity product that was offered was a "reversionary annuity," which was slightly different than the above-mentioned ones. The reversionary annuity allowed the existing owner of a 14% single-life annuity to pay an additional "top up premium" and convert their life annuity into a ninety-six-year period certain annuity. The cost of this reversionary annuity was a one-time payment of 4.5 year's purchase. Technically speaking a £14 life annuity could be extended to ninety-six years (from the date of purchase) in exchange for a payment of £63. Without getting into the historical or actuarial minutiae, the idea was to allow investors to continue the payment (from their date of death, continuing to an heir) all the way to the year 1790. If you think about it, the reversionary annuity is a combination of life insurance and life annuity. It is triggered by death, but paid as lifetime income. In fact, the reversionary annuity could be purchased on a stand-alone basis and contingent on the life of a complete stranger. If, for example, Joe owned a 14% life annuity that terminated upon his death, Frank could purchase the reversionary annuity [on Joe] that would pay Frank 14% for life if-and-when Joe died. Frank and Joe didn't have to be related, or even know each other.

According to the historian J. J. Grellier, who compiled a record (in 1810) of the national debt from the Glorious Revolution (1688) and onward, the government issued or sold £107,847 in 14% (single-life) annuities, £170,917 in 12% (double-life) annuities, and £21,235 in 10% (triple-life) annuities. So, it seems that the double-life annuity was the most popular of the three (for which there was data in the mid-1690s). But, these reversionary annuities were the most popular of them all. See Lewin (2003) for additional history and context.

In the following section I'll examine which of the three was the best deal of the three life annuities available. Main question: 14% for one, 12% for two, or 10% for three?

SOLVING FOR THE INTEREST AND MORTALITY RATE

The first step in comparing the three different choices is to solve for the implied mortality and interest rate, based on the (simplest) single 14% life annuity. Since the (14%) life annuity was offered to everyone irrespective of age, one must assume that (they assumed) a constant force of mortality, leading to an exponential survival probability with decay (force of mortality) denoted by: μ. Using the notion I introduced in Appendix B and used in Chapter 7, $\ln[s_x(t)] = -\mu t$, where the Gompertz portion is absent when the instantaneous mortality rate is constant.

Under a constant interest (discount rate) denoted by r, the annuity factor is:

$$\bar{a} = \int_0^\infty e^{-(r+\mu)t}\,dt = \frac{1}{r+\mu} = \frac{1}{0.14} = 7.143,$$

which is also the "number of years purchase" according to the terminology used at the time.[1] Nothing complicated here, but from the 14% annuity alone it is impossible to disentangle or separate the interest from the mortality. It could be 4% interest plus 10% mortality, or 8% interest and 6% interest, or vice versa.

[1] See Promislow (2011), Cannon and Tonks (2008), or Milevsky (2006) for more on the actuarial valuation. See also Milevsky and Young (2007) for related work on the optimal timing of annuitization, that is the best age at which to purchase a life annuity. Note that when $r = 0$ the annuity factor is life expectancy.

Recall that holders of the (single-life) 14% annuity were able to exchange or convert their life annuity into a ninety-six-year term annuity, in exchange for an additional payment of 4.5 years purchase. This was the reversionary annuity mentioned earlier. So, after having paid £100 for a £14 life annuity, they could pay an additional £63 and extend it. This then enables me to solve for the implied (constant) interest rate using the following equation:

$$63 = 14\left(\int_0^\infty e^{-rt} dt - \frac{1}{r+\mu} \right) = \frac{14}{r} - 100,$$

where the ninety-six-year (term) annuity is approximated by a perpetuity, to keep things clean and simple. Stated differently, you pay £163 for a £14 perpetuity.

Either way, we have two equations for the unknown (embedded) interest rate and mortality rate, leading to $r = 8.6\%$, $\mu = 5.4\%$. Based on the above (two) contracts, the government was assuming a life expectancy of 18.5 years and an interest rate of 8.6%, which, by the way, is reasonably close to estimates by various historians for the rate at which the English government could borrow in the aftermath of the Glorious Revolution (in 1688).

Now, let us examine the pricing of the double-life annuity. Since age is not a factor and the annuity pays as long as "both are not dead," the relevant survival probability in the integrand is one-minus the probability both are dead. In an exponential model this leads to:

$$\bar{a}(2) = \int_0^\infty e^{-rt} \left[1 - \left(1 - e^{-\mu t}\right)^2 \right] dt = \frac{2}{r+\mu} - \frac{1}{r+2\mu}$$

After substituting the earlier-derived $r = 8.6\%$, $\mu = 5.4\%$ into the double-life annuity factor, the yield that would be consistent with the 14% single-life annuity is 10.95%, which is 9.131 years' purchase. Alas, it seems that the 12% annuity yield offered by the Exchequer was 1% higher (and better) than what constant mortality rate model would dictate. Whereas the Exchequer were offering this at 8.33 years purchase, the internally consistent price should have been 9.0 years' purchase. The double life was a relatively better deal than the single life.

Now, using the same logic for the triple-life annuity, namely, that the annuity continues to pay as long as "all three are not dead," the relevant (theoretical) annuity factor becomes:

$$\bar{a}(3) = \int_0^\infty e^{-rt} \left[1 - \left(1 - e^{-\mu t}\right)^3 \right] dt = \frac{3}{r+\mu} - \frac{3}{r+2\mu} + \frac{1}{r+3\mu}$$

Finally, substituting the same interest (8.6%) rate and mortality (5.4%) rate parameters into the triple-life annuity factor derived above leads to a yield of 10% (to three digits), which is ten years' purchase and exactly what the Exchequer was charging! In other words the *single*-life and *triple*-life annuity were perfectly consistent with each other – again, assuming constant mortality – but the double-life annuity was *underpriced*. In sum, it was the best (relative) deal of the three life annuities available.

Coincidentally, recall from the sales numbers listed by Grellier, the Exchequer sold 50% more double-life annuities compared with the single life, and almost eight times more than the triple-life annuity. One might speculate that the majority (of buyers) knew the relative values of the three annuities and invested their money accordingly.

Indeed, a strong argument can be made that Edmond Halley's article published in 1693 in the *Philosophical Transactions* – in which he provided a methodology from pricing life annuities with multiple lives – helped the market arrive at this insight. Of course, the question remains why the Exchequer sold life annuities with the same yields regardless of age, when clearly (another) one of the insights from Halley's (1693) article was that mortality rates depend on age. Alas, perhaps the market was aware of his paper but the technocrats and politicians at the Exchequer were not.

Source Notes and Guide to Further Reading

The original tontine proposal by Lorenzo de Tonti appears in French in Tonti (1654) and was translated and published in English in the wonderful collection of actuarial history articles edited by Haberman and Sibbett (1995). The encyclopedia with ten volumes contains a number of the articles I mentioned, such as the one by Halley (1693), Finlaison (1829), and de Moivre (1725). It should be the first collection in your library if you are serious about historical research on insurance and actuarial matters.

The Haberman and Sibbett (1995) collection also includes details of the proposed (but never launched) tontine scheme for the City of London somewhere around the year 1674. It was sent to Sir William Hooker who was Lord Mayor at the time, and had elements that were quite similar to Tonti's 1654 version. But, again, it was localized to London and never got off the ground. It is worth noting however that this was in the aftermath of the infamous "Stop of the Exchequer" when Charles II decided to stop payments (aka default) on over a million pounds of financial liabilities in January 1672. All of this is described in Horsefield (1982) in particular and more generally in Roseveare (1991). Remember that prior to 1693 there was no National Debt to speak of or Exchequer to bail him out. This was King Charles II's personal financial problem.

As far as tontines are concerned, the review articles by Hendriks (1861), Kopf (1927) and the book by O'Donnell (1936) are quite dated, but they do a wonderful job of documenting how historical tontines operated, discussing their checkered history and providing a readable biography of some of their earliest promoters in Denmark, Holland, France, and England. In that (historical) context, see Trenerry (1911) and especially Clark (1999).

The monograph by Cooper (1972) is devoted entirely to the American tontine principle and foundations of the nineteenth-century (U.S.) tontine insurance industry. See Bowers (2012) for an off-beat update on American's current view of tontines. As I discussed in Chapter 6, tontine insurance is based on "tontine thinking" but is somewhat different because of the savings and lapsation component. You can certainly blame nineteenth-century tontine insurance for the bad reputation and legal problems of tontines in America. The Jared tontine proposed in this book would be a very distant and "tame 2nd cousin" of nineteenth-century tontine insurance, although they would obviously share a family name.

During the historical period covered in this book, a number of pamphlets and brochures were published in which the promoters expressed (strong) opinions about tontines or annuities (both for and against) and others suggested better or alternative designs. See, for example, Briton (1808), which argues that investing in common stocks provides a better yield than a life annuity. Another interesting pamphlet is Compton (1833), in which "tontine thinking" is used to suggest more efficient designs. Anonymous (1700) is yet another example of an (unknown) author commenting on the design, marketing, and rationale of various annuities in the last decade of the seventeenth century.

With regards to the same decade, and specifically the year 1693, one can't help but wonder whether the most famous scientist in England – and possibly in history – Sir Issac Newton, had any involvement with King William's tontine and the valuation of annuity options offered at the time. His contemporaries, who were personal friends and fellow Royal Society members Edmond Halley and Abraham De Moivre were certainly involved in the tontine and annuity business – possibly as consultants to investors. Where was Professor Newton in the story? As most Newton enthusiasts know, in 1696 he became Warden of the Mint, so he certainly had an affinity and interest in financial matters.

Well, it turns out – quite coincidentally – that 1693 were a very bad year for him personally. According to a variety of contemporary sources, he simply went mad or insane. Today his behavior might be labeled a nervous breakdown or clinical depression. This episode didn't last very long and he emerged from this "odd behavior" 18 months later, going on to live until 1727, when he died at the grand old age of 84. Some have claimed that his odd behavior in 1692 and 1693 was the result of mercury poisoning from his alchemistry experiments, while others have diagnosed him as having Asperger's syndrome. Either way he certainly wasn't available for consulting engagements when King William's tontine was launched in January and February 1693. He was battling his own set of demons. For those readers interested in this rather stressfull and peculiar period in Newton's methodically scrutinized life, see the recent article by Keynes (2008).

Moving on by a few centuries to some modern source, in a very readable article, Ransom and Sutch (1987) provide the background and story of the banning of tontine insurance in New York State, and then eventually the entire United States. The comprehensive monograph by Jennings and Trout (1982) reviews the history of European tontines, with particular emphasis on the French period, while carefully documenting payout rates and yields from most known tontines. It is a classic in the (albeit small) field and is a primary source for anyone interested in the history of tontines. In a separate article, Jennings, Swanson, and Trout (1988) delve into the details of Alexander Hamilton's tontine proposal, and its similarities to British tontines of the same period.

For those interested in the pricing of general mortality-contingent claims during the seventeenth and eighteenth centuries, as well as the history and background of the people involved, I recommend Alter (1983, 1986), Poitras (2000), Hald (2003), Poterba (2005), Ciecka (2008a, 2008b), and Rothschild (2009), as well as Bellhouse (2011) and Homer and Sylla (2005) for the relevant historical interest rates and the delightful collection of lectures by E. S. Pearson (1978). Two excellent books on the history of risk (in general) and investments (in general) is Bernstein's (1992) classic *Capital Ideas* and (the lesser-known) Rubinstein's (2006) *History of the Theory of Investments*. A related article on the history of the law of large numbers, which is at the mathematical heart of tontine schemes, is Sheynin (1968), who traces its origin to the by-now familiar Abraham de Moivre.

For more information about the (general) history of England during the mid to late seventeenth century and early eighteenth century (which is the period covered in this book), there is the classic Hume (1778), as well as Pincus (2009), Somerset (2012), and Vallance (2006) as well as Weil (2013). For a list of "who was who" as well as their roles within English society and the different arms and functions of government around the Glorious Revolution, see Gregory and Stevenson (2007); a source which is quite helpful for historical research novices (like me).

The economic history and impact of financial institutions that arose during the same period is covered by Sussman and Yafeh (2006). The Dutch financial influence on England is discussed in Marjolein (1991). Another important reference for the history – as well as the future – of the Bank of England is Francis (1847) and the edited volume by Capie, Fischer, Goodhart, and Schnadt (1994).

For a more lighthearted (and rather enjoyable) novel set in the period between the founding of the Bank of England and the South Sea Bubble, I recommend the book *A Conspiracy of Paper* by Liss (2000) as well as

Levenson's (2009) book *Newton and the Counterfeiter*. On a related note, I am rather embarrassed to admit that I enjoyed the various (historical fiction) novels by Jean Plaidy (1965, 1992) which is the pen name of the prolific author Eleanor Hibbert, which offered a vivid and intimate portrait of what was (or might have been) going on behind the royal scenes.

On the same lighthearted note, Kopczuk and Slemrod (2005) provide some compelling evidence that people can actually extend their life – just slightly – to avoid dying in years during which estate tax [in the U.S.] was higher. Likewise, Louge and Blank (2011) argue that civil war army veterans who were entitled to and received a pension lived longer than those without pensions. Add the two results together and the key to a long life is a lightly taxed pension.

From fiction to fact, another important reference within the history of mortality-contingent claim pricing is Finlaison (1829), who – as I mentioned in a number of chapters and I emphasize here again – was the first to document (and name) the mortality experience of King William III's 1693 tontine participants. He argued that life annuities sold by the British government – at the same price for all ages! – were greatly underpriced. Note that the life annuities were underpriced but not the tontines. The standard actuarial textbooks, such as Promislow (2011) or Pitacco et. al. (2009), for example, have a few pages devoted to the historical tontine principal.

For some interesting applications of "tontine thinking" to health insurance, see Baker and Siegelman (2010), as well as Lange, List, and Price (2007). A relatively recent, concise, and very readable history of tontines is available in the non-actuarial review article by McKeever (2009). He focuses on selective parts of the history as well as some of the legal (and estate-planning) aspects of tontine plans. It is another great source.

The Duke of Gloucester, the son of Queen Anne and the most famous nominee in King William's tontine died two years before his mother was crowned. But, according to a recent medical analysis conducted by Holmes and Holmes (2008), he wasn't chronically ill and "could have ruled Great Britain" had he survived the pneumonia that killed him. Indeed, modern history would have unfolded very differently.

References

Anonymous. (1700), *The Acts for Annuities Reviewed and Compared*, London.

Anonymous. (1730), *A List of the Surviving Nominees on the Fund of Survivorship at Midsummer 1730 and Their Descriptions to That Time*, printed by Henry King at the Three Crowns in Grace-Church-Street, London.

Anonymous. (1749), *A List of the Names of the Several Nominees with Their Ages Subscribed*, England Laws and Statutes, VIII.

Anonymous. (1885), *Papers Relating to Tontine Insurance Issued by Connecticut Mutual Life Insurance Co. 1885-1886*, Lockwood & Brainard Company Printers, Hartford, CT.

British History Online, available at www.british-history.ac.uk.

London Gazette, July 30, 1700, "His Highness the Duke of Gloucester was taken ill on Thursday last. And his distemper proved to be a violent fever with a rash. All proper remedies were applied but without success. And about one this morning this young Prince departed this life to the unexpected grief of their Royal Highness and sensible sorrow of the whole Kingdom."

National Archives [catalogue # 30/8/277], Chatham Papers.

Articles and Books

Alter, G. (1983), "Estimating Mortality from Annuities, Insurance and other Life Contingent Contracts." *Historical Methods* 16 (2): 45-58.

(1986), "How to Bet on Lives: A Guide to Life Contingent Contracts in Early Modern Europe." *Research in Economic History* 10: 1-53.

Baker, T., and P. Siegelman (2010), "Tontines for the Invincible: Enticing Low Risks into the Health-Insurance Pool with an Idea from Insurance History and Behavioral Economics." *Wisconsin Law Review* 79: 80-120.

Bearman, R. (2002), "Was William Shakespeare William Shakeshafte? Revisited." *Shakespeare Quarterly* 52 (1): 83-95.

Belenkiy, A. (2013), "The Master of the Royal Mint: How Much Money Did Isaac Newton Save Britain?" *Journal of the Royal Statistical Society* 176 (2): 481-498.

Bellhouse, D. R. (2011), *Abraham De Moivre: Setting the Stage for Classical Probability and Its Applications.* New York: CRC Press.

Bernstein, P. L. (1992), *Capital Ideas: The Improbable Origins of Modern Wall Street*. New York: Free Press.

Benartzi, S., A. Previtero, and R. H. Thaler (2011), "Annuitization Puzzles." *Journal of Economic Perspectives* 25 (4): 143–164.

Bengen, W.P. (1994), "Determining Withdrawal Rates Using Historical Data." *Journal of Financial Planning*, October: 171–180.

Biggs, J. H. (1969), "Alternatives in Variable Annuity Benefit Designs." *Transactions of Society of Actuaries* 21 (61): 495–517.

Blake, D. (1999), "Annuity Markets: Problems and Solutions." *Geneva Papers on Risk and Insurance* 24: 358–375.

Bowers, T. (2012), "American's Addiction to Tontines." *Business Horizons* 55 (3): 313–318.

Bravo, J. M., P. C. Real, and C. P. Silva (2009), "Participating Annuities Incorporating Risk Sharing Arrangements." Working paper.

Briton, A. (1808), *Annuities to Fools or Madmen: Plain Statements to Convince Those Persons of Credulity Who Are Willing to Surrender Hundreds and Purchase Tens by Way of Annuities*. London.

Cannon, E., and I. Tonks (2008), *Annuity Markets*. Oxford: Oxford University Press.

Capie, F., S. Fischer, C. Goodhart, and N. Schnadt (1994), *The Future of Central Banking: The Tercentenary Symposium of the Bank of England*. Cambridge: Cambridge University Press.

Carlos, A. M., E. Fletcher, and L. Neal (2014), "Share Portfolios in the Early Years of Financial Capitalism: London, 1690–1730." *Economic History Review* 67: 1–26.

Carswell, J. (1960), *The South Sea Bubble*. Stanford, CA: Stanford University Press.

Castle, S. (2014), "The Debt from 1720? Britain's Payment is Coming." *New York Times*, December 28, 12.

Chancellor, E. (2001), "Live Long and Prosper." *Spectator*, March 24.

Chung, J., and G. Tett. (2007), "Death and the Salesmen: As People Live Longer, Pension Funds Struggle to Keep Up, which Is Where a New, Highly Profitable Market Will Come In – One That Bets on Matters of Life and Death." *Financial Times*, February 24, 26.

Ciecka, J. E. (2008a), "Edmond Halley's Life Table and Its Uses." *Journal of Legal Economics* 15 (1): 65–74.

(2008b), "The First Mathematically Correct Life Annuity Valuation Formula." *Journal of Legal Economics* 15 (1): 59–63.

Clapham, J. (1945), *The Bank of England: A History (Vol. I & II)*. Cambridge: Cambridge University Press and the Macmillan Company.

Clark, G. (1999), *Betting on Lives: The Culture of Life Insurance in England: 1695–1775*. Manchester: Manchester University Press.

Claydon, T. (2002), *William III*. Edinburgh: Pearson Education.

Compton, C. (1833), *A Treatise on Tontine: In which the Evils of the Old System Are Exhibited and an Equitable Plan Suggested for Rendering the Valuable Principle of Tontine More Beneficially Applicable to Life Annuities: With an Account of the Successful Operation of the General Annuity Endowment Association*. London: J. Powell.

Cooper, R. (1972), *An Historical Analysis of the Tontine Principle with Emphasis on Tontine and Semi-Tontine Life Insurance Policies*. Philadelphia: S. S. Huebner Foundation for Insurance Education, University of Pennsylvania.

Costain, T. B. (1955), *The Tontine*. Garden City, NY: Doubleday.

Christie, A. (2011), *4:50 from Paddington: A Miss Marple Mystery*. New York: William Morrow Paperbacks.

Dale, R. (2004), *The First Crash: Lessons from the South Sea Bubble*. Princeton, NJ: Princeton University Press.

Deaton, A. (2005), "Franco Modigliani and the Life-Cycle Theory of Consumption." *Banco Nazionale del Lavoro Quarterly Review* (Italian version in Moneta e Credito). 58: 91–107.

Dellinger, J.K. (2006), *The Handbook of Variable Income Annuities*. Hoboken, New Jersey: John, Wiley and Sons.

Denuit, M., S. Haberman, and A. Renshaw (2011), "Longevity Indexed Life Annuities." *North American Actuarial Journal*. 15 (2): 97–111.

De Moivre, A. (1725), *Annuities upon Lives: The Valuation of Annuities upon any Number of Lives; as also of Reversions, to which is added an Appendix concerning the Expectation of Life and Probabilities of Survivorship*. London: William Pearson.

Deparcieux, A. (1746), *Essai sur les probabilités de la durée de la vie humaine*. Paris: Les Fréres Guérin.

Dickson, P. G. M. (1967), *The Financial Revolution in England A Study in the Development of Public Credit, 1688–1756*. London: MacMillan.

Direr, A. (2010), "Flexible Life Annuities." *Journal of Public Economic Theory* 12 (1): 43–55.

Donnelly, C., M. Guillen, and J. P. Nielsen (2013), "Exchanging Mortality for a Cost." *Insurance: Mathematics and Economics* 52 (1): 65–76.

(2014), "Bringing Cost Transparency to the Annuity Market." *Insurance: Mathematics and Economics* 56 (1). 14–27.

Duncan, R. M. (1952), "A Retirement System Granting Unit Annuities and Investing in Equities." *Transactions of the Society of Actuaries* 4 (9): 317–344.

Ezra, D., B. Collie and M. X. Smith (2009), *The Retirement Plan Solution: The Reinvention of Defined Contribution*. Hoboken, New Jersey: John, Wiley and Sons.

Finke, Michael S. Wade D. Pfau, and David Blanchett, The 4 Percent Rule is Not Safe in a Low-Yield World (January 15, 2013). Available at SSRN: http://ssrn.com/abstract=2201323 or http://dx.doi.org/10.2139/ssrn.2201323

Finkelstein, A., and J. M. Poterba (2002), "Selection Effects in the United Kingdom Individual Annuities Market." *Economic Journal* 112: 28–50.

Finlaison, J. (1829), *Report of John Finlaison, Actuary of the National Debt, on the Evidence and Elementary Facts on Which the Tables of Life Annuities Are Founded*. London: House of Commons.

Forman, Jonathan Barry and Michael J. Sabin, Tontine Pensions: A Solution to the State and Local Pension Underfunding Crisis (March 1, 2014). University of Pennsylvania Law Review, Vol. 163. Available at SSRN: http://ssrn.com/abstract=2393152 or http://dx.doi.org/10.2139/ssrn.2393152

Francis, J. (1847), *History of the Bank of England: Its Times and Traditions (Vol. I & II)*. London, UK: Willoughby and Company, reprinted by Elibron Classics.

Gavrilov, L. A. and N. S. Gavrilova (2011), "Mortality Measurement at Advanced Ages: A Study of the Social Security Administration Death Master File." *North American Actuarial Journal* 15(3): 432–447.

Geisst, C. R. (2013), *Beggar thy Neighbor: A History of Usury and Debt*. Philadelphia: University of Pennsylvania Press.

Goldsticker, R. (2007), "A Mutual Fund to Yield Annuity-Like Benefits." *Financial Analysts Journal* 63 (1): 63–67.

Gompertz, B. (1825), "On the Nature of the Function Expressive of the Law of Human Mortality, and on a New Mode of Determining the Value of Life Contingencies." *Philosophical Transactions of the Royal Society of London* 115: 513–583.

Gregory, J. and J. Stevenson (2007), *Britain in the Eighteenth Century: 1688–1820*. Milton Park, Oxon, UK: Routledge Companion to History.

Grellier, J. J. (1810), *The History of the National Debt from the Revolution in 1688 to the Beginning of 1800: With a Preliminary Account of the Debts Contracted Previous to That Era*. New York: Burt Franklin.

Haberman, S. and T. A. Sibbett, eds. (1995), *History of Actuarial Science: Volume I to X*. London: William Pickering.

Hald, A. (2003), *History of Probability and Statistics and Their Applications Before 1750*, Wiley Series in Probability and Statistics. Hoboken, New Jersey: John Wiley & Sons.

Halley, E. (1693), "An Estimate of the Degrees of the Mortality of Mankind, Drawn from the Curious Tables of the Births and Funerals at the City of Breslaw." *Philosophical Transactions* 17: 596–610.

Hamer, D. (1970), "Was William Shakespeare William Shakeshafte?" *Review of English Studies* 21 (81): 41–48.

Hargreaves, E. L. (1966), *The National Debt (1st edition, 1930)*. London: Frank Cass.

Hart, M.T. (1991), "'The Devil or the Dutch': Holland's Impact on the Financial Revolution in England, 1643–1694." *Parliaments, Estates and Representation* 11 (1): 39–52.

Hayashi, F., J. Altonji, and L. Kotlikoff (1996), "Risk-Sharing between and within Families." *Econometrica* 64 (2): 261–294.

Hendriks, F. (1861), "Notes on the Early History of Tontines." *Journal of the Institute of Actuaries (1861–1863)* 10: 205–219.

Heyrick, R. (1694), *Accompt of the Moneys Paid into the Receipt of the Exchequer upon the Late Million Act for the Benefit of Survivorship: Containing the Names of Several Nominees, Their Ages, Places of Abode, the Sums Paid upon Each Nominee's Life: As Also, the Deaths of Such Nominees as Were Certified into the Office of the Receipt of Exchequer before the 24th of December, 1693*. Examined by Sir Robert Howard in London. Printed at Grays-Inn-Gate in Holbourn, 54 pages. [514.k.2.23] British Library, London.

——— (1695), *Accompt of the Moneys Paid into the Receipt of the Exchequer Upon the Late Million Act for the Benefit of Survivorship: Containing the Names of the Several Nominees, Their Ages, Places of Abode, the Sums Paid upon Each Nominee's Life: As Also, the Deaths of Such Nominees as Were Certified into the Office of the Receipt of Exchequer before the 24th of December, 1694*. Examined by Sir Robert Howard in London. Printed at Grays-Inn-Gate in Holbourn, 54 pages. [RKN: 40006] Institute and Faculty of Actuaries, London.

Holmes, G. E. F. and F. F. Holmes (2008), "William Henry, Duke of Gloucester (1689–1700), Son of Queen Anne (1665–1714), Could Have Ruled Great Britain." *Journal of Medical Biography* 16: 44–51.

Homer, S. and R. Sylla (2005), *A History of Interest Rates*, 4th ed. Hoboken, New Jersey: John Wiley & Sons.

Horsefield, J. K. (1982), "The Stop of the Exchequer Revisited." *Economic History Review* 35: 511–528.

Hu, H. T. C. and T. Odean (2011), "Paying for Old Age." *The New York Times*. February 25, 15.

Hume, D. (1778), *The History of England from the Invasion of Julius Caesar to the Revolution in 1688* (11 volumes). Reprint 1983; Indianapolis: Liberty Fund.

Huntington (1792), *A List of the Nominees Appointed by the Contributors to the Tontine of the Year 1789, in Pursuance of an Act of Parliament Made and Passed in the Twenty-Ninth Year of the Reign of Our Most Gracious Sovereign King George the Third*. Gale ECCO, Print Editions (November 20, 2010), Hampshire, UK, reproduction of the original published in London, UK, by the Offices of Exchequer.

Holmes, G. E. F. and F. F. Holmes (2008), William Henry, Duke of Gloucester (1689–1700), son of Queen Anne (1665–1714), could have ruled Great Britain, *Journal of Medical Biography* 16: 44–51.

Impavido, G., C. Thorburn, and M. Wadsworth (2004), "A Conceptual Framework for Retirement Products: Risk Sharing Arrangements between Providers and Retirees." World Bank policy research working paper #3208.

Jordan, D. and M. Walsh (2013), *The King's Revenge*, UK: Abacus Press.

Jennings, R. M, D. F. Swanson, and A. P. Trout (1988), "Alexander Hamilton's Tontine Proposal." *William and Mary Quarterly* 45 (1): 107–115.

Jennings, R. M. and A. P. Trout (1982), *The Tontine: From the Reign of Louis XIV to the French Revolutionary Era*. Philadelphia: S. S. Huebner Foundation for Insurance Education, Wharton School, University of Pennsylvania.

JHC. (1803). "An Account Shewing the Total Number of Nominees of Life Rents Dying Annually Since 1693." *Journals of the House of Commons* 25. Reprinted by Order of the House of Commons, page 91.

Jordan, D. and M. Walsh (2013), *The King's Revenge*. London, UK: Abacus Press.

Keynes, M. (2008), "Balancing Newton's Mind: His Singular Behaviour and His Madness of 1692–1693." *Notes and Records of the Royal Society of London* 62 (3): 289–300.

Kindleberger, C. P. and R. Aliber (2005), *Manias, Panics and Crashes: A History of Financial Crises*, 5th ed. Hoboken, New Jersey: John, Wiley & Sons.

King. (1730). *A List of the Surviving Nominees on the Fund of Survivorship at Midsummer 1730 and Their Descriptions to that Time*, Printed by Henry King at the Three Crowns in Grace-Church-Street, London 1730. The British Library reference # 8285.ee.48.

Kiste, J. (2003). *William and Mary: Heroes of the Glorious Revolution*. Gloucestershire, UK: Sutton Publishing.

Kopczuk, W. and J. Slemrod (2005), "Dying to Save Taxes: Evidence from Estate-Tax Returns on the Death Elasticity." *Review of Economics and Statistics* May 85 (2): 256–265.

Kopf, E. W. (1927), "The Early History of the Annuity." *Proceedings of the Casualty Actuarial Society* 13 (28): 225–266.

Lange, A., J. A. List, and M. K. Price (2007), "A Fundraising Mechanism Inspired by Historical Tontines: Theory and Experimental Evidence." *Journal of Public Economics* 91 (9): 1750–1782.

Leeson, F. (1968), *A Guide to the Records of the British State Tontines and Life Annuities of the 17th & 18th Centuries*. Isle of Wight: Pinhorns, Shalfleet Manor.

Levenson, F. (2009), *Newton and the Counterfeiter: The Unknown Detective Career of the World's Greatest Scientist*. London, UK: Faber and Faber Limited

Lewin, C. G. (2003), *Pensions and Insurance before 1800: A Social History*. East Lothian: Tuckwell Press.

Liss, D. (2000), *A Conspiracy of Paper*. New York: Ballantine Books.

Louge, L. M. and P. Blanck (2011), "There Is Nothing That Promotes Longevity Like a Pension: Disability Policy and Mortality of Civil War Union Army Veterans." *Wake Forest Law Review* 39: 101–118.

Macleod, C. (1986), "The 1690s Patents Boom: Invention or Stock-Jobbing?" *Economic History Review* 39: 549–571.

Mackenzie, G. A. (2006), *Annuity Markets and Pension Reform*. New York: Cambridge University Press.

Marjolein, T. H. (1991), " 'The Devil or the Dutch': Holland's Impact on the Financial Revolution in England, 1643–1694." *Parliaments, Estates and Representation*, 11 (1): 39–52.

McKeever, K. (2009), "A Short History of Tontines." *Fordham Journal of Corporate and Financial Law* 15 (2): 491–521.

Milevsky, M. A. (2006), *The Calculus of Retirement Income: Financial Models for Pension Annuities and Life Insurance*. New York: Cambridge University Press.

Milevsky, M. A. (2012), *The 7 Most Important Equations for Your Retirement: The Fascinating People and Ideas behind Planning Your Retirement Income*. Toronto: Wiley.

Milevsky, M. A. (2013), "Want Financial Security? Look to the Renaissance," *Wall Street Journal*, Monday, April 22nd, page R4.

Milevsky, M. A. (2014), "Portfolio Choice and Longevity Risk in the Late 17th Century: A Re-Examination of the First English Tontine." *Financial History Review* 21 (3): 1–34.

Milevsky, M. A. and T. S. Salisbury (2014), "Optimal Retirement Income Tontines." http://ssrn.com/abstract=2271259.

Milevsky, M. A. and V. R. Young (2007), "Asset Allocation and Annuitization." *Journal of Economic Dynamics and Control* 31 (9): 3138–3177.

Milevsky, M. A., V. R. Young, and S. D. Promislow (2006), "Killing the Law of Large Numbers: Mortality Risk Premiums and the Sharpe Ratio." *Journal of Risk and Insurance* 73 (4): 673–686.

Mitchell, O.S., J. Piggott, and N. Takayama (2011), editors, *Securing Lifelong Retirement Income: Global Annuity Markets and Policy*. New York: Oxford University Press.

Murphy, A. L. (2005), "Lotteries in the 1690s: Investment or Tamble?" *Financial History Review* 12 (2): 227–246.

(2009), *The Origins of English Financial Markets: Investment and Speculation before the South Sea Bubble*. Cambridge: Cambridge University Press.

Newfield, P. (2014), "The Tontine: An Improvement on the Conventional Annuity?" *Journal of Retirement* 1 (3) :37–48.

Nichols, G. O. (1971), "English Government Borrowing: 1660–1688." *Journal of British Studies* 10 (2): 83–104.

O'Donnell, T. (1936), *History of Life Insurance in Its Formative Years; Compiled from Approved Sources*. Chicago: American Conservation.

Pearson, E. S. (1978), *The History of Statistics in the 17th and 18th Century: Against the Changing Background of Intellectual, Scientific and Religious Thought*. London: Charles Griffin.

Pechter, K. (2007), "Possible Tontine Revival Raises Worries." *Annuity Market News*, May 1.

Petram, L. (2014), *The World's First Stock Exchange*. New York: Columbia Business School Publishing.

Pfau, Wade D. (2012), An Efficient Frontier for Retirement Income (September 24, 2012). Available at SSRN: http://ssrn.com/abstract=2151259 or http://dx.doi.org/10.2139/ssrn.2151259

Piggott, J., E. A. Valdez, and B. Detzel (2005), "The Simple Analytics of a Pooled Annuity Fund." *Journal of Risk and Insurance* 72 (3): 497–520.

Pincus, S. (2009), *1688: The First Modern Revolution*. New Haven, CT: Yale University Press.

Pitacco, E., M. Denuit, S. Haberman, and A. Olivieri (2009), *Modeling Longevity Dynamics for Pensions and Annuity Business*. Oxford: Oxford University Press.

Plaidy, J. (1965), *The Three Crowns: The Story of William and Mary*. London: Robert Hale Limited.

(1992), *William's Wife*. London: Robert Hale Limited.

Poitras, G. (2000), *The Early History of Financial Economics: 1478–1776*. Cheltenham: Edward Elgar.

Poterba, J. (2005), "Annuities in Early Modern Europe." In *The Origins of Value: The Financial Innovations that Created Modern Capital Markets*, 207–224, edited by William N. Goetzmann and K. Geert Rouwenhorst. New York: Oxford University Press.

Promislow, S. D. (2011), *Fundamentals of Actuarial Mathematics*, 2nd ed. West Sussex, UK: John Wiley & Sons.

Raithby, J. (1819). *William and Mary, 1692: An Act for Granting to Their Majesties Certain Rates and Duties of Excise upon Beer Ale and Other Liquors for secureing Certain Recompences and Advantages in the Said Act Menc[I]Oned to Such Persons as Shall Voluntarily Advance the Su[m]me of Ten Hundred Thousand Pounds towards Carrying on the War against France [Chapter III Rot. Parl. pt. 2.nu. 2.]*. Statutes of the Realm, volume 6: 1685–94: 372–378. British History Online.

Ransom, R. L. and R. Sutch (1987), "Tontine Insurance and the Armstrong Investigation: A Case of Stifled Innovation, 1868–1905." *Journal of Economic History* 47 (2): 379–390.

Reinhart, C. M. and K.S. Rogoff (2009), *This Time is Different: Eight Centuries of Financial Folly*. Princeton: Princeton University Press.

Richter, A. and F. Weber (2011), "Mortality-Indexed Annuities Managing Longevity Risk via Product Design." *North American Actuarial Journal* 15 (2): 212–236.

Roseveare, H. (1991), *The Financial Revolution: 1660–1760*. Essex, UK: Longman Group.

Rotemberg, J. J. (2009), "Can a Continuously-Liquidating Tontine (or Mutual Inheritance Fund) Succeed Where Immediate Annuities Have Floundered?" Harvard Business School working paper, 9–121.

Rothschild, C. G. (2003), "Adverse Selection in Public Finance: Life-Contingent Contracts in Early Modern Europe." MIT working paper.

Rothschild, C. G. (2009), "Adverse Selection in Annuity Markets: Evidence from the British Life Annuity Act of 1808." *Journal of Public Economics* 93 (5–6): 776–784.

Rubinstein, M. (2006), *A History of the Theory of Investments: My Annotated Bibliography*. Hoboken, NJ: John Wiley & Sons.

Sabin, M.J. (2010), "Fair Tontine Annuity." SSRN abstract #1579932.

Sandel, M.J. (2012), *What Money Can't Buy: The Moral Limits of Markets*. New York: Farrar, Strauss and Giroux.

Scott, J. S., J. G. Watson, and W. Hu (2011), "What Makes a Better Annuity?" *Journal of Risk and Insurance* 78 (1): 213–244.

Sheshinski, E (2008), *The Economic Theory of Annuities*. Princeton: Princeton University Press.

Sheynin, O. B. (1968), "On the Early History of the Law of Large Numbers." *BIOMETRICA* 55 (3): 459–467.

Smith, A. (2000), *The Wealth of Nations: with Introduction and Notes by Robert Reich*, New York: Random House.

Somerset, A. (2012), *Queen Anne: The Politics of Passion*. Hammersmith: Harper Press.

Stamos, M. A. (2008), "Optimal Consumption and Portfolio Choice for Pooled Annuity Funds." *Insurance: Mathematics and Economics* 43:56–68.

Stevenson, R.L. and L. Osbourne (1889), *The Wrong Box*. New York: Charles Scribner's Sons.

Stoddert, B. (1805), *Remarks on the Washington Tontine: Including the Constitution of the Washington Tontine Company*. Georgetown: Early American Imprints.

Sussman, N. and Y. Yafeh (2006), "Institutional Reform, Financial Development and Sovereign Debt: Britain 1690–1790." *Journal of Economic History* 66 (5): 906–35.

Temin, P. and H. Voth (2004), "Riding the South Sea Bubble." *American Economic Review* 94 (5): 1654–1668.

   (2013), *Prometheus Shackled: Goldsmith Banks and England's Financial Revolution after 1700*. Oxford: Oxford University Press.

Tonti, L. (1654), *Edict of the King for the Creation of the Society of the Royal Tontine*. Translated by V. Gasseau-Dryer. Published in *History of Actuarial Science*, volume 5, edited by S. Haberman and T. A. Sibbett. London: William Pickering.

Trenerry, C. F. (1911), *The Origin and Early History of Insurance: Including the Contract of Bottomry*. Clark, New Jersey, Lawbook Exchange

Valdez, E. A., J. Piggott, and L. Wang (2006), "Demand and Adverse Selection in a Pooled Annuity Fund." *Insurance: Mathematics and Economics* 39 (2): 251–266.

Vallance, E. (2006), *The Glorious Revolution: 1688 & Britain's Fight for Liberty*. Imprint of Little, Brown Book Group, London, UK: Abacus Press.

Vega, Josef de la (1688), *Confusion de Confusiones*. Portions Reprinted by Martino Publishing in 2013.

Warshawsky, M. J. (2012), *Retirement Income: Risks and Strategies*. Cambridge: The MIT Press.

Wadsworth, M., A. Findlater, and T. Boardman (2001), *Reinventing Annuities*. Presented at the Staple Inn Actuarial Society, London.

Wagstaffe, T. (1674), "Proposals for Subscription of Money." In *History of Actuarial Science*, 19, edited by S. Haberman and T. A. Sibbett, London, William Pickering.

Walford, C. (1871), *The Insurance Cyclopaedia, Volume 1*. London: Charles and Edwin Layton.

Webb, A. (2010), "The United States Longevity Insurance Market." Pension Research Council working paper No. 2010–17. http://ssrn.com/abstract=1706899 or http://dx.doi.org/10.2139/ssrn.1706899.

Weil, R. (2013), *A Plague of Informers: Conspiracy and Political Trust in William III's England*. New Haven, CT: Yale University Press.

Weir, D. R. (1989), "Tontines, Public Finance, and Revolution in France and England." *Journal of Economic History* 49 (1): 95–124.

Wennerlind, C. (2011), *Casualties of Credit: The English Financial Revolution 1620–1720*. Cambridge, MA: Harvard University Press.

Wrigley, E. A. and R.S. Schofield (2002), *The Population History of England from 1541–1871*. Cambridge: Cambridge University Press.

Yaari, M. E. (1965), "Uncertain Lifetime, Life Insurance and the Theory of the Consumer." *Review of Economic Studies* 32 (2): 137–150.

Zwecker (2010), *Retirement Portfolios: Theory, Construction and Management*. Hoboken, New Jersey: John, Wiley and Sons.

Index

CPSIA information can be obtained at www.ICGtesting.com
Printed in the USA
LVOW06*2130140815

450172LV00003B/16/P